Alamance

Alamance

THE HOLT FAMILY AND
INDUSTRIALIZATION IN A
NORTH CAROLINA COUNTY,
1837–1900

BESS BEATTY

LOUISIANA STATE UNIVERSITY PRESS

BATON ROUGE

HD
9880
.H65
B4
1999

Designer: Rebecca Lloyd Lemma
Typeface: Trump Mediaeval
Typesetter: Crane Composition, Inc.
Printer and binder: Thomson-Shore, Inc.

Library of Congress Cataloging-in-Publication Data:
Beatty, Bess, 1947–
    Alamance : the Holt family and industrialization in a North
Carolina county, 1837–1900 / Bess Beatty.
        p.   cm.
    Includes bibliographical references (p.   ) and index.
    ISBN 0-8071-2373-0 (alk. paper). — ISBN 0-8071-2449-4 (pbk. :
alk. paper)
    1. Holt, Edwin Michael, 1807–1884.   2. Holt family.
3. Industrialists—United States Biography.   4. Cotton textile
industry—United States—History—19th century.   5. Cotton textile
industry—North Carolina—Alamance County—History—19th century.
6. Industrialization—North Carolina—Alamance County—History—19th
century.   I. Title.
HD9880.H65B4   1999
338.7'67721'0975658—dc21   99-23181
                                                              CIP

The paper in this book meets the guidelines for permanence and durability of
the Committee on Production Guidelines for Book Longevity of the Council on
Library Resources. ⊚

For my mother,
Eleanor Spratt Hacker,
my aunt Elizabeth Spratt,
and in memory of my aunts
Frances Spratt and Bess Rankin

CONTENTS

ILLUSTRATIONS

following page 122

Edwin Michael Holt

Emily Farish Holt

Postcard of the Alamance Factory

Locust Grove

Lynn Banks Holt

James N. Williamson and
Mary Elizabeth Holt Williamson

Governor Thomas Michael Holt

The Alamance Factory rebuilt

Workers at the Granite Factory

Home of Lynn Banks Holt

James Holt Sr. and his seven sons

Caswell Holt

*All illustrations courtesy of
Alamance County Historical Museum,
Haw River, North Carolina*

ACKNOWLEDGMENTS

Annual additions to the list of people I can thank are some recompense for the too many years it has taken to write this book. My work on southern textile workers began in a year-long NEH seminar at Brown University. I thank the members of that seminar, especially Joan Scott, who directed it, for my first critiques and encouragement. An NEH Fellowship for College Teachers, as well as a Sullivan Award from the Merrimack Valley Textile Museum and an Archie K. Davis Fellowship from the University of North Carolina made further research possible. Wilson Hall, my colleague at Shorter College, listened to early ideas and helped me on my way. I have been fortunate to meet and serve on panels with many of the best scholars working on the history of the southern textile industry. David Carlton, Douglas Flamming, Jacquelyn Hall, Melton McLaurin, and Alan Tullos have all shared their expertise.

Descendants of the Holts offered another kind of experise. Joan Carrigan, a descendant of Banks Holt, and Mary Stalter, a granddaughter of Banks Holt, shared both information and interest in the family. Bill Vincent, director of the Alamance County Historical Society, was equally generous with his considerable knowledge of the Holts.

It was my great good fortune to spend two years while I worked on this manuscript at the University of Iowa. For offering me a scholarly home that always combined high standards with good humor, I thank all members of the Department of History who were there in the mid-1980s. I especially thank David Schoenbaum for the best of academic friendships. Access to the Laboratory for Political Research made it possible for me to computerize and analyze census data for Alamance County from 1860 to 1900. John Kolp, especially, and Chi-hsing Lu were more than generous with their time and expertise.

At Oregon State University a fellowship from the Humanities Center, a Library Research Grant and assistance from the History Department have facilitated my completion of this project. Darold Wax long offered encouragement and more recently read four rough chapters to their considerable benefit. Bill Husband and David LaFrance read every chapter, and David the introduction as well; as usual they gave me no quarter. Their careful readings were of great benefit to the manuscript, and all those coffees of great benefit to me.

me. Bob and Mary Jo Nye arrived at OSU late in the life of this project; their generous encouragement nevertheless helped move it toward completion.

The History Department of the University of Oregon has always offered me a scholarly base in my hometown. During a sabbatical year, they generously offered me a courtesy appointment that greatly facilitated my work. They (with help from the English Department) also proved the best of care-givers when I took time off for a broken leg.

Jeff Ostler asked good questions in Iowa and read very rough chapters in Oregon. Jack Maddex answered innumerable inquiries on the Civil War. Daniel Pope taught me a lot about computers (or tried to) and read the chapter on the postbellum mills. Randy McGowen, who first met the Holts at Brown, must have been more than a little surprised to see them cross the Rockies into Oregon. He has maintained amused interest for more than fifteen years now.

My family has offered aid and encouragement even longer. I thank my mother, Eleanor Hacker, and my aunts, Elizabeth Spratt and Frances Spratt, for a great deal. My sister, Nell Cant, was considerate enough to move to Durham about the time I began this work. The Holts and C.L.J. have a history in common.

INTRODUCTION

In 1837 the United States suffered the worst financial collapse in its short history. Edwin Michael Holt may have been unaware of the financial reverse, or perhaps he was undaunted. The thirty-year-old, fourth-generation North Carolinian was raised to do as his ancestors had always done: support his family by cultivating his land. Yet that year he borrowed money from his older brother, a successful cotton planter, and went north to buy machinery for a small spinning mill built on his family's land along the Haw River in rural Orange County. Eight years after his death in 1884, a leading paper in the state claimed that "North Carolina is more indebted to Edwin M. Holt for substantial benefits than to any other citizen she has produced—benefits flowing directly from him and through the family of which he was the progenitor."[1] Today Alamance County, which divided from Orange County in 1849, is best known as the home of Burlington Industries, founded by J. Spencer Love almost a century after Edwin Holt built the Alamance Factory. Building on the foundation of the Holt family's mills, Love developed the largest textile corporation in the world.

Edwin Holt dominated the economic history of Alamance County in the nineteenth century much as J. Spencer Love did in the twentieth. This is the first in-depth study of the nineteenth-century builder as well as his family and the people who were hired to operate their mills. Edwin Holt lived all of his life on land first settled by his great-grandparents in the 1740s. Yet he veered sharply from their pattern. With the founding of the Alamance Factory, Edwin Holt became an industrialist and began the industrial transformation of Alamance County.

Edwin Michael Holt, whose life spanned more than three-fourths of the nineteenth century, was born into a slaveholding family. From the time he was a young man he claimed legal title to black men and women who worked acreage extensive enough to earn their master the designation planter; in 1860 he owned over a thousand acres and fifty-one slaves. He supported the Confederate States of America, which several of his sons fought for and a number of his relatives died for. After the war Holt joined the Democratic Party, the white man's party in the South; he also joined in the deter-

1. *Charlotte Observer*, October 22, 1892.

mination to assure white supremacy. He seems to fit well, in other words, the image of a wealthy nineteenth-century white southerner.

In important ways, however, Holt and his progeny are hard to reconcile with images of the southern past. For nearly half a century, from the mid-1830s to his death in 1884, Edwin Holt's primary economic interest was in manufacturing yarn and cloth. Personal and family profit and success, not regional development or social betterment, were his primary motivations. He inspired his sons, his sons-in-law, and eventually his grandsons to become success-driven manufacturers as well. There is little evidence that many of them were particularly concerned about the lives of the people who ran their machines. They were businessmen. The family marketed goods in the North to the eve of the Civil War and resumed sales there within months of its end. Yankees ceased being enemies as soon as the guns were silent and again stood as models to emulate. Edwin Holt was a southern manufacturer sharing much in common with his northern counterparts. He was, in the words of historian Clement Eaton, "a hard-driving capitalist."[2]

A study of this nineteenth-century southern industrialist and his extended family fills a gap in the history of North Carolina. More important, it contributes to the effort to answer oft-repeated questions about the nineteenth-century South. Howard Rabinowitz, in a recent survey of the New South, acknowledges the importance of questions about continuity and change in southern history by pointing out that "although it is now fashionable among historians to challenge the value of this approach, in one way or another everyone working in this field comes back to it."[3] A similar argument can be made concerning questions about southern distinctiveness. How much the South differed from the North, and how much the New South differed from the Old, form perennial questions of southern history, perennial because of the volume of contradictory evidence as well as the perceived consequences for contemporary society.

Eugene Genovese has been especially convincing in his claims that there were profound differences between the bourgeois capitalistic modernizing North and the aristocratic plantation premodern South. He has forcefully argued that slavery marked the South, made it different socially, politically, and economically. For example, according to Genovese slavery precluded large-scale industrial development. Genovese does recognize some antebellum southern indus-

2. Clement Eaton, *A History of the Old South* (New York, 1949), 376.
3. Howard Rabinowitz, *The First New South, 1865–1920* (Arlington Heights, Ill., 1992), 3.

try; Edwin Holt is one of the southern industrialists he acknowledges. But industry, he claims, was always subordinated to the needs
of a plantation society; Holt, for example, is one of the industrialists
he describes who "owned plantations of substantial farms and maintained relationships of interest and affection with their rural neighbors." Genovese adds as further evidence of Holt's rural mooring
that he "had received important financial assistance from his friend
Thomas Ruffin and was much in his debt."[4] Genovese was not
wrong; Edwin Holt owned a plantation, maintained good relations
with his rural neighbors, and borrowed money from successful
planters, including Judge Ruffin. But the limited information available circumscribed Genovese's analysis. I argue in this detailed
study that after 1837 the Holts were fundamentally capitalists committed to industrial development and were evolving into a bourgeois
family.

Genovese has not gone unanswered. James Oakes effectively
challenges Genovese's "monolithic image of the Old South," argu-
ing instead for recognition of "a diverse slaveholding class, along
with a general tendency away from paternalism and toward an acceptance of liberal democracy and free-market commercialism."[5] In
other words, the Old South was both more varied and more American than Genovese acknowledged. Oakes draws especially on
evidence of planter geographic mobility to challenge Genovese's depiction of southern seigneurialism in opposition to northern capitalism. Because most of them remained rooted in Alamance County,
the Holts are not a perfect fit for Oakes's model. However, my study
of this family reinforces Oakes's demand for more attention to
southern diversity and to those social and economic features the
South held in common with the North.

Genovese has arguably been the most provocative historian in-
terpreting the Old South; C. Vann Woodward's work has been central in framing debate about the New South. Almost half a century
after it was published, *Origins of the New South, 1877–1913*, remains the point of departure for any historian interested in postbellum southern history. It was a "new" South, Woodward argues,
because "no ruling class of our history ever found itself so completely stripped of its economic foundations as did that of the South
in this period." As a result, a middle class unfettered by the planter

4. Eugene Genovese, *The Political Economy of Slavery: Studies in the
Economy and Society of the Slave South* (New York, 1961), 191.
5. James Oakes, *The Ruling Race: A History of American Slave Holders*
(New York, 1982), xii.

ethos was able to build a new industrial South.[6] Edwin Holt does not conform perfectly with Woodward's thesis any more than with Oakes's; this study of his life, however, also suggests only its modification. Holt was one of the ruling class members divesting themselves of a planter ethos even before the war came.

Woodward's middle-class thesis has been widely accepted, but it has also been challenged. Dwight Billings, one of the dissidents, argues that at least in North Carolina planters and agrarians, not a new middle class, controlled industrial development. Billings concludes that "the majority of North Carolina mill owners who were operating during the period of 1865 to 1884 were prominent planters and agrarians (Type I)." To exemplify his Type I agrarian mill builders, Billings chose Thomas M. Holt; his example of Type II mill owners who "were members of prominent landed families even though they were not active farmers themselves" is Holt's nephew William Holt Williamson. Like Genovese, Billings acknowledges that the Holts were industrialists; also like Genovese, he claims that their southern plantation roots made them fundamentally different from their northern counterparts. According to Billings, Edwin Holt's son and grandson were among those who led the South down a Prussian road launching a "revolution from above." He claims that "under the leadership of the landed class, textile manufacturing was incorporated into the traditional social structure when the paternalistic ethos of the plantation was extended into mill villages." According to this interpretation, the textile industry brought to North Carolina "conservative modernization," and "the hallmark of conservative modernization is preservation of traditional agrarian social relations." The New South, according to Billings, was "hardly new at all." Billings based his conclusions about the two Holts he profiled on biographical studies, hagiographies really, written by their contemporaries.[7] My more detailed research reveals that Billings missed a great deal. Both Thomas Holt and William Holt Williamson were sons of textile manufacturers; both recalled that as young boys they determined to follow the leads of their industrial-minded fa-

6. C. Vann Woodward, *Origins of the New South, 1877–1913* (Baton Rouge, 1951), 29.

7. Dwight Billings, *Planters and the Making of a 'New South': Class, Politics and Development in North Carolina, 1865–1900* (Chapel Hill, 1979), 29. Billings repeats a number of errors from the dated sources he used. For example, he claims that Thomas Holt graduated from the University of North Carolina (he attended for only one year) and that he served in the U.S. Congress (he served in the North Carolina legislature).

thers. A thorough study of their lives reveals them as questionable leaders of the "revolution from above."

Gavin Wright has been one of the most effective critics of the Prussian Road School; his work also calls for qualification of Woodward's thesis. Wright argues that while there may have been continuity of ruling individuals as Billings claims, there was still, as Woodward counters, a new class "because the interests associated with their property had changed." In his study of one postbellum Georgia mill, Douglas Flamming concurs, responding to "brutal debates over whether Dixie's postbellum business leaders were in fact a different breed—both genetically and ideologically—" by claiming that "wealthy postbellum southerners had to behave differently in the economic arena than their antebellum counterparts, and new forms of behavior required new ways of thinking." Alan Kulikoff, in an important analysis of "the agrarian origins of American capitalism," warns that "only with great difficulty can historians prevent an unambiguous description of early American social and economic relations."[8]

This study of the Holts argues the need to acknowledge this ambiguity but does not fundamentally challenge the work of Wright or Flamming. I argue that as the sons of Edwin Holt took over the family mills after the war, they were compelled to think in new ways. Limits to their new ways of thinking, however, ultimately led to the collapse of the Holt dynasty.

Did the new ways of thinking involve an erosion of antebellum paternalism? Numerous scholars, writing before and after Billings, have claimed the hallmark of traditional agrarian social relations, southern style, was paternalism. Billings's conclusion that "the plantation was the model for social relations in the mill villages" echoes Melton McLaurin's earlier one that "the mill village was an almost completely paternalistic system." Both echo W. J. Cash, whose overly impressionistic and overly influential *Mind of the South* identified "what the Southern factory almost invariably was: a plantation, essentially indistinguishable in organization from the familiar plantation of the cotton fields." All three writers inherited the assumptions of Broadus Mitchell, whose 1921 work *The Rise of the Cotton Mills in the South* historicizes the very image nine-

8. Gavin Wright, *Old South, New South: Revolutions in the Southern Economy Since the Civil War* (New York, 1986), 48; Douglas Flamming, *Creating the Modern South: Millhands and Managers in Dalton, Georgia, 1884–1984* (Chapel Hill, 1992), 46; Alan Kulikoff, *The Agrarian Origins of American Capitalism* (Charlottesville, 1992), 17.

teenth-century mill owners and their allies worked so hard to promote: that they were benevolent paternalists whose efforts were rewarded with the gratitude of the poor and docile white men, women, and children they saved from a wretched life on the land.[9]

Like many American historians interested in working people, E. P. Thompson's extraordinary scholarship inspired me to take another look at the power called paternalism. Thompson warned that "paternalism is a description of social relations as they may seem from above," and that "we may call a concentration of economic and cultural authority 'paternalism' if we wish. But if we allow the term, then we must also allow that it is too large for discriminating analysis." Thompson also pointed out "that deference could be very brittle indeed and made up of one part of self-interest, one part of dissimulation, and only one part of the awe of authority." In a 1984 article on southern mill workers, I argued that "the written history of the early Southern textile industry is filled with assumptions of owner paternalism and worker docility"; southern labor historians, I was claiming, had not read Thompson closely enough. The assumption, however, did not survive the decade. In 1987 Jacquelyn Dowd Hall and a team of historians at the University of North Carolina, Chapel Hill, published *Like a Family*, a study that took the overly inbred debate about southern mill folk as far as the *New York Times Book Review*. "Family" here does not refer to paternalistic owners shepherding their flocks but to a community of resilient mill folk striving to live lives of dignity. Two years later I. A. Newby and Allen Tullos published important contributions to this revision, and in 1992 Douglas Flamming added his rich study of one Georgia mill. Hall and Newby put textile workers from across the Piedmont at the center of their studies. Tullos presents individual stories representative of Piedmont owners and workers alike. Flamming's coverage of one mill during a more than one-hundred-year period enabled him to offer a case study of southern economic development and its impact on social relationships.[10]

9. Billings, *Origins of the 'New South,'* 102; Melton McLaurin, *Paternalism and Protest: Southern Cotton Mill Workers and Organized Labor, 1875–1905* (Westport, Conn., 1971), 102; Broadus Mitchell, *The Rise of the Cotton Mills in the South* (Baltimore, 1921).

10. Bess Beatty, "Textile Workers in the North Carolina Piedmont: Mill Owner Images and Mill Worker Response, 1830–1900," *Labor History* 25 (1984): 485; Jacquelyn Dowd Hall et al., *Like a Family: The Making of a Southern Cotton Mill World* (Chapel Hill, 1987); Allen Tullos, *Habits of Industry: White Culture and the Transformation of the Carolina Piedmont* (Chapel Hill, 1989); I. A. Newby, *Plain Folk in the New South: Social Change*

Writing history involves a constant struggle to reconcile the specific and the general. Like Flamming's work, my work on the Holt family is a specific study designed to shed light on general questions about economic and social development in the nineteenth-century South. Following the lead of these four authors, I have attempted to put the mill workers and their relationships with the mill owners at the center of my work. Unfortunately, there are few sources available to flesh out the stories the census figures suggest. There is, however, enough for me to join in the revision of a scholarship that long described mill workers as essentially docile and grateful. The Alamance strike of 1900 makes clear that many of the county's cotton mill people were neither.

The Alamance strike was a class struggle. As in the rest of the industrializing world, class division grew alongside southern industrial development. More than any recent historian, E. P. Thompson has taught about class as a historical relationship. "Class," he pointed out, "happens when some men, as a result of common experiences (inherited or shared) feel and articulate the identity of their interests as between themselves, and as against other men whose interests are different from (and usually opposed to) theirs."[11] Much in southern society—notably slavery, a civil war, and an extreme and violent version of the dogma of white supremacy—mitigated against class "happening" in the South in the same ways that it did elsewhere. The nineteenth-century South was different. But obsession with difference can obscure shared experiences. In this book I have explored the social consequences of industrial transformation in one southern county and tried to understand how white men and women (the latter largely overlooked by Thompson) began to first feel and then articulate the identity of their interests much as men and women did throughout the industrializing world.

The book covers the years of the Holt dynasty from the founding of the Alamance Factory in 1837 to the strike of 1900, the class revolt that closed the family's mills. Chapter 1 includes background and then carries the story of industrial development to 1860. Chapter 2 considers the impact of industrialization on familial and social relations. Chapter 3 draws heavily on the 1860 federal manuscript census to draw a profile of workers in the antebellum Holt mills.

and Cultural Persistence, 1880–1915 (Baton Rouge, 1989); Flamming, _Creating the Modern South._

11. E. P. Thompson, _The Making of the English Working Class_ (New York, 1966), 241

Chapters 4 and 5 look at both owners and workers during the tumultuous decades of the Civil War and Reconstruction. Chapters 6, 7,
and 8, covering the postbellum years, repeat the themes of the first
three chapters. Chapter 9 covers the Alamance County strike of
1900. The epilogue concludes the book with a description of the
demise of the Holt family and the rise of Burlington Industries,
founded by J. Spencer Love.

Alamance

1

A Man of Chance

EDWIN HOLT AND
THE ALAMANCE FACTORY,
1 8 3 7 – 1 8 6 0

In 1807 Edwin Michael Holt was born in a part of the North Carolina Piedmont traditionally known as the Haw Old Fields; he was born in a place little changed from the time his great grandparents had settled there more than half a century earlier. Holt and his descendants built textile mills where yeomen had farmed since first European settlement. Few of their farms were large enough to be called plantations. North Carolina's plantation belt was in the eastern part of the state; well into the nineteenth century only the eastern planter elite played a significant role in the emerging transatlantic market economy. Throughout the Piedmont most farm families continued to aspire to little more than self-sufficiency. Local exchange of goods and labor generally sufficed to supplement family production. An ideal of Jeffersonian yeomanry rather than one of Hamiltonian mercantile industrial capitalism or of the Tidewater South's slave plutocracy prevailed.

Geography did not ordain for the Haw Old Fields a significant role in the new economic order. Central North Carolina enjoyed neither the geographical advantages that prompted the Northeast to become the cradle of industrialization in the United States nor those that promoted plantation agriculture in the Deep South. One historian has written of the eighteenth-century Piedmont that "by neither soil nor climate was it well adapted to the staples of the day. Far worse than this were the difficulties in the way of transportation." Until railroads were built in the mid–nineteenth century, water offered the only feasible means of transporting bulk produce and goods long distance. Most rivers in North Carolina run west to east, where they are blocked from the Atlantic Ocean by a chain of barrier islands. The Cape Fear, the state's most navigable river, flows from

Fayetteville to Wilmington, the state's best port. In the early nine-teenth century, Piedmont farmers who wanted to send their goods to distant markets had to carry them over rough roads to Fayetteville. The scarcity of local markets and the barriers transportation im-posed on exploiting a larger market mandated that most landhold-ings remain small. As a result, many white families had little incentive to produce more than they could consume. The limited commerce was generally carried out locally or in adjacent counties. Most colonies and then states found profit by exploiting expanding markets for their staple crops or from commerce, but North Car-olina foundered. Historians have described nineteenth-century North Carolina as "so underdeveloped, backward and indifferent to its condition that it was often called . . . the 'Rip Van Winkle' state" and as a place "sunk into vegetative indolence."[1]

The majority of the first European settlers in the Piedmont, the land between the Appalachian Mountains and the Tidewater, were descendants of Scotch-Irish and Germans, most of them immigrat-ing there between 1730 and 1750. Michael Holt I and his wife Eliza-beth Scheible, two of the Germans, lived for twenty years in a Lutheran community in Virginia, then joined the migration into the North Carolina Piedmont.

In the Alamance portion of the new county of Orange, created in 1752, Scotch-Irish Presbyterians settled east of the Haw River and German Lutherans to the west. The Germans, a minority in the county, included some of the most prosperous families; among the most prosperous of all were the Holts. Throughout the eighteenth century these German settlers tried to preserve their native language and customs, although intermarriage and assimilation made this in-creasingly difficult. By the nineteenth century, German was rarely spoken as the Holts and other German families intermarried with non-Germans, primarily the Scotch-Irish.[2]

1. Quoted in Tullos, *Habits of Industry*, 45; Hugh Lefler and Albert Ray Newsome, *North Carolina: The History of a Southern State* (Chapel Hill, 1953), 317, 314; Guion Griffiths Johnson, *Ante-Bellum North Carolina: A Social History* (Chapel Hill, 1937), 20.
2. "Before Germanna," 17, W. C. Rankin Papers, Southern Historical Collection, Wilson Library, University of North Carolina at Chapel Hill [hereinafter cited as SHC]. In the twentieth century several members of the Holt family have claimed that their family is of English origin. The available written evidence, however, is convincing that Michael Holt I was German; James G. Leyburn, *The Scotch-Irish: A Social History* (Chapel Hill, 1962), 216. Samuel A. Ashe, ed., *Biographical History of North Carolina: From Colonial Times to the Present*, vol. 7 (Greensboro, 1905–1917), 160–61;1;

Africans were the third and smallest group of immigrants coming into the Piedmont, in their case involuntarily. The enslavement of Africans was not as extensive as elsewhere in the South; few whites owned slaves and most who did owned few. But slavery was generally accepted by whites here as it was throughout the colonies. Although human bondage was unknown in their homeland, German settlers showed little hostility to this form of labor. The peculiarity of enslaved men and women speaking German was occasionally noted by people passing through the region, but to Germans living in this premodern society, where a concept of individual freedom awaited the revolutionary era, slavery itself was not peculiar.[3]

In 1759, Michael Holt I became one of Orange County's largest and wealthiest landholders when he received a royal grant of 739 acres (a previous ban on landholding larger than 660 acres in the northern portion of Carolina had inhibited the creation of large estates). When he died in 1767 he left his son Michael Holt II adequate wealth to assure his place among the county's gentry and as a representative of the king.

Wealth and royal privilege divided white men in this isolated agrarian society. If "class" in the modern sense awaited the occupational stratification of industrialization, in this colony as elsewhere there existed a profound sense of social hierarchy. As Gordon Wood has explained, the "difference between aristocrats and commoners, between gentlemen and ordinary people, made manifest the unequal and hierarchical nature of the society."[4] Michael Holt II lived in one of the more isolated parts of the English colonies; he was a crude man by the standards of more cosmopolitan areas, but in Alamance he was an aristocrat, a gentleman.

The revolutionary concept of equality profoundly challenged a hierarchical society that privileged men like Michael Holt. One of the earliest battlegrounds of this social revolution was on the land he won by royal decree. The Battle of Alamance was fought in the spring of 1771 after Governor William Tryon suppressed an uprising of "regulators," aggrieved yeomen demanding relief from a govern-

Johnson, *Ante-Bellum North Carolina*, 12. The area that became Alamance County was part of Orange County until 1849. When discussing the future Alamance County in the years before the division I refer to it as "Alamance."

3. William S. Powell, *North Carolina Through Four Centuries* (Chapel Hill, 1989), 110.

4. Gordon S. Wood, *The Radicalism of the American Revolution* (New York, 1992), 25.

ment they condemned as oppressive. Calling themselves "poor industrious peasants" and "poor Inhabitants," they clearly distinguished themselves from rich men like Michael Holt II. He was among those roughed up when his poorer countymen broke into the Orange County Courthouse. A judge there reported to Tryon that it was a "barbarous riot" and included Holt as among those who were "severely whipped." The governor responded by dispatching troops to confront the regulators; wounded defenders of the status quo were taken to Holt's home, which the governor had turned into a military hospital.[5]

Defeat of the regulators assured that wealthy men, including Michael Holt, would maintain power. Yet the conflict that left him severely whipped was one of the early indications that the common folk were shedding the "consciousness of humility"; in Wood's words, this new awareness of rights was something "the American Revolution brought about."[6] It is ironic, however, that one of the first battlegrounds where poor industrious peasants tried to assert their rights was in the southern part of the new republic where a defense of slavery would long retard the emerging concept of individual freedom.

Growing conflict between the colonies and England soon overshadowed the struggle of aggrieved white men that culminated in the Battle of Alamance. Although the regulators and the wealthy men they had so recently challenged now fought together, some as loyalists and others as patriots, past grievances were not easily dismissed. When war broke out in 1775, Michael Holt II first remained loyal and helped raise troops to suppress the rebellion in North Carolina. But while leading men to join the king's army he had a change of heart, disbanded them, and returned home. The patriots arrested him as a loyalist anyway and for a short time he was imprisoned in Philadelphia. Friends successfully petitioned the Continental Congress to release Holt on the grounds that "he did actually return home." He remained at his home for the duration of the war, occasionally supplying the Americans but not fighting for either side. Apparently Holt ultimately found it impossible to tolerate an alliance with former regulators who had become loyalists. When he disbanded the men he led in support of King George III, he explained

5. Kulikoff, *Agrarian Origins of America Capitalism,* 131; William S. Powell et al., *The Regulators in North Carolina: A Documentary History, 1759–1776* (Raleigh, 1971), 246; Ashe, *Biographical History of North Carolina,* vol. 7, 162–64; Walter Whitaker, *Centennial History of Alamance County, 1849–1949* (Burlington, N.C., 1949), 64.

6. Wood, *Radicalism of the American Revolution,* 30.

"I cannot persuade myself to be so loyal to my king as to consort with this crowd."[7]

Among Michael Holt's descendants, a heritage of loyalty to England paled as rapidly as ties to Germany. He was remembered not as a defender of royalty or class privilege but as a patriotic American. In a university thesis he wrote three-quarters of a century after Michael Holt refused to fight the British king, a great-grandson deplored "British oppression."[8]

Despite his questionable allegiance, Holt was able to buy 380 acres of land from the new state of North Carolina; this additional property combined with his previous holdings assured his sons a landed inheritance. Michael Holt II married twice; with his second wife, Jane Lockhart, who was from the Scottish side of the river, he had seven children. The third of them, Michael Holt III, was born in 1778 into one of the wealthiest families in Orange County. Two decades before his birth, the county was described as a place with "no schools, no churches or parson, or doctors or lawyers; no stores, grocers or taverns." Only slowly did this isolated place emerge from such backwardness. Wealth, held primarily in land and slaves, continued to assure status for men like Michael Holt III, but it did not assure the amenities of middle-class life that were becoming essential in more cosmopolitan parts of postrevolutionary America. Despite the family's wealth, the Holt offspring received only the rudimentary education available. One son moved west, but the other children remained close by, farming and raising families much as their parents and grandparents had done for decades. When Michael Holt II died in 1799, he had already divided much of the land he owned among his children and had also given them title to some of his slaves; in his will each one received in addition "one negro man, one negro woman, one horse, one cow, one calf, one feather bed and furniture."[9]

---

7. William Saunders, *The Colonial Records of North Carolina* (Raleigh, 1886–1890), vol. 10, 828; Ashe, *Biographical History of North Carolina*, vol. 8, 165.

8. Ashe, *Biographical History of North Carolina* vol. 7, 181; Robert Carrigan, "Richard Caswell" (senior thesis, University of North Carolina at Chapel Hill, 1855).

9. Rachel Holt, "Edwin Michael Holt, 1807–1884" (M.A. thesis, University of North Carolina at Chapel Hill, 1969), 4; Description of Orange County quoted in Wood, *Radicalism of the American Revolution*, 131; Ashe, *Biographical History of North Carolina*, vol. 7, 170; Orange County Wills, Will of Michael Holt II; Sallie Walker Stockard, *The History of Alamance* (1900; reprint Haw River, N.C., 1986), 124–25.

Michael Holt III was twenty-one when his father died. The year before he had married Rachel Rainey, the eldest of the eleven children of Benjamin Rainey, a prosperous Piedmont farmer, and his wife, Nancy. A biographer of Rachel's youngest son described her as "a woman of queenly beauty coupled with strong common sense."[10] Otherwise she has almost disappeared from the historical record.

Between 1798 and 1809 Michael and Rachel Holt had six children. Polly died at the age of twelve and Alfred, Jane, and Nancy when they were young adults. William and Edwin both lived more than seventy years and died after the Civil War; the different courses the lives of these two brothers took symbolize the differences between the Old South they were born into and the New South emerging before they died.

Their father, Michael Holt III, was one of the wealthiest men and largest slaveholders in the North Carolina Piedmont. His descendants remembered him as a versatile and mechanically minded man, and claimed that his youngest son, Edwin, took after him. In 1810 Michael Holt owned ten slaves; ten years later he owned thirty and by 1830, forty. He held fewer slaves when he died in 1842 because some of the people he claimed as property were given to his children and grandchildren. In addition to his plantation, he ran a stage coach stop, store, gristmill, woodworking shop, sawmill, distillery, and a blacksmith shop.[11]

Concerned with "the improvement of our much exhausted soil of this my native land," he was a pioneer in promoting scientific farming in North Carolina, the first to introduce clover and blooded cattle into Orange County. After several trial-and-error experiments, Holt developed a comprehensive agricultural plan in 1824, which he encouraged Thomas Ruffin, the state's preeminent jurist and a close family friend, to try on his "Allemance" plantation as well.[12]

Michael Holt III was also a politician, serving a term in the North Carolina House of Representatives a few years before Edwin was born and later in the state senate in 1820 and 1821, where he championed legislation to improve education and finance internal improvements. In 1825, while a candidate for the state senate, he ad-

10. Ashe, *Biographical History of North Carolina*, vol. 7, 181.
11. Third, Fourth, Fifth, and Sixth Censuses of the United States, 1810, 1820, 1830, 1840, Orange County, North Carolina; Ashe, *Biographical History of North Carolina*, vol. 7, 160–71.
12. Rachel Holt, "Edwin Michael Holt," 6; Michael Holt to Thomas Ruffin quoted in J. G. de Roulhac Hamilton, ed., *The Papers of Thomas Ruffin* (Raleigh, 1918), 59; Michael Holt to Thomas Ruffin, May 10,1832, Ruffin Papers.

vocated "not only the great improvement of roads to our market towns, and the improvement of our rivers from thence to the ocean, but also the improvement of the human intellect by providing suitable school funds for the establishment of schools for the instruction of the rising youth of the country, that the poor, as well as the rich, may have opportunities afforded them to improve the talent which nature has given them."[13]

Holt combined his advocacy of internal improvements with a defense of slavery that was becoming commonplace and increasingly shrill all over the South through the first half of the nineteenth century. In 1842 he insisted that "our slaves are the most Happy people amongst us," and "in the General they live sumtuiously[.] our good slave Holders, keeps the meal Tub well replenished, the old Bacon often have to be removed to give Room for the new, few Masters knows their own slaves at church, oweing to their Dress, often they wares as good a coat as the Master, and the slave delights to Honour the Master in his attention & service." Holt even claimed that the slaves were better off than "our poore white population often scarce of Bread." It was for these poor whites that he now defended developing mills in North Carolina as a means of "gieveing good births of employment to the poore Orphan, who has to begin the world without plough or Hoe, or wherewith to lay his head." In old age he described himself as a Republican Whig who hoped that "in a few years N Carolina may bost of Their independence, spin all our cotton, give employment to the poore white labourer, a kind of seperation of Slave Labour and free labour."[14]

Michael Holt wrote his defense of the dignity of free white labor distinct from black slave labor five years after his son Edwin founded a textile mill and began the industrial transformation of Alamance. The capitalist transformation of Alamance developed, of course, much more slowly than in the Northeast, which by the 1840s rivaled England as the most industrial place in the world. The emergence of a proletarian working class and the clash of class identities that resulted had by the 1840s compelled intense debate in the North about the role of wage laborers in a republican society. Free labor was, as Eugene Genovese has written, "a revolution in human

13. Rachel Holt, "Edwin Michael Holt," 5; Stephen Weeks, Scrapbook History and Biography of North Carolina, vol. 6, p. 201, North Carolina Collection.
14. Michael Holt to Willie P. Mangum, January 25, 1842, reprinted in Henry T. Shanks, ed., *The Papers of Willie Pearson Mangum*, 5 vols. (Raleigh, 1950–56), vol. 3, pp. 276–77.

values."[15] Marxist historians have long contended that because this revolution of values occurred in the North under the leadership of an industrial and commercial bourgeoisie far more than in the South, where a landed aristocracy continued to command the labor of slaves, the two parts of the new republic diverged so profoundly that the result was a civil war. Broad generalizations understandably demand that the North and the South be sharply demarcated—the one reordering a society based on wage labor, the other finally willing to destroy the Union in a defense of its increasingly archaic slave labor. But the words of Michael Holt, owner of slaves in a part of the upper South where slavery was common but large plantations were not, reveal that some southerners, especially in areas marginal to plantation agriculture, reached in both directions. Slaves he claimed as "the most happy people amongst us," but poor whites could only be saved by sharing with northern workers the chance to earn a wage. His youngest son grew up on one of the largest plantations in Alamance, but from an early age Edwin Holt was as eager to pursue northern-style capitalism as southern-style plantation agriculture.

Edwin Michael Holt, described as much like his father, was born January 14, 1807, in his grandfather's home on the site of the Battle of Alamance; he never moved more than a thousand yards away. He bore his father's and grandfather's names and remained rooted to their land, symbolizing his place in an agrarian, premodern world ordered by place and familial relationships. It was a world that this Holt would never entirely leave even as he led in the transformation of that world into a modern industrial society.

Edwin's boyhood was similar to the early years of many white males raised in Alamance since first European settlement there. By the 1830s the people scattered along Alamance Creek called their village, which included little more than a store and a few grinding mills, Holt's Store. Edwin's father was praised by a biographer as "a zealous lover of knowledge and promoter of all our institutions for the education of the young" and was credited with "educating at the best schools of our country both his male and female children." No record of the schools Edwin and his siblings attended survives; these best schools may have offered them no more than a rudimentary education. Generally white children in the Piedmont were educated haphazardly at best, although opportunities for formal education did slowly improve after the Revolution as new academies opened.

15. Genovese quoted in Michael Perman, *The Coming of the American Civil War* (Lexington, Mass., 1993), 137.

Edwin may have attended the one founded in 1800 near his home by Herr Johannis Scherer, where German was spoken until 1812. A grandson wrote that "from all accounts he went to work almost immediately after learning to read, write, and do a little simple arithmetic." Clearly Edwin had less formal education than either of his brothers. It was common for the state's gentry elite to counsel careers in law and medicine for their sons; Michael Holt sent William and Alfred to the University of North Carolina to pursue these professions.[16] William received an A.B. in 1817 and then an M.D. at the Jefferson Medical College in Philadelphia. After a year in Chapel Hill, Alfred read law and practiced until his death in 1825 at the age of twenty-one. After preparing his older sons for professions, perhaps Michael Holt decided that the youngest should be trained to run his plantation, and probably Edwin concurred; in time he would encourage his own sons to forgo university educations for practical training.

Edwin Holt grew up on one of the largest plantations in Alamance. As a child he probably played with slave children. Stephen Holt was born the same day Edwin was and remained close to the Holt family until his death in 1892.[17] But although Stephen Holt may have been at times a playmate, he was also a slave. The presence of slavery blunted the erosion of hierarchical society demanded by the regulators and fostered by the Revolution. The small society of the Holt plantation enforced hierarchical relationships of the most profound kind. Michael Holt's son Edwin questioned the primacy of plantation agriculture, but he never questioned his own privileged and patriarchal position.

At age fourteen Edwin began overseeing his father's supply wagons to Fayetteville, a rough trip of over one hundred miles. As late as 1834 the *Hillsborough Recorder* complained that because the road was so inadequate many had to abandon goods en route and all returned with broken-down horses.[18] Despite the difficulties, for a fourteen-year-old boy the trips were a reprieve from the isolation of a plantation and an introduction to the potential of a market economy.

Edwin was also introduced at an early age to the idea of an in-

16. Michael Holt to Thomas Ruffin, May 10, 1832, Ruffin Papers; *Hillsborough Recorder*, May 5, 1842; Gena Church and Elizabeth Grant, "The History of Education in Alamance County," *North Carolina Education* 10 (1943): 126; Eugene Holt, *Edwin Michael Holt and His Descendants, 1807–1948* (Private Printing, 1949), 5; Paul D. Escott, *Many Excellent People: Power and Privilege in North Carolina, 1850–1900* (Chapel Hill, 1985), 4.

17. *Alamance Gleaner*, January 7, 1892.

18. Ashe, *Biographical History of North Carolina*, vol. 7, 181–82; Johnson, *Ante-Bellum North Carolina*, 27.

dustrial economy. In 1813, when he was six years old, his father joined a group of wealthy men from Orange County "for the purpose of establishing a COTTON and WOOLEN Factory in the town of Hillsborough or its vicinity." The mill, planned as an economic weapon to be used against the British during the War of 1812, never materialized.[19]

That same year, however, Michael Schenck built the first cotton mill in North Carolina in Lincolnton, approximately one hundred miles south of Hillsborough. In the next two decades more small spinning plants appeared along the streams of the Piedmont. In 1817 Henry Humphreys established the Mount Hecula Mill near Greensboro; it was Humphreys more than anyone who inspired Edwin Holt to become a mill man.

It was not an obvious choice. A newspaper editor later claimed that in the first decades of the nineteenth century "manufacturers were so odious" in North Carolina that few men of wealth would consider investing in factories.[20] Widespread opposition to industrialization, however, was never as strident in that state as it was in South Carolina and other parts of the cotton belt South where planters feared the rise of a white working class that might oppose slavery or of a black working class that might become difficult to hold in slavery. Extreme opposition to industrial development was rarely heard in the Piedmont by the 1830s, although such development remained stymied, in part because until that decade many of the state's political leaders, particularly those from the powerful plantation belt in the east, were opposed to state investment in the necessary internal improvements.

Textile mills were generally favored in the Piedmont; area newspapers, frequent advocates of industrial development, pointed to those established both in North Carolina and elsewhere as models to emulate. In 1843 the *Greensboro Patriot*, dismissing any suggestion that its state was too backward for industrial development, yet perhaps still intimidated by northern superiority, bragged that the central Piedmont would soon beat Richmond, Petersburg, and anywhere else in the South "for quality, excellence and cheapness of domestic cotton goods." Little spinning mills like the one Humphreys built,

19. Richard W. Griffin and Diffie W. Standard, "The Cotton Textile Industry in Ante-Bellum North Carolina, Part I: Origin and Growth to 1830," *North Carolina Historical Review* 34 (1957): 21–22.
20. Richard W. Griffin and Diffie W. Standard, "The Cotton Textile Industry in Ante-Bellum North Carolina, Part II: An Era of Boom and Consolidation, 1830–1860," *North Carolina Historical Review* 34 (1957): 133–34.

however, were dwarfed by those being built in eastern Massachusetts. By 1830 the Lowell plants were producing more yarn and cloth than the rest of the country combined. Textile historian Richard Griffin has described North Carolina's early mills as "a comparatively small beginning" made in years when "the New England textile industry seemed to blossom overnight into full flower."[21]

Until the Whig era began in 1835, the state was dominated politically by the eastern counties, where powerful planters opposed internal improvements as well as government support for education and a more regionally balanced political system. Nathaniel Macon, described by Thomas Jefferson as the last of the Romans and more recently as one who "typified conservative North Carolinians," was the state's most powerful and famous delegate to the United States Congress from his election to the House of Representatives in 1791 to his retirement from the Senate in 1828. A dogmatic agrarian, Macon predicted that the country would never become an industrial nation "whilst the present Constitution remained to the United States."[22] Until his death in 1837 he continued demanding that North Carolina remain exclusively agrarian, but by then he had become the shrill advocate of a minority position.

Yet widespread lethargy continued to undermine innovative investment. William Powell suggests that in the first half of the century "North Carolina seemed unaware of much that was going on anywhere." A number of newspaper editors in the Piedmont tried constantly to challenge this isolation and apathy; according to two textile historians, they seemed to be "vying with each other to demonstrate their enthusiasm" for mill building. This enthusiasm, however, was not always sustained through the next two decades. Particularly in the 1850s, as cotton prices rose, support for cotton mills accordingly waned.[23]

Industrial development found its most forceful political advocate in Archibald Murphy, who represented Orange County in the North Carolina legislature through the second decade of the nineteenth century. Born in 1777, a year before Michael Holt III, Murphy lived in Hillsborough until his death in 1832. Holt and Murphy had

21. Griffin and Standard, "Cotton Textile Industry in Ante-Bellum North Carolina, Part I," 27, 32; *Greensboro Patriot*, September 30, 1843.
22. Richard B. Creely, *Grandfather's Tales of North Carolina History* (Raleigh, 1901), 88; Powell, *North Carolina Through Four Centuries*, 235; Lefler and Newsome, *North Carolina*, 303.
23. Powell, *North Carolina Through Four Centuries*, 245; Griffin and Standard, "Cotton Textile Industry in Ante-Bellum North Carolina: Part II," 141–42.

ties through intermarriage and the exchange of real estate. Chronically in debt, Murphy eventually had to sell much of his land to Michael Holt, who wanted property that had once belonged to his father-in-law back in the family. When Murphy fell behind in payment, Holt initially accepted "two small negroes in part satisfaction of his judgment" but soon returned them out of concern for Murphy's financial crisis, which included a $34,000 debt to Thomas Ruffin, his uncle by marriage.[24] These kinds of kinship and financial entanglements could create conflict, but they also served to bind the elite together. Despite his debt, Archibald Murphy remained on good terms with Michael Holt and was his ally on most political issues. Murphy used his position in the North Carolina Senate to fight Macon and the eastern conservatives; he demanded that the state develop public education, finance internal improvements, and revise the constitution to give more power to the western counties. Most likely as a young man Edwin Holt knew Murphy, his father's friend and political ally, and was influenced by his ideas.

In the 1830s the Whig Party, formed in opposition to President Andrew Jackson's states' rights Unionism as well as his commanding personality, offered men like Holt and Murphy a new political vehicle with which to pursue their goals. Historian Charles Sellers credits Whigs, politicians as well as industrialists, with doing "much to pave the way for industrial development after the Civil War." Powell describes the Whig era between 1835 and 1850 as "the most progressive North Carolina had known since its first permanent white settlers arrived more than two hundred years before." In 1835 the efforts of men like Archibald Murphy and Michael Holt resulted in a state constitutional convention that established more equitable distribution of power among white men, although it disfranchised free black men. But Whig defeat of conservative agrarianism should not be interpreted as a victory for democracy. Jackson, Sellers explains, "was stirring up a democratic challenge to bourgeois / middle-class hegemony."[25] Ultimately it was that very bourgeois / middle-class hegemony, not a more equitable distribution of political power, that the state's Whigs demanded.

24. Ashe, *Biographical History of North Carolina*, vol. 7, 167; Herbert S. Turner, *The Dreamer: Archibald DeBow Murphy, 1977–1832* (Greensboro, 1972), 19, 138–41.
25. Charles Sellers, "Who Were the Southern Whigs," *American Historical Review* 54 (1954): 343; Powell, *North Carolina Through Four Centuries*, 282; Charles Sellers, *The Market Revolution: Jacksonian America, 1815–1846* (New York, 1991), 313.

Not all enterprising young men of Edwin Holt's generation, however, were as convinced as he was that Whig success would reverse North Carolina's record of stagnation; many of them joined the movement west, at its peak in the 1830s and 1840s. In the thirties North Carolina grew by only 2.1 percent compared to a 175 percent population increase in Mississippi. One migrant concluded, "I have given up my state—and shall hereafter associate 'imbecility' and 'impotency' as terms synonymous with North Carolina." Even a North Carolinian as successful as Paul C. Cameron, the largest land- and slaveholder in Alamance, considered relocation to the rich lands of the Mississippi Delta in the 1830s because he feared that if he remained in North Carolina he would never rise above "common mediocrity." Cameron did buy delta land in the 1850s but continued living in North Carolina; many other whites, including Edwin Holt's brother-in-law and mill partner, William Carrigan, chose to leave and forced slaves to go with them. In her monumental history of antebellum North Carolina, Guion Griffiths Johnson concluded, "It is undoubtedly true that emigration took from the State many of its best citizens and left behind the reactionary and the conservative."[26]

This drain of talent, however detrimental to the state at large, created opportunity for ambitious men who remained behind. None of them was as farsighted or ultimately as successful as Edwin Michael Holt. He was inspired by the ideas of political leaders like Archibald Murphy as well as his own father, and the successes of industrialists like Henry Humphreys, rather than persuaded by the opposition of planter conservatives like Nathaniel Macon or by those who despaired of North Carolina altogether. In 1837, the year Macon died, Holt went north for the first time, to Paterson, New Jersey, where he bought 528 spindles for his Alamance Factory. Despite the continuing opposition of powerful men, industrialization was slowly transforming the Piedmont.

Holt lived with his parents and helped run their plantation until 1828, when he married Emily Farish, the third of thirteen children born to a prosperous planter and his wife from an adjoining county.[27] Michael Holt gave the couple land and slaves, and Emily's family

26. Johnson, *Ante-Bellum North Carolina*, 38–41; James C. Cobb, *The Most Southern Place on Earth: The Mississippi Delta and the Roots of Regional Identity* (New York, 1992), 9.

27. Wade Hampton Hadley, *Chatham County, 1771–1971* (Durham, N.C., 1976), 266; Farish family record in the possession of Mary Stalter Family; Seventh Census of the United States, 1850, Caswell County, North Carolina. The census records Frances Farish's birthplace as North Carolina whereas the Farish family record claims it was Virginia.

may have contributed a dowry as well. Edwin built a small two-room house across the road from his boyhood home. For the first nine years of their marriage Edwin and Emily Holt's lives were closely patterned after those of their parents; Edwin ran their plantation, which by 1840 included 1,200 acres and nineteen slaves, and operated a small store. Emily had their first child, who was named Alfred Augustus for his deceased uncle, in 1829. Their second son, born in 1831, was named Thomas Michael after both of his grandfathers. By 1837, the year Holt founded the Alamance Factory, the family included two more sons, James Henry, born in 1833, and Alexander, born in 1835. The Holts' first daughter, Frances Ann, born the year the mill began operation, was named for her maternal grandmother.

Holt named his fifth son, born in 1839, William Edwin, combining his own name with that of his older brother. Honoring his brother this way may have been in recognition of the financial support William Holt gave him to launch the mill. William loaned Edwin money but had no similar desire to become a manufacturer himself. Although trained as a physician, he rarely practiced medicine, concentrating instead on running Linwood, his plantation in Davidson County; his interests were almost exclusively agrarian. Both William and Edwin inherited their father's interest in innovative scientific farming. William's improved land and herds of Durham and Devon cattle and Southdown sheep were so impressive that planters interested in scientific farming from all over the South and even the prominent historian and agriculturalist George Bancroft came to have a look. William Holt was an early advocate of the North Carolina Agricultural Society and followed Thomas Ruffin as its president. His plantation, on the edge of the state's cotton belt, produced much of the cotton used in the Alamance Factory in its early years. By 1860 he owned 2,500 acres of land, which along with his livestock and other assets were valued at more than $100,000, and fifty-nine slaves.[28] William Holt's plantation and slaves made him a rich man, but when he died, three years after the Civil War ended, he was bankrupt.

Following the example of both his father and older brother, Edwin Holt also sought the most efficacious scientific methods and commanded enslaved black men and women to cultivate his land. In

28. Ashe, *Biographical History of North Carolina*, vol. 7, 175–77; William H. Gehrke, "The Ante-Bellum Agriculture of the Germans in North Carolina," *Agricultural History* 9 (1935): 159–160; Eighth Census of the United States, 1860, Davidson County, North Carolina.

1850 he owned thirty-five slaves who worked 500 improved acres. His total holding of 950 acres was worth twelve thousand dollars. Ten years later he owned fifty slaves, the gain probably entirely through natural increase. The purchase of family land from his brother-in-law increased his plantation to 1,600 acres, three-fourths of them cultivated, with a total value of twenty thousand dollars. On the eve of the Civil War, Edwin Holt was the second largest planter in Alamance County. Too many days below freezing inhibited growing cotton in Alamance; Holt grew primarily corn, oats, and wheat, much of it for home consumption or barter. Some of his grain was distilled into whiskey, or ground into flour and sent to Fayetteville for sale.[29]

Commercial farming was profitable, but it was manufacturing that made Edwin Holt a rich man. He perceived the potential of industrial development when most North Carolinians, including his brother, saw it as only a side show to agriculture. At the time of his death, Edwin Holt was possibly the richest man in North Carolina.

When he founded the Alamance Factory in 1837, Holt joined a small protobourgeois class developing in the North Carolina Piedmont. In 1830 there were only four textile mills in the state, but by the time his mill began operating, at least twelve more had been built. In 1832 John Trolinger, whose German ancestors had settled near the Holts along the Haw River, built the first textile mill in Alamance on the site of his grandfather's gristmill. Within five years Trolinger and his sons had 1,000 spindles successfully spinning yarn for the local market. Holt would also have been familiar with the chronically unsuccessful Cane Creek Manufacturing Company, incorporated in Orange County in 1836, which he watched struggle to pay dividends for twenty years; in 1857, convinced of its profitability if properly managed, he bought it. Charles Mallett's Phoenix Mill, built in Fayetteville in 1836 with 4,500 spindles and 100 looms, making it the largest mill in antebellum North Carolina, was profitable from the beginning. Also in 1836, Francis Fries joined a group of men in Forsyth County who invested in the Salem Cotton Manufacturing Company. Benjamin Elliott established Cedar Falls in Randolph County the following year. John M. Morehead, a college classmate and lifelong friend of William Rainey Holt, built a factory

29. Seventh and Eighth Censuses of the United States, 1850, 1860, Alamance County, North Carolina. Edwin Michael Holt Diary, February 10, March 11, April 26, December 14, 1844, and similar entries between 1845 and 1854, Alamance Cotton Mill Collection, SHC.

in Rockingham County in 1838. Governor from 1841 to 1845 and long one of the most influential men in the state, Morehead offered a powerful affirmation of industrialization.[30]

Holt developed close personal and professional ties with all of these men, especially with Henry Humphreys. One of Holt's sons later recalled that "my father made it convenient to visit Greensboro often, and whenever he went he always made it his business and pleasure to call on Mr. Humphries [sic]. The two soon became good friends. The more my father saw of the workings of Mr. Humphries' mill the more convinced he became that his own ideas were correct."[31]

In the fall of 1836 Charles Danforth, part owner of the New Jersey machine company that had set up Humphreys' mill, returned to North Carolina to consult with him and others interested in developing a textile industry in the state. Owners of the Salem mill, including Francis Fries, "induced by the large dividends declared by cotton manufacturing," interviewed Danforth concerning the best arrangement for a mill and the prices of northern machinery.[32] Edwin Holt was also aware of the potential for profit and possibly consulted with Danforth as well. He was convinced that the Alamance Creek falls running his father's gristmill would also be adequate for running a small cotton mill.

Although he had long supported economic diversification in the state, Michael Holt initially opposed his son's plan to build a spinning mill, perhaps because he had seen his own effort fail twenty-five years before. Despite his father's opposition, in the spring of 1837 Edwin traveled by steamer to New York City, then overland the fourteen miles to Paterson, New Jersey, and bought enough machinery to run a small mill. Previously Holt had known industrialization only as a few scattered mills dotting a rural landscape. In Paterson he saw vividly industrializing America. A European visiting the same year wrote, as he stood at the falls of the Passaic River, that "a more beautiful wildspot can hardly be conceived" and marveled at finding himself "in the midst of such a strange combination

30. Griffin and Standard, "Cotton Textile Industry in Ante-Bellum North Carolina: Part II," is the best general treatment of these early mills. Also see Burton Alva Konkle, *John Motley Morehead and the Development of North Carolina, 1796–1866* (Philadelphia, 1922).
31. Eugene Holt, *Edwin Michael Holt and His Descendants*, 7.
32. Ibid.; Salem Manufacturing Company Minute Book, Oct. 1, 1836, Salem Manufacturing Company Papers, Moravian Archives, Winston-Salem.

of nature and art." Looking away from the falls he encountered the sharp contrast of factories, "art in full activity."[33]

Paterson was a small industrial city by northern standards but larger than any city in North Carolina. Good water power, as well as proximity to New York City, had attracted twenty cotton mills there by 1832, although by the time of Holt's visit the city was falling behind in competition with New England. Textile machine companies, including Godwin, Clark, and Rogers, the company that equipped first Humphreys and then Holt, had followed the mills to Paterson.[34] Holt ordered spindles from them and hired one of their mechanics to come to Alamance long enough to set up the mill and train him and his workers to run it.

On his way home Holt stopped in Philadelphia where he dined with Thomas Ruffin, a prominent jurist in North Carolina and a close friend of the Holts, who was also in the North on business. During their conversation Ruffin became convinced that the mill Holt described could succeed and offered to form a partnership as well as allow use of a site he owned on the Haw River. Holt borrowed money from Ruffin but rejected the partnership.[35]

Many of the small mills in the South were either nonfamilial partnerships like the one Ruffin proposed or financed by subscribers and run by a board of directors. Holt, however, determined from the outset that ownership of his mill would be exclusively within his family. Even as he was launching his own industrial career he was planning similar careers for his sons. Still, Ruffin's endorsement, coming from one of the most prominent men in the state, was important in giving his idea credibility. It may have prompted Michael Holt to reconsider his opposition, although Edwin remained determined not to obligate his father financially; he did purchase water power from him for a nominal fee.[36]

Ruffin's support may have also helped persuade William Carrigan, who had married Edwin's sister Nancy in 1827, to enter into a partnership. Less familiar than Holt with industrial development and never as convinced of its future potential, Carrigan may have

33. Ashe, *Biographical History of North Carolina*, vol. 7, 183–84; Miriam J. Studley, *Historic New Jersey Through Visitors' Eyes* (Princeton, 1964), 101–103.

34. W. B. Goebbel, "A History of Manufacturing in North Carolina Before 1860" (M.A. thesis, Duke University, 1925–26), 124. Charles Danforth bought the company soon after Holt bought his machinery.

35. Ashe, *Biographical History of North Carolina*, vol. 7, 183–84.

36. Ibid.

been difficult to persuade. Born in Georgia in 1797 into humble circumstances, as a young man he worked as a farmhand and then as a school teacher. Years later he described his hard beginnings to a nephew and warned him not to change his vocation too often.[37] Carrigan's marriage into the Holt family was economically advantageous, establishing him as one of the most prosperous farmers in Alamance. Once Edwin Holt had convinced him to enter into a partnership to produce yarn, the two men agreed that Carrigan would run their store and keep the mill books while Holt would oversee the plant's daily operation.[38]

In late 1837, as a severe financial panic swept across the country, the Alamance Factory began spinning small quantities of yarn, most of which local women bought to weave into cloth for their families' needs. The machinery from Paterson arrived, accompanied by a mechanic who remained with Holt for eighteen months. For the first eight years Michael Holt's old water wheel was used to run the spindle frames as well a sawmill and a gristmill. Local people, apparently most of them teenage girls, were hired to run the frames. Training inexperienced workers who had never seen, let alone operated, factory machines would remain time consuming and frustrating for mill owners and machine company representatives throughout the nineteenth century. But slowly the machines and the workers came together. In March 1839 Holt's father-in-law could write him, "I am glad to here you have started your new machinery and it done well."[39]

Major Abram Godwin, a partner in Godwin, Clark, and Rogers, most likely inspected the Alamance Factory in the fall of 1837 while visiting a number of mills in the state. Northern machine companies competed in the South for new customers and accordingly were generous with their time and advice. Their expertise was critical to Holt and other southerners interested in building mills. The historian of a northern machine company correctly recognized that "the great debt of South to North was not for capital but for skill." In 1842 Francis Fries, one of Holt's closest business associ-

37. William Carrigan to nephew, July 27, 1850, Carrigan Papers, Manuscripts Division, Perkins Library, Duke University.
38. Ashe, *Biographical History of North Carolina*, vol. 7, 183–85; Goebbel, "History of Manufacturing in North Carolina Before 1860," 194–95.
39. Griffin and Standard, "Cotton Textile Industry in Ante-Bellum North Carolina: Part II," 145; Andrew Pierpont, "Development of the Textile Industry in Alamance County, North Carolina" (Ph.D. dissertation, University of North Carolina at Chapel Hill, 1953), 32; Thomas Farish to Edwin M. Holt, March 10, 1839, Alamance Cotton Mill Records.

ates, advertised that "I flatter myself that I will be able to do ample justice to my customers hereafter, having just returned from the North, and there discovered where I erred in this [an unexplained problem] as well as in some other branches of the business."[40] Good relations between southern mill men and their northern advisers generally survived through the 1850s despite the escalating sectional conflict.

Although dependent on northerners for technical advice, Holt looked almost exclusively to men he knew in North Carolina, most of them planters, for financial support. Industrial endeavors such as Holt's mill were hampered by the paucity of banks in the South. As a result, Holt was forced to seek more traditional ways to build capital. His brother loaned him money and also sold him cotton. In the spring of 1844, Edwin sent William a quarter of the four thousand dollars owed him packed in a barrel of flour. During the first years that he operated the mill, Holt continued financing it with loans from relatives and close friends. In addition to his brother, his major source of capital, creditors included Francis Fries, the Ruffin family, and several other farmers or planters from Alamance.[41]

Holt continued to oversee his plantation, but his greatest priority was to make the Alamance Factory profitable. Years later his son Thomas recalled that

> the mill ran 12 hours a day. I was a little fellow—only six years old—when the cotton factory started, and well do I remember sitting up with my mother waiting for my father to come home at night. In the winter time the mill would stop at 7 o'clock, and after stopping he would always remain in the mill for half an hour to see that all the lamps were out and the stoves in such a condition as there would be no danger of fire. Then he would ride a mile and a quarter to his home. In the morning he would eat his breakfast by daylight and be at the mill by 6:30 o'clock to start the machinery going. He kept this habit up for several years and until his mill was paid for. In the meantime he engaged the services of a bright young man from the country and taught him how to run the mill. After this young man be-

40. Bess Beatty, "Lowells of the South: Northern Influences on the Nineteenth-Century North Carolina Textile Industry," *Journal of Southern History* 53 (February 1987): 39; George S. Gibbs, *The Saco-Lowell Shops: Textile Machine Building in New England, 1813–1849* (Cambridge, Mass., 1950), 248; Francis Fries Letterbook, "1842 advertisement," Francis Fries Papers, Moravian Archives, Winston-Salem.

41. Edwin Michael Holt Diary, March 27, April 1, 1844, April 20, June 8, 1846, March 29, May 18, 1847, May 12, 1849, January 7, February 15, 1851.

came competent to run the mill, it was turned over to him and run by him under the supervision of my father.[42]

Once his superintendent had been adequately trained, Holt spent much less time overseeing day-to-day operation of the mill. His diary, covering the years between 1844 and 1854, indicates that in those years he gave nearly equal time to his mill and plantation. In the fall and winter of 1843 he was sick with a fever and went to the factory only once in four months, but typically during this ten-year period he went three or four times per month. In addition he traveled to buy cotton for the factory and goods for his store, oversaw repairs and new building, including houses for his workers and other matters related to his textile production.[43]

The original Alamance Factory was a frame building with a brick foundation illuminated by whale oil lamps and heated by wood-burning stoves. For the first eight years it produced only undyed yarn, which was packed in five-pound bundles and sold locally in the company store, commissioned to peddlers, or taken by wagon to towns in North Carolina and the surrounding states for sale to women as hand-knitting or weaving yarn. In 1845 power looms were added and the factory began producing cloth for sale as well.[44]

Many of the small spinning mills built in the antebellum southern Piedmont never outgrew local markets. Edwin Holt wanted to compete in a much larger arena, even in the North, but the limited infrastructure in North Carolina, particularly the inferior transportation system that precluded extensive development, hampered his ambition. Generally goods sold further north than southern Virginia were sent by wagon to Fayetteville, downriver from there to Wilmington or another port, and then shipped north. A sizable market was necessary to absorb the high transportation costs, but it was not easy for small southern mills to compete with those in the North. To gain entry into distant markets, Holt had to become well known and to establish a reputation for producing a superior product. When Holt began he was largely unknown outside of Alamance. In 1838, when a Fayetteville paper attempted to name all of the factories in the state, the *Hillsborough Recorder* needed to correct their omission of "the Allemance Factory."[45]

42. Stockard, *History of Alamance*, 93–94.
43. Edwin Michael Holt Diary.
44. Julian Hughes, *Development of the Textile Industry in Alamance* (Burlington, N.C., 1965), 3.
45. Goebbel, "History of Manufacturing in North Carolina," 136; *Hillsborough Recorder*, July 26, 1838.

Beginning with a network of family and friends, Holt did gradually develop a regional reputation and an increasingly larger market. Emily's father, Thomas Farish, and at least one of her brothers bought supplies for Holt and Carrigan's store when they traveled in the North and helped sell their yarn in Caswell County. In the forties, Holt formed a partnership with Stephen Moore and opened a second store in Hillsborough. The rural county, however, offered only a limited clientele; in 1848 one of Holt's sons reported that the store was of "very little value to them," because it sold few goods even though he concluded that it attracted more customers than other small stores. In 1852 Holt liquidated the eight thousand dollars worth of stock in the Hillsborough store; soon after the original store was sold as well.[46]

In more distant markets, where Holt and Carrigan were not well known, it was especially difficult to build a reputation for honesty and reliability. A potential customer in Virginia agreed to place an order only if he could be assured that the Alamance Factory would not send a mix of good and bad yarn as another mill had done, and that the goods ordered would arrive promptly. North Carolina's backward transportation system made promptness of delivery especially difficult to guarantee. Another manufacturer reminisced that Holt and Carrigan sold much of their cloth from covered wagons, that "they'd drive them all over North and South Carolina and into Tennessee, selling the cloth known as Alamance plaid." Holt made some trips himself but more often depended on finding friends who were willing to carry his goods when they traveled to Petersburg or elsewhere. In 1839 an agent reported that he could find no wagons going to Petersburg so would ship to Fayetteville instead. Poor transportation also meant that acquiring cotton was difficult and expensive. Initially William Holt supplied the factory, but as their demand grew Holt and Carrigan had to seek reasonably priced cotton elsewhere. In 1854 one of Edwin's sons reported that "cotton ranges from 9 to 10c, we have bought our stock, got it in Fayetteville & Raleigh costing in those markets 9 to 9 1/2 c some few bales as high as 10c."[47]

46. Thomas Farish to Edwin M. Holt, March 10, 1839, G. J. Farish to Edwin M. Holt, September 5, 1841, Alamance Cotton Mill Records; Alfred A. Holt to William A. Carrigan, April 5, 1848, Carrigan Papers; Dun and Bradstreet Credit Ratings for Hillsborough, 1850–1852, Dun and Bradstreet Papers, Baker Library, Harvard University.
47. J. D. Watkins to Holt and Carrigan, March 13, 1839, Archibald Smith Papers, SHC; Manufacturer quoted in Hall et al., *Like a Family*, 26; Griffin and Standard, "Cotton Textile Industry in Ante-Bellum North Carolina: Part II," 138; Eli Smith to Gentlemen, March 23, 1830, Alamance Cotton Mill Records; Thomas M. Holt to uncle, February 18, 1854, James W. White Papers, SHC.

By the mid-forties, as Holt turned much of the daily operation of the Alamance Factory over to men he had trained, he began spending more time working with other industrialists in the state, promoting and developing the infrastructure necessary for their mutual progress. Camaraderie and cooperation among members of the industrial class emerging in North Carolina were essential for the textile industry to become more than a string of small and scattered local mills. Holt and Carrigan both traveled on business several days a month, primarily to the towns and small cities in the North Carolina Piedmont and southern Virginia. Sometimes Holt went to consult with other mill men and to inspect the operation of their mills. He also traveled to oversee marketing, consult with creditors, and purchase cotton. Beginning in 1849 he traveled several times a year to attend meetings of the North Carolina Railroad. Both Holt and Carrigan went frequently to Hillsborough and, after Alamance became a separate county in 1849, to Graham, the new county seat. In both Orange and Alamance, Holt often served as a magistrate or judge.[48]

Both men also traveled north on business. "The early forces on the frontiers of change," Thomas Cochrane has written, "were created by men who in expanding their markets or traveling on business affairs saw new things and accepted new ideas. Sometimes they saw, simply, better machines; more often they observed more efficient ways of conducting routine business." David J. Jeremy, in his study of technology transferral from Britain to the United States, explains that for the developing northern states "only European immigration could provide the textile mill managers, skilled operatives, and machine makers needed for the new technology."[49]

The process Jeremy described was repeated, North to South. For southerners, northern contact was essential if they were going to learn about the new technology. The most successful southern mill owners commonly employed one or more northern or European mechanics and superintendents to teach them. Going north also facilitated the requisite industrial education of would-be owners. Between 1844 and 1854 Holt recorded four trips that he made north and one that Carrigan made. In March 1845, for example, he returned to Paterson to buy new spindles and to Philadelphia for store

48. Edwin Michael Holt Diary.
49. Thomas C. Cochran, *Frontiers of Change: Early Industrialization in America* (New York, 1981), 17; David John Jeremy, *Transatlantic Industrial Revolution: The Diffusion of Textile Technologies Between Britain and America, 1790–1830s* (Cambridge, Mass., 1981), 10–11.

goods. He traveled with Stephen Moore by train to Richmond where the two men took a steamboat to Philadelphia. Holt recorded in his diary that he "dined on board the Steam Boat on the Potomac—passed through Washington City about 5 oclock—Baltimore 8 oclock and arrived in Philadelphia at 3 1/2 oclock—went to church." In Philadelphia he bought goods, including hats, hardware, books, and leather. After a day in New York City, he continued on to Paterson where he "bought of C. Danforth 528 spindles and preparation and returned." After several more days in New York and Philadelphia, Holt arrived home on April 6. He recorded no more trips north for six years, although gaps in the diary may have been during periods of travel. Over a twelve-month period in 1851 and 1852, Holt went three times to Philadelphia, where he introduced his oldest sons to the contacts he had there.[50]

Less than a decade after the Alamance Factory was founded, Holt and Carrigan had a solid reputation in the Quaker city and were selling a sufficient quantity of yarn to work through the commission house of A. W. Adams there. They had become prosperous enough to absorb occasional losses, as they did in 1848 when Adams failed. Carrigan went to "get things fixed," repossessed what he could of their inventory, and agreed to forgo pay for goods worth about $2,500.[51]

Despite occasional losses, Edwin Holt, enhanced by his father's legacy, prospered. In 1842 Michael Holt died, leaving his youngest son one-fourth of his estate. This inheritance, combined with the profitability of the Alamance Factory, prompted Edwin to consider building or buying a second mill. In the spring of 1846 he discussed a joint endeavor with Francis Fries, but it never materialized. Around the same time Holt visited the Cedar Falls Mill in Randolph County but turned down an offer to buy it from Benjamin Elliott for $28,000. He also considered but rejected a site near his brother's home in Lexington.[52] It was not until 1857 that Holt finally acquired his second mill, the bankrupt Cane Creek Factory, which three years later he turned over to his son Thomas.

By 1850, although North Carolina's textile production was minuscule compared to that of some northern states and even lagged behind production in Georgia and South Carolina, it was extensive enough for some mill men in the state to meet in Raleigh and orga-

50. Edwin Michael Holt Diary, March 17–April 5, 1845 and other entries.
51. William Carrigan to nephew, February 7, 1848, Carrigan Papers.
52. Dun and Company Credit Ratings for Alamance County, 1852; Edwin Michael Holt Diary, May 2, 22, 1846. Fries also discussed building a cotton mill in Alamance County with John Trolinger.

nize a society to promote a textile industry. Although John Morehead was chosen president and Benjamin Elliott gave the main address, Edwin Holt was not persuaded by his friends and business associates to attend. He always maintained close ties with mill men, but it was his sons, coming of age in the fifties, whom he looked to for professional collaboration. He also recognized that while other industrialists in the state were potential allies, they were also potential competitors.

Mill men had reason to promote their common interests, but competition for both local markets and skilled workers often created conflict. In the summer of 1846 Holt recorded that "Rominger quit work and will goe to Trolingers tomorrow." In 1852 he again recorded losing a skilled worker to Trolinger. In the late fifties Fries tried to intervene when Holt clashed with a mill owner in Caldwell County concerning which one of them was entitled to the services of a northern mechanic. Fries assured Holt that the man had sought additional employment only after he finished work at the Alamance Factory and that "if Mr. Patterson finds that Mr. J.[ordan] has not been acting in good faith towards him and you, I know that he will much regret having anything to do with him, and if he can honorably do so, will refuse to give him work." Years later the Fries family lost the service of Thomas Siddall, one of the most skilled northern textile men working in the state, to the Holts. Siddall, whose family had immigrated from England, built looms in Pennsylvania before coming to work for Fries in the late thirties. He was skilled but not particularly deferential, and Fries eventually fired him.[53] There is no evidence that his employment with Holt many years later caused conflict between the two close friends, but the competition for skilled workers often did.

North Carolina mill men also competed for local markets. In the late thirties Francis Fries accused Henry Humphreys of underselling him in Forsyth County and admonished that he did not "think it very gentlemanly for Humphreys to send his yarn into our neighborhood." Fries considered a price war as a means of retaliating. In 1839, at a manufacturers convention held in Greensboro to consider regulating prices, William Carrigan represented the Alamance Factory and, according to Fries, "agreed in the opinion that we ought to rise 10 cts on old prices." Fries feared, however, that most other textile manufacturers would demand free competition. For the next two

53. Edwin Michael Holt Diary, August 31, 1846, September 10, 1852; Francis Fries to E. M. Holt, November 11, 1859, Patterson Papers; Beatty, "Lowells of the South," 49.

years he continued to advocate uniform prices and worked to assure the "good wishes of all owners of rival establishments." By the fall of 1841, however, Fries determined that because of "yarns being in brisk demand at fair prices at the North" price fixing was no longer desirable, a decision possibly influenced by the death of Humphreys the year before.[54] There is no evidence that Holt intervened in the quarrel between the two men. After Humphreys's death, Fries became Holt's closest professional associate.

Holt had a more limited background in business than did Fries, who had trained in the North as a young man, but he proved to have business acumen equal to anyone in the state. When the price of yarn was low he held his off the market until he could command a higher return. In the mid-forties he invested in twelve looms and began weaving his surplus yarn for sale. Initially he lost five dollars a day on the cloth he produced, but he held it off the market until he was able to sell at a profit. Holt later recalled buying new machinery "as fast as I made money." This kind of investment strategy may explain the occasional letters received at the Alamance Factory reminding Holt and Carrigan that some payment was overdue. But whether delayed payments were due to carelessness or design, they didn't erode Holt's growing reputation as a reliable businessman. By the mid-1850s his cloth was so popular in Philadelphia that he could not meet the demand.[55]

Holt's success demonstrated that in the North Carolina Piedmont investing in factories could be profitable, at least for an individual as dedicated and sagacious as Edwin Holt. But building the economic infrastructure necessary for industry to flourish was beyond the capacity of individual effort. Following the lead of his father, Edwin Holt became a Whig, the party that most advocates of industrialization in the state joined to foster their economic agenda. In 1844 Holt campaigned for Henry Clay, Whig candidate for presi-

54. Salem Manufacturing Company Minutes, April 28, 1838, Salem Manufacturing Company Papers; Francis Fries to John Butrum, February 20, 1838, Fries Papers, Moravian Archives; Francis Fries Diary, October 30, 1841, Francis Fries Memorandum Book, February 18–19, 1839, Francis Fries to Mallett, June 12, 1839, Fries Papers, Moravian Archives.

55. Adelaide Fries, "Introductory Sketch to Francis Fries Diary," Fries Papers, Moravian Archives; William Bryce to Edwin M. Holt, April 30, 1850, December 16, 1851, Browning Brothers to E. M. Holt and Sons, June 5, 1868, Alamance Mill Papers; Edwin M. Holt to James W. White, October 22, 1873; E. M. Holt to William A. Carrigan, February 18, 1854, White Papers; Hughes, Development of the Textile Industry in Alamance, 3; Stockard, History of Alamance, 89–95; Edwin T. Freedly, Philadelphia and Its Manufacturers (Philadelphia, 1859), 236–37.

dent, whose American System included federal support for state internal improvements. When Clay campaigned in Raleigh, Holt camped nearby for two nights in order to hear him speak. On April 12 he recorded that "Mr. Clay arrived about sundown amidst the shouts of the People and was escorted to the governors Palace by an immence concourse of People," and the next day that "Mr. Clay addressed the people about 2 hours and 25 m in his usual plain and happy style which was listened to with marked attention and gave universal satisfaction both to Whigs and Democrats."[56] Clay lost to Jacksonian Democrat James K. Polk (whose war with Mexico resulted in orders for Alamance cloth), but the North Carolina Whigs remained in power until 1850.

Holt and like-minded North Carolinians supported the Whig's American System particularly because of the promise it offered for developing a system of railroads in the state. In 1849, in the wake of Clay's defeat, which signaled that national aid was unlikely, enough Democrats joined the Whigs in the North Carolina legislature to charter a state railroad to be paid for by a combination of state aid and private subscription. Senate President Calvin Graves, a Democrat from Caswell County (whose daughter Thomas Holt was courting at the time) cast the tie-breaking vote. The railroad was promoted as essential for North Carolina to compete in manufacturing; accordingly manufacturers were among its earliest and most ardent supporters. On June 14, shortly after the successful vote, a convention to promote the railroad, described in a recent history as an assembly of "who's who of North Carolina business and politics," was held in Salisbury. Despite the railroad's obvious importance for his ambitions, Edwin Holt remained at home and "commenced mowing" that day. By the end of the summer, however, he was actively involved in promoting the railroad; in 1851 he was elected a director.[57] Four years later the North Carolina Railroad was completed through Alamance County with stations in Mebane, Haw River, Graham, and in a new town, Company Shops, founded to house maintenance facilities.

The year the railroad came to Alamance County a resident observed that almost immediately farmers began sending their crops by "this easy and cheap mode of conveyance" to nearby cities and predicted "that a brighter day has dawned on the old H's [Hawfields]

56. Edwin Michael Holt Diary, April 9–13, 1844.
57. Allen R. Trelease, *The North Carolina Railroad, 1849–1871, and the Modernization of North Carolina* (Chapel Hill, 1991), 20–21; Edwin Michael Holt Diary, June 14, August 16, 1849, July 11, 1851.

at last." Four years later he claimed that improvement in the county was "all attributable to railroads." Thirty years after the railroad was completed, Giles Mebane, a prominent politician in the state before the Civil War (and after 1865 Banks Holt's father-in-law), described it as "the greatest blessing ever conferred on the county and [one that] has done more than any other one thing to aid in her material development and promote her manufacturing interest."[58]

Possibly no one in the county benefited as much from the railroad as Edwin Michael Holt. It did not save all of the small spinning mills that dotted the Piedmont; as many failed as succeeded. The Alamance Factory, however, grew more profitable year after year. Early in his manufacturing career Edwin confided to his wife that the mill had earned over six thousand dollars in one year. After 1851 the profit was his alone. William Carrigan had never been as convinced as his brother-in-law that the little mill would prosper, nor as patient. In the summer of 1850 he pessimistically reported to a relative "we are still running the factory it pays very bad, we have about 50 bales of cotton & when we run that out I think we will stop till the new crop comes in, the price of cotton is too high for the price of goods."[59] Shortly after, Carrigan sold his share in the mill to Edwin Holt.

In 1857 Holt ignored a national recession as he had done twenty years before and bought his second mill, the Cane Creek Factory, which the Trolingers were forced to sell at auction. Acquiring additional property was an integral part of bringing his sons into textile manufacturing. In 1860 he sold Cane Creek, presumably for only a nominal amount, to Thomas, who renamed it the Granite Factory. It was this son who first began producing the dyed cloth known as Alamance plaids that proved extremely popular in the Philadelphia market and gave the Holts a national reputation. Years later Thomas recalled the happenstance that resulted in the Holt family trademark:

> In the year 1853 there came to our place of business on Alamance Creek a Frenchman, who was a dyer, and who was "hard up" and out of money and without friends. He proposed to teach me how to color cotton yarn if I would pay him the sum of one hundred dollars and give him his board. I persuaded my

58. S. A. White to John M. Allen, July 28, 1855, December 27, 1859, John Mebane Allen Papers, SHC; George Beecher, *Science and Change in Alamance County* (Graham, N.C., 1938), 13.
59. Eugene Holt, *Edwin Michael Holt and His Descendants*, 37; William Carrigan to Nephew, July 27, 1850, Carrigan Papers.

father to allow me to accept his proposition, and immediately went to work with such appliances as we could scrape up, which were an eighty-gallon copper boiler (which my grandfather used for the purpose of boiling potatoes and turnips for his hogs), and a large cast-iron wash-pot which happened to be in the store on sale at the time. With these implements I learned my A B C's in dyeing.

Here was industrial progress still clinging to rural roots. Improvising with his turnip boiler, Thomas also procured various herbs and flowers found in nearby woods to use along with indigo to dye his plaids.[60]

By 1850 the Alamance Factory was valued at $80,000; ten years later, primarily because William Carrigan withdrew his capital, its worth had dropped to $57,000. The value of the yarn and cloth produced rose in this ten-year period from $37,000 to $45,000 and profits from $8,618 to $13,704. Plaids continued to sell especially well. In 1854 Thomas reported "we have been very much presed for goods during the winter, have scarcely been able to supply the demand. Fine yarns no 18 are worth 23c in Philadelphia." Dun and Bradstreet, the northern firm that evaluated businesses all over the country, consistently made positive entries, for example, the "factory always dgy [?] well." The store owned by Holt, Carrigan, and Moore in Hillsborough was also credited as "vy steady." In 1859 Dun and Bradstreet described Edwin Holt as "a man of chance."[61]

According to Gavin Wright, "under slavery, the South lacked the creative tensions which generated a manufacturing sector in the North: specifically, the impulse to mechanization in agriculture; the development of an industrial labor force; the funneling of entrepreneurial talent into manufacturing; and the promotion of cities, towns, and internal improvements by landowners."[62] A study of Edwin Holt's antebellum textile mill demands only that Wright's generalization be qualified. What comprised "the South" was steadily changing through the first six decades of the nineteenth century. The purchase of Louisiana in 1803 and the annexation of Texas in 1847 facilitated the large-scale migration of people from the upper South into lands more suitable for the growing of cotton. The

60. *Raleigh News and Observer,* April 12, 1896; Goebbel, "History of Manufacturing in North Carolina," 132.
61. Thomas Holt to William Carrigan, February 18, 1854, White Papers; Dun and Company Credit Ratings for Alamance County, 1850–1860.
62. Gavin Wright, *The Political Economy of The Cotton South: Households, Markets, and Wealth in the Nineteenth Century* (New York, 1978), 8.

upper South, including the North Carolina Piedmont, accordingly became less "southern" and more receptive to the creative tension necessary to build a manufacturing section. Edwin Holt owned slaves until they were emancipated in 1865, but from 1837 on his talent was increasingly put to developing textile mills, building an industrial labor force, and promoting the internal improvements necessary to make Alamance a manufacturing sector.

Industry brought profit to Edwin Holt, and it brought a kind of progress to Alamance County. It also brought disruption in traditional ways of life and generated new forms of class conflict. The regulators of eighteenth-century Alamance would find their ideological descendants working in the Holt mills a century later.

2

Worthy of Their Sire

AN INDUSTRIAL FAMILY IN
ANTEBELLUM NORTH CAROLINA

In 1850, in response to a census taker's query, Edwin Holt identified himself as both manufacturer and farmer; diary entries he made from 1844 to 1854 make clear that he was both.[1] This decade-long record of succinct daily accounts is less useful for answering questions about how economic change shaped his social relationships or the degree to which those relationships were peculiarly southern. Unfortunately, although generally women wrote more detailed diaries than men, no diary written by Emily Holt or her daughters survives. Extant letters and other sources, however, make it possible to make some observations about the social, familial, and gender relations of this elite family and how they were changed by the patriarch's industrial success.

How gender roles were affected by economic change has provoked considerable debate at least since Friedrich Engels's work offered a materialist theory to explain the subordination of women. But as Elizabeth Fox-Genovese points out, "The debate over the impact of capitalism on American women in general remains inconclusive, and the subject has barely been raised for southern women in particular."[2]

In trying to understand what this antebellum North Carolina family was like and how it was affected by industrial success, Jane Turner Censer's *North Carolina Planters and Their Children, 1800–1860* is especially useful. Censer analyzed 168 planters, most of them from the eastern part of the state, who owned seventy or more slaves in 1830. Edwin Holt's ownership of fifty-one slaves in

1. Seventh Census of the United States, 1850, Alamance County, North Carolina.
2. Elizabeth Fox-Genovese, *Within the Plantation Household: Black and White Women of the Old South* (Chapel Hill, 1988), 58.

1860 put him just below the designation of great planter; in many ways his family was similar to the wealthier North Carolinians. Censer describes her great planters not as seigneurs, a term Eugene Genovese has used to describe them, but as people who in their familial relations "markedly resemble northerners of similar social status." Censer convincingly rejects the assumption that these wealthy parents raised their children to leisurely lives full of conspicuous consumption; instead she argues that they were concerned that their children work hard and succeed.[3] She acknowledges, of course, that the southerners were in some ways distinct. Her conclusions fit well with a study of the Edwin Holt family. It was possible for them to fit comfortably among the North Carolina elite while at the same time evolving into a bourgeois family that was at ease with northern middle-class ways as well.

The ten Holt children, like their parents before them, were born in a place dominated by agriculture. After the Alamance Factory was founded in 1837, however, they were not exclusively an agrarian family. Edwin Holt's commitment to industrial development is clearly revealed by his relationship with his seven sons. When they became successful industrialists in their own right, the sons were praised as "worthy of their sire." Thomas later reminisced that "my father trained all of his sons in the manufacturing business. I attribute the success which has crowned the efforts of his sons in the manufacturing of cotton goods to the early training and business methods imported to them in boyhood by their father, Edwin M. Holt." Ultimately Holt was so persuasive in promoting careers in manufacturing that his three sons-in-law gave up farming to become mill men, and most, perhaps all, of his twenty-six adult grandsons became involved in textile manufacturing as well.[4]

Alfred Holt, the oldest of Edwin Holt's seven sons, was only eight years old when his father built the Alamance Factory. When his three youngest brothers were born, their father was already an established manufacturer. Lynn Banks, named for his mother's family, was born in 1842. The Holts' seventh son and youngest child, Lawrence Shackleford, was nearly ten years younger than Banks. In contrast to most (and perhaps all) of his older siblings who were

3. Jane Censer, *North Carolina Planters and Their Children, 1800–1860* (Baton Rouge, 1984), xix, 152.

4. B. H. Mebane, "Address at Unveiling of Portrait of L. Banks Holt," typescript, 1927, copy in North Carolina Collection; Ashe, *Biographical History of North Carolina*, vol. 7, 185; Eugene Holt, *Edwin Michael Holt and His Descendants*.

named for family members, Lawrence was named for the Philadelphia businessman training his brother Thomas in 1851, the year he was born. The youngest son's name symbolized the shift his family was making from a traditional rural world centered on family ties to a modern industrial world centered on functional relationships that tied individuals less to family and more to class.

The Holt daughters, like their mother, remained more firmly rooted to the traditional roles mandated for females in an agrarian world. Frances was followed by two more girls—Mary Elizabeth, born on Christmas day 1844, and Emma Virginia, in 1847. They were not as profoundly affected as their brothers were by their father's industrial ambition; for the most part their parents and teachers trained them for the traditional roles of females in an agrarian, preindustrial society. The introduction of mills into their rural world influenced their girlhoods less profoundly than it did the daughters of the area farmers or widowed mothers who became workers in the factories the Holts built. But Edwin Holt's three daughters grew up in a family being transformed by industrial development, a transformation that had important consequences for their adult lives. Like most nineteenth-century white women, they were raised to believe that marriage was their first priority. Although the Holt daughters married men who began their adult lives as farmers, their husbands were convinced by the example and persuasion of their father-in-law to become mill men.

The transition of the Holts from an preindustrial agrarian family into a modern bourgeois family was eased by the intertwining of economic and familial relations. Both Edwin and Emily Holt had large and close families in Alamance and adjacent Caswell counties. Their family relationships were primarily affective, but they were reinforced by economic interest. When Edwin Holt decided to build a textile mill, he had to confront his father's opposition, but eventually Michael Holt supported his son. The mill's early success was made possible by access to his father's land, a loan from his brother, and a partnership with his sister's husband. A niece was married to James Newlin, whose family also owned a mill in Alamance; Holt and Newlin maintained close business ties as well as familial ties. Several members of Emily's family helped sell factory goods. Edwin Holt always stressed the importance of family in professional life; his practice of choosing relatives as business partners was adopted by his sons and grandsons through the nineteenth century.

Family relationships remained primary, but industrial development gradually transformed upper-class society in Alamance from one based on kinship to one based on class. Edwin Holt had learned from his father how water power could be harnessed to run a grist-mill and also something of the ways of a market economy. As he matured, however, he increasingly associated with pioneer mill-builder Henry Humphreys, whose example he determined to follow. Over time his industrial interests manifested more in common with Humphreys and other industrialists in the state than with his father, his brother William Rainey Holt, or eventually even with his brother-in-law and partner William Carrigan. William Holt supported his younger brother's mill, but the success of the Alamance Factory never prompted him to question his own commitment to staple crop agriculture based on slave labor. Carrigan was a mill man for more than a decade but was never completely convinced of manufacturing's future; he finally gave it up in the early fifties and moved with his five sons to seek their fortune growing cotton in Arkansas. Edwin Holt always remained close to his brother and brother-in-law, but the outcome of the Civil War underscored the divergences in their lives. After the war his grown sons, trained from youth to be mill men, became his closest associates, while William Holt and William Carrigan struggled to survive the destruction of their plantation way of life.

Women endured the choices their husbands made. Descendants recalled Edwin Holt giving credit for his success to his wife; if his tribute was anything more than empty hyperbole, it was likely a reflection on how well she discharged the responsibilities of her traditional sphere. In the South the dogma of social hierarchy that a slave society mandated overwhelmed the bourgeois individualism that in the North fostered, however slowly, a concept of women's rights. Unfortunately not enough evidence survives to closely analyze how Emily Holt, a woman from the upper South whose husband eagerly embraced the new economic order, responded to events such as the Seneca Falls convention, which in 1848 demanded that this new order include rights for women. No diary and very few letters written by her survive. The limited extant evidence indicates that Emily Farish imbibed at an early age the tenets of ideal womanhood. Unlike her husband, she rarely moved beyond a traditional society centered on kinship. Emily was never involved in her husband's mills and probably knew little about them. Edwin mentioned her in his diary several times a month, usually in reference to visits with relatives, her health, and the birth of her last three children.

In family size the Holts proved to be southern and traditional. Effort to limit family size was more common in the more urban areas of the North than in the South in the first half of the nine-teenth century. Great planters in North Carolina averaged seven children; Emily gave birth to ten. She oversaw their upbringing until they were old enough for their father to supervise their formal edu-cation. Edwin recorded several prolonged illnesses of his wife during the ten-year period he kept a diary, but usually she enjoyed excellent health and gave birth easily. A month before the arrival of her ninth child, Edwin recorded that "Emily planted Peas radishes & onions & sowed cabage." As Elizabeth Fox-Genovese has rightly warned, how-ever, historians must be as quick to recognize the use of metaphor in describing women's work as men's. Emily Holt oversaw a household that included (by 1860) fifty-one slaves. Most likely it was some of them who actually planted and sowed the vegetables while their mistress supervised.[5]

Jane Censer describes "short visits, parties, weddings and church attendance" as the primary means of diversion for the great planters. These were also primary sources of entertainment for the Holt family. Emily Holt's responsibility for overseeing the domestic life of a large family and extended household was demanding, but having slave women constantly available as servants made travel possible even when her children were small. For most elite women, women who for the most part had no involvement in the affairs of their husbands, travel was an integral part of their social lives, a means to maintain an extended network of kinship and friends and break the isolation of a rural farm or plantation. To be sure, in this rural society travel for Emily Holt meant relocating in homes simi-lar to her own. She never accompanied Edwin north, so only learned secondhand about places like New York City, Philadelphia, and Washington, D.C. Emily usually visited family, especially with her parents and siblings in Caswell County, but occasionally with close friends like the Ruffins as well. Sometimes she traveled with Edwin, particularly for family occasions such as weddings and fu-nerals, but more often she went without him, although always with male escort. Her husband's diary suggests that she was more likely to take her daughters visiting than her sons. In December 1843, for example, Emily took six-year-old Frances to visit the Farishes, leav-ing her sons, the youngest only eighteen months, at home. On an-

5. *Ashe, Biographical History of North Carolina*, vol. 7, 12; Censer, *North Carolina Planters and Their Children*, 24; Fox-Genovese, *Within the Plantation Household*, 128–29; Edwin Michael Holt Diary, February 15, 1847.

other occasion Frances went with both of her parents to visit their relatives in Lexington while her brothers and one-year-old sister remained at home.[6]

There is no evidence that until after the Civil War Emily traveled out of North Carolina. For women to travel far or for purposes other than to visit kin or close friends was rare, although not unknown. Two of Edwin's nieces took a trip to New York City in 1844 and on their return stopped in Alamance to tell their aunt and uncle about their journey there.[7]

These two nieces were among the numerous relatives and friends who assured the Holts a steady stream of company. They also had an extended family living close by. Until his mother died in 1839 and his father three years later, Edwin's parents resided across the road in the family's ancestral home. The Carrigans lived on the portion of the family estate that Nancy had inherited. In 1841 she died, survived by her husband and their five sons—Alfred, William, Robert, John, and James. Emily Holt, whose five oldest sons were close in age to the Carrigan boys, assumed the role of surrogate mother. Alfred Carrigan later recalled that "the two families were almost as one; my mother being dead, dear sweet Aunt Emily was reverenced and adored by both families as a mother."[8]

The extended Holt and Carrigan family that Emily Holt mothered included twelve boys and three girls. Edwin Holt mentioned his young children in his diary only at the time of their birth or when one was ill or injured. When an ox cart ran over four-year-old William and, the next year, a horse ran over ten-year-old Alexander and "knocked out two teeth and hurt him verry much," their father sent for the doctor and for several days carefully monitored their recovery. He was equally solicitous when two-year-old Lawrence contracted scarlet fever and frequently noted the health of the Carrigan boys as well.[9]

Holt assumed more responsibility for his children's upbringing when they began their formal education. Throughout the antebellum period the instruction of young children in Alamance was generally left to parental improvisation. Until they reached their early teens,

---

6. *Censer, North Carolina Planters and Their Children*, 2; Edwin Michael Holt Diary, January 1, 1844, April 31–May 8, 1846, and other entries.

7. Edwin Michael Holt Diary, October 28, 1844.

8. Rachel Holt, "Edwin Michael Holt," 16.

9. Edwin Michael Holt Diary, February 21–22, 1844, September 11–13, 1845, December 11–19, 1853, and other entries.

the Holt and Carrigan children were usually educated together in "old field schools" that their fathers helped to establish on a term-by-term basis. In 1844 they attended classes at Saint Paul's Church, which were taught by a young man Carrigan boarded and described as *"pious."* The next year Carrigan arranged for his nineteen-year-old nephew and namesake, William A. Carrigan, to teach an English school concentrating on reading, writing, and arithmetic. The Holts, Carrigan, and other parents paid two dollars for each child enrolled and also supplied firewood and anything else needed to run the facility. Almost half of the "scholars," who ranged in age from approximately six to fourteen, were Holts or Carrigans. Possibly because boys considerably outnumbered girls, after she spent a year at this school, Frances was sent to Caswell County, where she had a number of female cousins. The boys also attended a variety of schools. In 1848 some of the younger ones rode horseback to nearby Mebane to study in a field school there. James Holt, at fifteen too old to join them, was sent to board in Hawfields, halfway between his home and Hillsborough. After James visited a brother and cousins at the Caldwell Institute in Hillsborough, one of them reported that he "dislikes his situation very much and that will deter anyone from learning though he studied under King Solomon himself."[10]

Soon after, James was enrolled at Caldwell as well. This Presbyterian boarding school was considered one of the most prestigious in the state. The oldest Holt boys went when they were fourteen or fifteen and remained for three or four years. Possibly because he was their sole parent and traveled frequently, Carrigan sent his sons at a younger age. The Holt and Carrigan boys, often accompanied by their fathers, went for the first session in early January, remained until June, and then returned for the second session from mid-July to late November. Rules published in 1835, a few years before these boys entered, required that all professors be Presbyterian, that students "attend social worship twice a day and preaching on the Sabbath," as well as study the Bible and catechism, and that faculty dismiss students who were "immoral or disorderly." Like most academies of the time, Caldwell particularly emphasized Greek and Latin classics as well as instruction in mathematics and philosophy. Required reading included Xenophon in Greek and Salust, Ovid, and Livy in Latin. To be admitted students had to submit testimonials to their character,

10. School records in Carrington Papers; William Carrigan to nephew, February 10, 1845; William Carrigan to William A. Carrigan, September 17, 1848, Carrigan Papers.

and to remain they had to refrain from visiting "taverns, tipling houses, theatrical exhibitions, dancing assemblies, horse racing, and circus."[11] But it was class privilege more than religious piety that elite boarding schools like Caldwell most effectively nourished.

Local and kinship networks were eroded, and regional and even statewide class ties grew as children from wealthy families all over North Carolina and occasionally from other southern states lived together and established ties they retained as adults. Social societies formed in the academies bound elite male students together in a commitment to common values. Thomas Holt praised the society he joined as one of "honor and happiness" where "manhood shall have taken its stand," with members who stood for "God, their country and its liberty."[12] Honor, Thomas clearly understood, was the privilege of white elite males. Along with piety and the classics, the Holt and Carrigan boys and their classmates learned their gender, race, and class privileges.

Boarding schools generally reinforced assumptions that girls, once grown up, would attend to traditional feminine roles. Christie Farnum's study of antebellum female academies in North Carolina suggests that socializing girls to their proper gender roles was a major preoccupation of these schools. But the very nature of boarding schools meant that proper roles were defined in the context of class and race. By bringing girls from elite white families together, academies also taught them to view themselves as members of a privileged class. Frances Holt was only twelve when she went to Mrs. Burwell's in Hillsborough. In time she switched to Mrs. Edgeworth's in Greensboro where she remained until she was nearly eighteen. Although, as Censer points out, "southern historians have probably overemphasized the 'ornamental' aspects of female instruction," these schools did offer girls a somewhat different curriculum from that of boys at schools like Caldwell. At Mrs. Burwell's girls studied academic subjects—including English composition, history, geography, mathematics, Latin, French, moral philosophy, and Christianity—in the morning and "ornamentals"—notably music, painting, and needlework—in the afternoon. The Holt girls received an education superior to that of most white boys in North Carolina at the time. Despite their mathematics and Latin, however, nothing

11. Charles L. Raper, *The Church and Private Schools of North Carolina* (Greensboro, 1898), 104–105; "Plan of the Caldwell Institute Presbytery of Orange County," October 1835; William Carrigan to William A. Carrigan, September 17, 1848, Carrigan Papers.

12. Thomas Holt to William A. Carrigan, April 20, 1848, Carrigan Papers.

in their boarding school experience challenged the dogma of their proper sphere.[13]

The girls at Mrs. Burwell's were closely supervised; they could go into Hillsborough on Saturday afternoons but only if chaperoned. The school's founder claimed that her intention was "to teach the young Ladies to 'think,' " but apparently she did not intend that they think much about challenging their ascribed sphere. Mrs. Burwell wrote one of her pupils of her hope that "you possess *that* which in the sight of God is of great price, a meek & quiet spirit."[14]

Edwin Holt and William Carrigan continued to closely supervise the educations of their children as they reached adolescence. They often took them to and from school, sat in on their examinations, and bought their books, clothes, and supplies. In 1847 Carrigan lamented that he had been unable to return from Philadelphia until shortly before Christmas and therefore had "only a few days to fix the boys to send them back to school." For the first session that year Holt spent three dollars on supplies for fifteen-year-old Thomas, including an arithmetic, a Morse geography, an English grammar, a comb, cowhide, soap, ink, shirt buttons, and steel pens. For Alfred he purchased a ready-made coat, a silk cravat, black ribbon, a geometry, a picture frame, matches, candle snuffers, fiddle strings, and a desk lock, and also gave him two dollars in cash. School books Holt and Carrigan bought for their children included a Greek lexicon and dictionary, a Morse dictionary, an English grammar, and a trigonometry book. Holt also bought books for his children to read at home, including a hymnal, a history by Wooster, *Paradise Lost,* and *Mitchell's Atlas.*[15]

Rules for the Caldwell Institute suggest an austere and strict environment. Letters written by the Carrigans and Holts while schoolboys there reveal, however, that in reality the school often had to cater to the demands of the wealthy boys it served. The Carrigans brought their dogs and firearms to school; in 1848 Robert accidentally discharged his gun, burning his eyes and nose. Although careless, he could count himself as "among the best in the class," while

13. Christie Anne Farnham, *The Education of the Southern Belle: Higher Education and Student Socialization in the Antebellum South* (New York, 1994), 2; Censer, *North Carolina Planters and Their Children,* 45–47; Pamphlet, "The Burwell School," Hillsborough Historical Society.

14. "Burwell School."

15. Edwin Michael Holt Diary, numerous entries; William Carrigan to nephew, February 7, 1848, Carrigan Papers; Store Ledger, vols. 1–3, Alamance Cotton Mill Records.

despairing that his younger brother John was "a very bad boy" who "goes his own way." When John complained that he was prevented from studying because of headaches caused by having no meat at breakfast, his father forced the school to provide the food he wanted by threatening to board him somewhere else. But meat did not make John a scholar; nearly two years later his father agreed that his fourth son could leave school before finishing and come home to work.[16]

Thomas Holt also came to hate school. When he was sixteen he described Hillsborough as "the dullest place almost on the globe," and a year later still found it "one of the dullest places in the Union and if I should use vulgarity the arse hole of creation." He elaborated his charge by claiming that "times here are dull, dull, verry dull." When his father was in Hillsborough for a session of court, he visited Thomas and promised him a gold watch if he would study. However, he allowed his oldest son to leave before the end of a term because he needed his help at home. When Alfred went to work in his father's store his younger brother reported "he is very well pleased with it, as he did not like to go to school."[17]

Alfred and Thomas found Caldwell dull, but their years there were significant in establishing them as members of a privileged class. Boarding schools also reinforced the sharp delineation of male and female roles. Adolescent boys and girls, living in isolation from one another, often established passionate same-sex relationships. Sixteen-year-old Thomas Holt struck up a friendship with William A. Carrigan (the schoolteacher mentioned earlier), five years his senior, so emotional that he wrote "my love for you is so great that it cannot be expressed in words." He offered this friend an arithmetic book "in rememberance of me" in which was written several times "the name of your most sincere and worthy friend."[18]

Friendships between young women and men outside of courtship were sharply proscribed. Because his Carrigan cousins were all male and his closest sister six years younger, Thomas was not even very experienced in pursuing friendships with female relatives. As a result he generally viewed females of his age and class as abstracted ideals to be pursued romantically. When he was sixteen

16. William Carrigan to William A. Carrigan, February 7, March 26, 1848, Robert Carrigan to cousin, February 5, 1849, Robert Carrigan to William A. Carrigan, February 26, 1851, Carrigan Papers.
17. Thomas M. Holt to William A. Carrigan, August 22, 1849, April 20, 1848, Carrigan Papers
18. Ibid., August 22, October 14, 1847.

Thomas wrote of a "fine time with a young lady" and recalled that he left the rest of the ladies "for the other boys to attend to and I confined myself to one particular one." Several months later he wrote "I am going with some ladys on the mountains to get flowers," the only indication that he socialized with a group of young women rather than pursuing a courtship with one. When he was nearly nineteen, Thomas reminisced with William A. Carrigan about the time the two of them "sat beneath the shady oaks of Alamance and cool[ed] our sweating brows talking and uterly lost in imagination about the lovely beings." Carrigan concluded "that T. Holt had his thoughts very much inclined toward the Feminine gender." During his year in Chapel Hill, however, Thomas concluded that he need look elsewhere for a suitable wife as "I do think they have a hard set of feminines there."[19]

Adolescent males like Thomas Holt may have thought a great deal about adolescent females, but their lives were starkly separate. Before they began working for their family's mill or stores, the activities of the Holts and their Carrigan cousins were fairly typical of young males growing up on southern plantations. During one of their vacations Carrigan wrote that his sons "had a fine time of it at hom, broke Leo to set Partridges very well and had their guns a going." With the hound dog Leo, they hunted possums at night and rabbits, squirrels, and turkeys by day. In 1849 the Carrigan boys acquired twin colts, which they trained, and a dog they named Bug who quickly grew "very large" and so "fierce" he "will bite anyone who comes into the yard." Robert described Bug as "a noble fellow" but lamented that since he was not well trained it was "almost impossible to prevent him following us to church and other such places."[20]

The Holts also grew up with horses and dogs and looked forward to hunting during vacation. When he was sixteen Thomas wrote William A. Carrigan, "I shall miss you verry much then in squirrel hunting and every thing else. Cad [Alfred] has got him a fine double barrel gun which I expect to slay the squirrel with." Around the time he left school to work for his father, Alfred joined a group of young men on a trip to Pilot Mountain; his brother explained, "They

19. Ibid., October 14, 1847, April 20, 1848, March 25, 1850, William M. Carrigan to cousin, May 13, 1849, Carrigan Papers; Thomas Holt to William L. Scott, May 4, 1851, William L. Scott Papers, Manuscripts Division, Perkins Library, Duke University.
20. William Carrigan to William A. Carrigan, February 7, 1848, March 26, 1849, Robert Carrigan to William A. Carrigan, March 12, 1849, William Carrigan to cousin, May 13, 1849, Carrigan Papers.

are going like wagoners with guns and they will make it somewhat a hunting excursion." Alfred was described "as lazy as ever bragging on *game cocks*." He more positively described his delight in raising thirty young chickens, which he thought were "of the best blood in the state."[21]

From an early age, however, Alfred Holt and his brothers were raised to spin cotton, not to raise chickens. Although the boys lived close together, were sent to the same schools, and enjoyed typical rural activities, there were significant differences in the ways William Carrigan and Edwin Holt raised their sons. In 1849 Alfred Holt wrote that during vacation the Carrigans "hunt most of the time," implying that hunting was less consuming for him and his brothers. More significantly, the Holts clearly imbibed from an early age their father's goal that they become mill men; none of them seriously questioned it. In contrast, none of the Carrigan boys seriously considered becoming manufacturers. Carrigan struggled to educate all five of his sons. In 1848, with one in college and three in boarding school, he complained that although he could not afford to send them all to school, "I dont see what else I can do with them I cant make them work." When Alfred Carrigan decided he wanted to farm, his brother William determined to train for a law career, which "calls in to active exercise humor and talent of the highest cast." He also concluded that "if this is to be my plough for life it cannot be in North Carolina. I cannot wish or expect to leave my native state but Pa has 5 sons all of whom he intends to give a Collegiate education and for the study of a profession it will be no use to them here. Could he without great sacrifice leave for Arkansas, I would gladly see him imigrate."[22]

His second son was persuasive. Soon after William Jr. despaired of North Carolina, William Carrigan sold his land and share in the Alamance Factory to Edwin Holt and moved his household to Arkansas. Typical of many North Carolinians but in sharp contrast to his brother-in-law, Carrigan was convinced that there was greater opportunity for his sons as cotton planters or professionals in the developing Southwest than in manufacturing in North Carolina. Although he had initiated the move, his son William temporarily

21. Thomas Holt to William A. Carrigan, October 4, 1847, Alfred Carrigan to cousin, March 29, 1848, Alfred Holt to William A. Carrigan, May 8, 1849, Carrigan Papers.

22. Alfred Holt to William A. Carrigan, May 8, 1849, William Carrigan to nephew, July 24, 1848, William Carrigan to William A. Carrigan, March, 1850, Carrigan Papers.

remained behind to finish his education at the University of North Carolina. In his senior thesis, "Beyond the Mississippi," he defended the West as "the eldorado for the young and enterprising," and condemned North Carolinians who tried to discourage young men from going there as "both selfish and ignoble."[23] It is at least possible that he had his uncle, Edwin Holt, in mind.

In contrast to Carrigan, Holt was not concerned that his sons acquire a college education or train for a profession; he wanted them to become mill men and to that end he viewed practical training as more efficacious than earning a college degree. He encouraged them when they were eighteen or nineteen to begin seriously training for a career in manufacturing. All seven heeded his advice.[24]

After he left Caldwell, Alfred began clerking in the mill store and traveling, often accompanying his uncle to Petersburg, Virginia, to gain experience in marketing. In 1851, Alfred established A. A. Holt and Company Dry Goods, the first of the numerous businesses formed by Edwin Holt's sons. In 1856 Dun and Bradstreet described Alfred as a "1st rate man & citizen."[25]

From an early age Thomas was also anxious to follow his father's example. While still at the Caldwell Institute he confided in William A. Carrigan a secret, previously shared only with his father, that he wanted "when I get old enough, to put up a store in Fayetvill" where he would merchandise for Holt and Carrigan; he arrogantly promised his older friend the position of assistant. After graduating from Caldwell, Thomas attended the University of North Carolina in Chapel Hill for over a year, until in 1851 his father sent him to Philadelphia to train in merchandizing. Although a few years earlier Thomas had been eager to leave boarding school and begin a business career, he was happy at the university. Not yet twenty years old, he clearly reflected the heavy hand of his father's sense of responsibility. While in Philadelphia he wrote a former college classmate, "I much prefer a college life to the one I am living at present, but I could not be at college always so I might as well commence at one time as another." Thomas sought news of college society from

23. William M. Carrigan, "Beyond the Mississippi" (senior thesis, University of North Carolina, 1852), n.p.

24. Alfred was just beginning his career in textiles and commerce when he died at the age of twenty-eight. Alexander, who struggled with alcoholism much of his adult life, never owned his own mill but did work for his father and was a "silent partner" with some of his nephews. Thomas, James, William, Banks, and Lawrence all became successful mill owners.

25. Edwin Michael Holt Diary, April 6, 1848; Dun and Company Credit Ratings for Alamance County, 1856.

the place he called "the Hill," because "these things greatly interest me. . . . It would afford me much pleasure to be at your commencement," he added "but as I am a business man now, & not a man of pleasure I must only go where my business directs." Thomas did find some pleasure in Philadelphia; when he heard Jenny Lind sing he enthused that "she can best anything I have ever heard," as "she jerked me smack out of my boots." But with business dull he also complained "I get the blues like hell." Perhaps a two-week visit from his father and then a visit home in May, arriving the day after his brother Lawrence was born, helped cheer Thomas up. He returned home from Philadelphia for good in the fall of 1851 and began working in the Alamance Factory.[26]

None of his brothers spent as much time training in the North as Thomas, but until the Civil War the family maintained close contacts there, especially in Philadelphia. Through the 1850s the older sons frequently traveled north together, usually in the spring and fall. Thomas and James went in September 1852 and again in March 1853. Alfred and Thomas made the next three trips together while James, seriously ill for months, remained at home. These experiences enabled Holt's sons to oversee marketing of their yarn and cloth and buy goods for their stores, and even more importantly, to establish and maintain close contact with northern entrepreneurs.[27]

When he acquired the Granite Factory in 1860, Thomas Holt had been married for three years. When he and his brothers entered their twenties, romantic musings on "the delicate beings" gave way to finding wives suitable to their social standing. Censer suggests that among North Carolina's elite "in marriage choices, as in career selection, parents continued to exercise authority over young adults increasingly by indirection." Extant letters written by the youngest Holt daughter and her future husband (discussed in a subsequent chapter) reveal that, at least in her case, the parents did not dictate the choice of a spouse. If the Holts did not dictate, however, none of their nine children who married made what they would have considered an unsuitable choice. Eight of the Holt children married people from within their parents' circle of interrelated families in Alamance and Caswell Counties. William, Mary, and Lawrence married

26. Thomas Holt to William Scott, May 4, 1851, William Scott Papers; Edwin Michael Holt Diary, May 18, 1851; William Carrigan to W. A. Carrigan Jr., June 27, 1853, Carrigan Papers.
27. Edwin Michael Holt Diary, numerous entries. For the years after Holt's diary ends in 1854 there is no documentation that his sons continued regular visits north but most likely they did.

first cousins, a practice, Censer points out, that did distinguish the great planters from northern elites; all but one of the other six who married were involved in a form of marriage anthropologists have called sibling exchange.[28] James and Thomas married sisters, Mary and Frances married cousins, and Banks married a niece of Alfred's wife. These marriage patterns reveal that although the Holts were in significant ways becoming a modern bourgeois family, kinship and family ties remained primary determinants of marital choices.

In the summer of 1850 an uncle reported that Alfred Holt "is to be married in Sept. to a Miss Mebane of the Hawfields who is an excellent woman." For over a week before their son's marriage, Edwin recorded "Emily making preparation for the wedding." Alfred's ceremony and that of a cousin the day before occasioned three days and nights of celebration. Thomas described the revelry in a letter that offers extraordinary insight into the assumptions of elite white males to an entitlement based on their race and gender. "Words cannot express," he wrote William A. Carrigan, "the pleasure and enjoyment I realized"; yet he proceeded to try. Named an attendant at his cousins' wedding, he "performed with Miss Caroline Graves, the daughter of the Hon. Calvin Graves from Caswell." Thomas effusively described the next day, the day of his brother's wedding, and the two days after:

> I took my gal in my buggy and had a glorious ride about 25 miles. I tell you Will, I chatted her from the ash corner to the loftiest sumit of the Alps and I stuck soft chat to her in style, I tell I was in hog heven eaten cold bacon, get out Gouge if I was not. Well we got to Old Mebane and brother Alf was married about 1/2 after 7 or 7 oclock, and we had a glorious party that night. Next morning came with it beautiful rays and we got something to put in our craws and then got in our buggy and [vehicles?] and went up home about 19 miles. I had my gal with me again, and went on with the same conversation I was upon the day before, it is the greates wonder in the world that I did not just bust rite open. I felt a d——d site happier than the married folks. Well we got to the old mans and had a fine dance very near all the night. I tell you I set to her like a pig upon a tater pelin, but morning came again but what a change it was drizzling rain.

A year before, a cousin had written of Thomas that, concerning women, "were I to meet with as much disappointment as he I would

28. Censer, *North Carolina Planters and Their Children*, 65, 87.

hang up my harp and bid its notes ever be attuned to those of the weeping willow." Thomas, however, had a rather higher opinion of himself, writing, "Bill I tell you I am a perfect stud monkey among the white gals, black ones too sometimes." He bragged that at his brother's wedding party "I come it over some of their yellow maids the night at Pa's. I had on white pants and I got tired dancing so I thought I would attend to the yellow ones some. I went out and come it and dirtyed the knees of my pants like h——l so I had to put on black ones, and every personed noticed it but I dident care a dam."[29]

Darlene Clark Hine's charge that the sexual vulnerability of black women is frequently observed but rarely analyzed is only beginning to be addressed. Melton McLaurin's study *Celia: A Slave*, for example, graphically reveals "the power of the white patriarch" over enslaved females. Thomas's letter speaks to this power as well. He revealed a climate not unique to the one night he described. This Holt son didn't hesitate to turn to the black women when he pleased, he made no effort to hide his activity, and his indifference to the response of his family and friends indicates their toleration. Perhaps only Emily Holt responded with more than indifference or amusement. Corroborating evidence that female slaves on the Holt plantation were vulnerable to the sexual demands of the men who enslaved them is provided by a story passed down through the generations of one black family. Alex Haley, a descendant of one of the Holts' female slaves, described in his family biography how she capitalized on the anger that Emily Holt and so many white women were forced to suppress to effect her own sale to the plantation of her intended husband.[30]

The different responses of Emily Holt and her son Thomas to the sexual exploitation of enslaved women reveals the hypocrisy of southern sexual morality. Thomas Holt had little reason to fear his parents' disapproval when he had sexual relations with slave women in the quarters; privately he could brag to a friend that he was "sometimes a stud monkey" who "come it over some of their yellow maids" and even offer a hint of his activities to his parents and

29. William Carrigan to William A. Carrigan, July 27, 1850, May 13, 1849, Edwin Michael Holt Diary, September 1850, Thomas Holt to William A. Carrigan, October 4, 1850, Carrigan Papers; Edwin Michael Holt Diary, September 2, 1850.

30. Darlene Clark Hine, "Rape and the Inner Lives of Black Women in the Middle West," *Signs* 14 (1989): 912–13; Melton A. McLaurin, *Celia: A Slave* (Athens, 1991), 137; Alex Haley, *Roots* (Garden City, N.Y., 1976), 500–505.

other relatives when he changed his soiled pants in the middle of a party. But when his mother was confronted with a broader public disclosure of her son's activities, a favored slave was dispensable.

Sexual morality was tightly racially bound. Only eight months after his brother's wedding party, Thomas wrote from Philadelphia that although "you can have fine times here with the women if one desires it . . . I never indulge in anything of kind." He insisted, "I am strictly moral," although conceding "the temptations are many and d——d strong."[31]

The party for Alfred was held in the Holts' new home, Locust Grove, which Edwin had built for his family the year before. Previously, even as the family grew to include nine children, they had lived in the small house he had built across the road from his parents when he married Emily. Locust Grove, built adjacent to this house, has been described by an architectural historian as "a significant new influence on the development of antebellum architecture," in the South. Holt was already acquiring timber from a neighbor when he saw a design by A. J. Davis, a prominent New York architect, featured in the *Horticulturist*. He wrote Davis, who had already designed a house for John M. Morehead, "I desire a plain building" and reminded the northern architect of southern peculiarities including the necessity of separating the kitchen from the main dwelling and building "our sleeping apartments to be more roomy and better ventilated than the North." The result was the first house built in Alamance not of the vernacular. Holt contracted Eli Denny, a local builder described by Alfred Holt as "much of a gentleman," to supervise the work. In contrast to the mansions his children would later build for conspicuous display, Edwin Holt's more modest dwelling was built primarily to accommodate a growing family. It has been described as "modern in design, yet modest in proportions and finish" and as "not a symbol of wealth and power but as residence suitable for the life of a country gentleman."[32]

Emily Holt may have been more eager to have the new home reflect her husband's financial success than he was. She took charge of much of the decorating, even drawing up sketches for decorative window grills. She had been impressed by the work of Tom Murray,

31. Thomas Holt to William L. Scott, May 4, 1851, William Scott Papers.
32. Carl R. Lounsbury, *Alamance County Architectural Heritage* (Graham, N.C., 1980), 33–34, 54; Edwin M. Holt to A. J. Davis, March 2, 1849, A. J. Davis Diary, February 3, 1844 (xerox copies at the Alamance County Historical Museum).

a skilled blacksmith enslaved nearby, and hired him to do the work. While working for the Holts, Tom began courting Reny, one of their slaves. It was in order to live with the skilled man who decorated the Holts' new home that this slave woman forced her mistress to confront the behavior of her sons.[33]

Edwin Holt's sons were disciplined by his ambition for them. That discipline did not preclude sexual exploitation of black women before they married, but it did demand that they marry into socially acceptable families. In October 1855 Thomas married Louisa Matilda Moore and a few months later James married her sister, Laura Cameron Moore, daughters of a wealthy landowner in Caswell County, and nieces of Holt's partner in the Hillsborough store. The marriages of their Carrigan cousins with two other Moore sisters further solidified the ties among the three families. Thomas assured economic as well as familial ties with his wife's family by making Louisa's brother, Adolphus (Dolph) Moore, a partner in the Granite Factory.

Marriage was the primary determinant of how adult females ordered their lives. While their brothers were raised for careers as mill men and as young men were sent north to learn the ways of bourgeois capitalism, the Holt daughters were raised for lives similar to those of their mother and even their grandmothers. There are no extant letters written by Frances, Mary, or Emma from their school years and little written about them survives. Clearly they were especially close to their mother and probably spent much of their time home from school with her. She sometimes took her daughters visiting and escorted them to and from school; there is no evidence that she was similarly involved with her sons. Because Edwin Holt's diary ends when Frances was only seventeen, it reveals little about his relationships with his daughters as they became adults. He occasionally bought things for Frances as she entered her teens, including shoes, a shawl, and a bible, but much less often than he purchased necessities for his adolescent sons. He did, however, play a major role in overseeing his daughters' educations, escorting them to school more frequently than their mother did and sitting in on their exams.[34]

After completing their formal education around the age of eighteen, the first priority for elite young women was to find a suitable husband. Frances did not marry until 1862 when she was twenty-

33. Haley, *Roots*, 500–505.
34. Alamance County Store Ledger, vol. 1, Alamance Cotton Mill Records; Edwin Michael Holt Diary, numerous entries.

five, an age by which almost 90 percent of the daughters of great planters in the state had married. In the North teaching was becoming an increasingly common way for well-educated young women to pass the years between school and marriage; elites in the South, however, generally remained opposed to any form of work for their daughters outside of the home. There is no hint that Frances or either of her sisters ever considered teaching or any paid work. Several extant letters, written in the summer of 1857 by a family friend whom Frances apparently considered a potential match, reveal something of her life-style during the time between school and marriage. In the spring of 1857 Frances visited for a week with the Mebanes, her sister-in-law's family, and left Frank Mebane convinced of her interest in a courtship. Two weeks later Frances met him in Graham and asked that he take her and Mary to Company Shops because, or at least he assumed, they wanted to buy "paint" (makeup). Neither her father's wealth nor close family ties with the Mebanes, however, assured Frances's success. Frank was secretly courting another at the time and kidded his sweetheart about this other flirtation. After seeing Frances in June, he wrote, "I have some mighty funny things to tell you when we meet." Apparently Frances was quite open about her religious beliefs, which to him were "funny and ludicrous." When he did not see Frances again that month, Frank joked, "I expect she will catch a beau while she is in the mountains."[35]

Frances did not catch a beau in the mountains and for five more years sought a suitable husband. Frank Mebane's letters offer hints about her activities during those years. In the three-month period covered she spent a week with friends and a month in the mountains, suggesting that visiting was for her, as it was for her mother, central to social life.[36] But the mountain trip reveals that, in contrast to her mother's generation, elite women of Frances's age also traveled for vacation, to spend time in a place chosen for desirability, such as the mountains in the summer, rather than exclusively to visit close friends or relatives.

Frances continued living at home until she married; during those years her closest ties remained within her family. Alexander,

35. Censer, *North Carolina Planters and Their Children*, 91; Fox-Genovese, *Within the Plantation Household*, 46; Frank Mebane to Cousin Fannie, May 11, 28, June 8, July 7, August 22, 1857, Mebane Family Papers, SHC.

36. Frank Mebane to Cousin Fannie, August 22, 1857, Mebane Family Papers.

who had the greatest difficulty conforming to his father's model, remained closer to his oldest sister than to any of his other siblings.[37] Frances named three of her own children for her youngest sister and her two youngest brothers, a hint that during these years between the end of her formal education around 1855 and her marriage to Thomas Slade in 1862 she assumed the role of surrogate mother to her younger siblings.

Women in the Holt family rarely visited the mills that so consumed their brothers and husbands. On one infrequent visit, Frances and Thomas's wife, Louisa, both "dressed fit to kill," approached Thomas while he worked in his dyehouse. When her husband, covered with the grime of the factory, started to embrace her, Louisa first told the "horrid man" she didn't recognize not to touch her. Clearly the reality of mill work was almost invisible to these elite women.[38]

Largely excluded from their business affairs, the Holt women did join the men in their family in religious activities. Religion, like family structure and distinct gender roles, served to tie people in antebellum Alamance County to a traditional premodern past even as that way of life was being eroded by industrialization. In the fall of 1854 Edwin Holt recorded in his diary that "Thomas, Alfred and Fanny professed Religion." The conversion of his three children at a camp meeting reveals the influence of evangelical religion on people still rooted in a rural world. When Alfred died four years later, he was described in an obituary as "a professed follower of Jesus Christ and a member of the Presbyterian Church."[39] By the time Thomas and Frances and their siblings reached middle age, however, they had shed the emotionalism of their youth to become members of churches that symbolized their elite status in Alamance County.

By the mid–nineteenth century, religion in the Piedmont was losing its ethnic identity and increasingly was organized by class. The first Holts were German Lutherans, an identity they had carried across the ocean. Intermarriage, however, particularly with Scotch-Irish Presbyterians, challenged theological dogmas. By the 1830s conversions were swelling the ranks of the Baptists and Methodists at the expense of both Lutherans and Presbyterians.

Until 1860 Edwin Holt was a member of Saint Paul's Lutheran Church near his home, but he frequently attended a variety of churches of different denominations elsewhere and worshiped with

37. Alamance County Wills, Will of Alexander Holt.
38. Hughes, *Development of the Textile Industry in Alamance*, 11–12.
39. Edwin Michael Holt Diary, October 11, 1854; *Hillsborough Recorder*, March 3, 1858.

a wide spectrum of white (and possibly sometimes black) society. Holt's church attendance was sporadic; some months he went every Sunday, but at other times he traveled on the sabbath or stayed at home. Diary entries reveal a religious sensibility. He concluded 1844, for example, by writing "may God in his mercy continue to bless and preserve us during the coming year and make us more deserving his bountiful blessings is my Prayer." But it was the tempered religion of a tempered man. Although he occasionally attended camp meetings, often highly emotional manifestations of the Great Revival that swept the country in the early nineteenth century, he never revealed in his diary that he was personally as affected by revivalism as his three children were. Some of the religious and educated elite in Alamance, as elsewhere, were critical of the excessive emotionalism and disorder generated at these meetings. A young woman attending the one where the Holt children professed religion reported that there were many moaners and many converts—she singled out Alfred Holt—and that "Mr. Hughes tried to keep excitement down, but could not."[40]

Camp meetings generally included all classes and sometimes both races, but religious democracy steadily eroded in organized churches. Elites like the Holts increasingly separated themselves from the religious practices of the poorer folk, and especially from their workers. In 1853, after John Carrigan attended a revival held at the factory with his brother, he wrote, "We went to the Factory to preaching & they got to shouting & praying about him [his brother Robert] & scared him half to death he could not get out of the house there is but three girls at the Factory but what have professed religion I was there last night Bud had prayer meeting and all the hollering I ever herd It is nothing more than a frolic to me."[41] John Carrigan represented young elite men who were beginning to relate religious behavior to class standing. The conversion of their Holt cousins the following year reveals, however, that the division was not as complete as it would become in the late nineteenth century.

Theories about class stratification in bourgeois societies have often associated religion with social control. Paul Johnson, in his study of industrialization in upstate New York, suggests that the bourgeoisie there used their position in churches to enforce temperance, a measure considered desirable for keeping workers sober and

40. Edwin Michael Holt Diary, December 31, 1844; Fannie Thompson to sister and brother, October 12, 1854, Allen Papers.
41. John Carrigan to William A. Carrigan, February 14 [?], 1853, Carrigan Papers.

reliable. There is no evidence that before the mid-fifties Edwin Holt was concerned about alcohol consumption; at least as late as 1854 he was proud of the "very superior" corn whiskey that he could supply his friends with. But the emergence of a working class affected the easy toleration of alcohol typical of rural premodern societies. In 1853 a "great temperance speaker" was brought to speak in the factory of Holt's kinsman James Newlin. The same year the father praised his whiskey, his son Alfred joined approximately one hundred men and women from Graham in signing a petition demanding that "since the use of intoxicating liquors is exceedingly injurious to good morals and by no means calculated to advance the cause of Education," the city refuse a license for anyone to sell it in the city. Alfred was influenced by his own emotional conversion and possibly also by his wife, who would spend the rest of her life trying to get her three sons to profess religion and refrain from drinking.[42] Already an ambitious businessman before his death at the age of twenty-eight, it is also possible that Alfred also perceived a relationship between temperance and a disciplined, and therefore profitable, work force.

Apparently it was the oldest son's influence that prompted his parents and most of his siblings to join the First Presbyterian Church in Graham; after he married, Lawrence followed his wife's example and became an Episcopalian. At least into the seventies, however, the family maintained ties with Saint Paul's Lutheran Church.[43] Only in the last decades of the nineteenth century did organized religion become for the Holts clearly tied to their class standing.

Richard D. Brown, in his study of modernization, argues that by the 1830s "an American variant of the modern personality syndrome" was fully in evidence. The chief characteristics of this type, he claims, were "belief in the capacity to improve the natural and social environments; openness to new experience; personal ambition for oneself and one's children, to be realized by time-thrift and planning; and an increasing independence from traditional authority figures."[44] The nineteenth-century modern type Brown describes is

42. Paul E. Johnson, *A Shopkeeper's Millennium: Society and Revivals in Rochester, New York, 1815–1837* (New York, 1978); Edwin Holt to Webb and Douglas, January 17, 1854, McLaws Papers, SHC; Fannie Thompson to brother, June 21, 1853, John Mebane Allen Papers; "Petition to the City of Graham," in Hamilton, ed., *Papers of Thomas Ruffin,* 506–507; Mrs. B. F. Meane to daughter, November 14, 1889, Mebane Family Papers.

43. Eugene Holt, *Edwin Holt and His Descendants,* 39; Ledger Book, 1872, Alamance Mill Collection.

44. Richard Brown, *Modernization: The Transformation of American Life, 1600–1865* (New York, 1976), 95.

generally associated with the North, but the type was not unknown in the antebellum South. The life of Edwin Holt, who by the 1830s fitted almost exactly Brown's description, suggests that studies of modernization and regions must be more nuanced, more willing to acknowledge and accommodate exceptions.

By the eve of the Civil War Edwin Holt had enjoyed over twenty years of profitable manufacturing in Alamance; his oldest sons were launching careers of their own as mill men. Although his wife and daughters remained more rooted in the ways of traditional rural society, their lives also were affected. Many associations remained largely agrarian and traditional, but the Holts were both creating and becoming part of a protobourgeois class in the Piedmont. In 1860 over three hundred men, women, and children worked for the Holts and other mill owners in Alamance. They too were early members of a new industrial class.

3

Those Who Might Otherwise Be Wretched

WORKERS IN THE ALAMANCE FACTORY, 1837–1860

In 1849 Benson J. Lossing, traveling around the country in search of material for a history of the American Revolution, passed through the little village that had grown up around the Alamance Factory. In his book he recalled crossing "the Allamance, at the cotton factory of Holt and Carrigan," where "around this mill quite a village of neat log-houses, occupied by the operatives, were collected, and every thing had the appearance of thrift. I went in, and was pleased to see the hands of intelligent white females employed in a usual occupation." Lossing praised the little North Carolina village as "a real blessing, present and prospective, for it gives employment and comfort to many poor girls who might otherwise be wretched."[1]

Mill villages were a novelty in this part of the country in the 1840s. Although Lossing concluded that the one across the "Allamance" was a refuge for poor girls, the limited extant evidence suggests that a variety of people, not all of them poor or potentially wretched, worked in the early Alamance Factory. In the early nineteenth century, factories were so new and rare in the Piedmont that rigid theories concerning who should work in them only slowly evolved and were not always translated into practice.

Southern mill men looked north for models of labor organization just as they did for technological expertise. They were most familiar with the Lowell system, one where young women were

1. Benson Lossing, *The Pictorial Field-Book of the Revolution*, vol. 2 (New York, 1860), 388.

ALAMANCE

lodged in carefully supervised boardinghouses. Lowell, however, was atypical in the North. Most northern mills followed the Rhode Island model, recruiting families that could contribute several members and housing them in single family units. These mill villages included men and boys, although women and girls made up the majority of residents. In the 1830s, for example, females accounted for more than two-thirds of the people in John Slater's East Village in western Massachusetts, and more than two-thirds of the workers lived in families that included at least one other worker.[2]

Most southern mill men, whose plants were more like Slater's and the other small ones in western Massachusetts than like Lowell, also came to prefer the Rhode Island or family system of labor. William Gregg, the most successful textile manufacturer in antebellum South Carolina, tried and failed to copy the Lowell system; one of his contemporaries concluded that "girls were unwilling to leave the home of their birth for strange places; and it was soon found that the boardinghouse plan would not be sustained." Gregg finally decided that the family system of labor was superior anyway for the "great moral restraint" it provided in contrast to one in which "large numbers of young females are collected together from a wide range of country, away from parents' care." Similarly, in North Carolina board members of the Salem Factory determined that although "families that can furnish 3 or 4 good hands will remain the most desirable help," they would also build a boardinghouse for single females. But their young female boarders also failed to live up to the idealized image of the Lowell girls. The Salem Factory owners frequently complained that these unattached women were prone to set their own hours and to leave whenever they wished; too often they quit altogether, leaving the mill chronically short of trained workers.[3]

Edwin Holt, perhaps profiting from his friend Francis Fries's failure to emulate Lowell, joined most southern mill men in turning to the Rhode Island system, recruiting families to live in the houses he built around the Alamance Factory and expecting them to furnish several hands apiece. A grandson remembered that "his general pol-

2. Jonathan Prude, *The Coming of Industrial Order: Town and Factory Life in Rural Massachusetts, 1810–1860* (New York, 1983), 86–87.
3. Broadus Mitchell, *William Gregg: Factory Master of the Old South* (Chapel Hill, 1928), 55–56; Salem Manufacturing Company Minutes, November 27, 1837, February 7, 8, April 28, May 8, June 19, November 26, 1838, September 11, 1839, September 25, October 31, 1840, July 1, November 10, 1841, Moravian Archives.

icy was not to hire an individual but a family, and he insisted that each member of the family old enough must do some kind of work."[4]

The majority of people working in North Carolina mills throughout the nineteenth century were young unmarried white women and children. The minority of adult male workers held the most highly skilled and supervisory positions. A desire to help the "girls who would otherwise be wretched" may have affected decisions about whom to hire, but clearly the primary consideration was to acquire the cheapest labor possible. Teenage girls could be paid less than adult men. In contrast to slaves, white workers, male and female, could be dismissed when mills were stopped as they frequently were for bad weather, construction and maintenance, and for various holidays. Furthermore, as Gavin Wright has explained, "an economic reason why such employment was limited and often temporary is that employers of slave labor were buying into a southern regional slave market and had no hope of locating a local supply of 'cheap' slave labor."[5] Even for an owner of a large number of slaves such as Edwin Holt, it made economic sense to use them in agriculture rather than in industry.

Although a general consensus was reached in the antebellum period concerning the most desirable type of labor organization, mill men did experiment more with the makeup of their work force than they would later in the century. Opposition to a racially mixed work force was heard in the antebellum Piedmont, but combinations of enslaved men and white women were sometimes tolerated. Several mill owners in North Carolina used slave labor, either exclusively or along with white workers. Henry Humphreys used enslaved black girls and free white girls working together to run the machines in his first mill. Fries sometimes had male slaves work in his mill along with local white females; he was considering turning exclusively to slave labor on the eve of the Civil War.[6]

Owners could experiment with their work force more because a greater variety of people were willing to try mill work in the indus-

4. Eugene Holt, *Edwin Holt and His Descendants,* 37.
5. Gavin Wright, "Cheap Labor and Southern Textiles Before 1880," *Journal of Economic History* 39 (1979): 665.
6. Griffin and Standard, "Cotton Textile Industry in Ante-Bellum North Carolina: Part II," 132; Carrie Fries to Henry Fries, May 25, 1860, Fries Papers, Moravian Archives; Carrie Fries wrote this letter for her father, Francis Fries.

try's early years. It was more common for married women, including some with small children, to work than it would be in the late nineteenth century. Before mills became stigmatized as refuges for lower-class whites, even women of some means occasionally worked in them.

Theories that blacks and whites could not and should not work together, and that mills were havens for poor whites and not suitable for members of respectable society, were not dogma in the 1830s; these were assumptions that evolved along with the early mills. In order to minimize opposition, however, advocates of industrial development needed to define the work force in a particular way, which meant they were not always entirely candid in reporting who actually worked. The depiction of southern mill men as motivated more by paternalistic benevolence than by economic ambition was well under way before the Civil War. Almost as soon as the first mills were built, the defense of southern mill villages centered on describing them as havens for poor whites, much as Lossing had described the Alamance village. In time this led to claims that these villages were only suitable for poor whites. When Humphreys turned to hiring only those he considered needy and deserving to run his machinery, he was praised for giving "employment for numerous hands hitherto doing nothing for the community, and but little for themselves." The same year that Holt founded the Alamance Factory, an article in the *Hillsborough Recorder* described another factory that "gives employment to 62 operatives, members of 15 or 16 families, who derive an ample support from it, and generally of a class who formerly suffered for want of even the common necessaries of life. Now they have a respectable occupation, live comfortably, are cheerful and contented." Eight years later an article singled out a mill in neighboring Randolph County as one where "the operatives are all white, and sustain a moral character equal to that of any portion of the surrounding population." The *Recorder* also published an article praising wage work as proof "that the encouragement of manufacturers in this country has no tendency to degrade the operative class." A decade later, a Raleigh paper propagandized for industrial development in North Carolina on the grounds that "many hundreds and thousands of poor men with families, who are existing upon half starvation from year to year . . . whose wives and children are suffering for the want of food and raiment" could be made into useful citizens. Michael Holt joined those who defended providing poor whites with a steady wage. Five years after opposing his son's plan to build a mill, he expressed hope that "in a few years N Carolina may bost of Their independence, spin all our cotton, give employment to the poore white labourer, a kind of separation of Slave Labour and free."[7]

Arguments such as these were intended to convince all segments of society that industry was beneficial; they were also intended to make wage work appear respectable. According to an Englishman traveling around the state, at least by 1855 there was no longer a stigma attached to mill work.[8] The presence of slavery, however, made it impossible to remove the stigma entirely. As abolitionism grew louder, defensive southerners increasingly defended slave labor by claiming its superiority to industrial wage labor.

Politicians, newspaper men, and other propagandists for mill work, even the father of one of the state's most ambitious mill men, could idealize a mission of uplift, but Edwin Holt like other owners had to be practical when hiring labor. Their primary concern was not to rescue poor whites but to make a profit. The cheapest workers available were young women and children, so southern mill men learned from their northern counterparts and recruited them for all but the most skilled or physically demanding tasks. In the 1840s George Makepeace, a Rhode Island mill man who had relocated in North Carolina, advised owners in his adopted state to "get all of the widow women that has got a family of girls or other families that are mostly girls as we do not want many boys."[9]

The North Carolinians did want boys and men for the most highly skilled and supervisory positions. A virtual ironclad taboo against women holding positions of authority over men grew inevitably from societal norms about natural male dominance and endured throughout the nineteenth century. In the 1830s Fries and his board of directors reprimanded their talented northern supervisor Thomas Siddall for giving Susan Crotch "more authority than is proper."[10]

---

7. Griffin and Standard, "Cotton Textile Industry in Ante-Bellum North Carolina: Part II," 133; *Hillsborough Recorder,* May 26, 1837, January 23, September 11, 1845; Raleigh paper quoted in Johnson, *Ante-Bellum North Carolina,* 67–73; Michael Holt to Willie P. Mangum, January 25, 1842, in Henry T. Shanks, ed., *The Papers of Willie Person Mangum,* 5 vols. (Raleigh, 1950–56), vol. 3, pp. 276–77.
8. Griffin and Standard, "Cotton Textile Industry in Ante-Bellum North Carolina, Part II," 155.
9. George Makepeace to Webb and Douglass, September 11, 1851, Webb Papers.
10. *Salem Manufacturing Minute Book,* May 14, 1842, Fries Papers, Moravian Archives.

But if the idea of women assuming improper authority was uniformly offensive to men, ideas about the relationship of women to work varied considerably. Makepeace recognized that female labor was essential to industrial development; Fries and virtually all mill men opposed giving females authority in the workplace. Their different emphases underscore that the impact of industrialization on gender roles was profoundly contradictory. Girls and women worked in factories. But the rapid change industrialization wrought also fostered a conservative ideology concerning women best described as a "cult of domesticity."[11] As men became increasingly independent of family and home, women were more rigidly defined as dependents whose sphere was exclusively family and home. Because the industrial revolution also required new types of labor, however, this new ideology had to be refined in order to exploit the potential of female workers. Two assumptions—that women should be dependent on men and that the poor should not be dependent on the state—framed debate about the propriety of women and work. A society that assumed white female dependency yet blamed the poor for their own plight had no simple solution for white female poverty. Views that young women were particularly suitable for industrial work needed to be reconciled with the cult of domesticity.

Building mill villages with a gloss of paternalism was one possible way to provide indigent women with proper work. The idea of mills serving as a source of self-support for widows and their children as well as a means of exploiting their idle labor had been associated with industrialization since the late eighteenth century when the first small factories appeared. During his tenure as secretary of the treasury in the Washington administration, Alexander Hamilton argued that the country should establish factories particularly to exploit "the employment of persons who would otherwise be idle." To Tench Coxe, who followed Hamilton in the Treasury Department, this idea specifically meant women and girls whose "aid in manufacturers prevents the diversion of men and boys from agriculture."[12]

Hamilton and Coxe were not much concerned with the propriety of white women working, but some elite southerners were. The image of the southern lady on her pedestal is a well-entrenched part of Old South mythology. A number of historians, drawing primarily on the writings of elite women, have concluded that southern white

11. See especially Barbara Welter, "The Cult of True Womanhood: 1820–1860," *American Quarterly* 18 (1966): 151–75.
12. Alice Kessler-Harris, *Out to Work: A History of Wage-Earning Women in the United States* (New York, 1982), 23–24.

women were distinct from northern women in their disdain for work. As Ann Scott has clarified, however, "The precise meaning of 'work' varied with station in society, economic condition, and geographic location, but women of leisure were hard to find."[13]

Editorials in Piedmont newspapers are especially revealing concerning their society's ambivalence about women and work. In 1845 the *Recorder* printed an article written by Lowell women challenging the idea that "it was derogatory to a lady's dignity, or a blot upon female character, to labour," which, the editor concluded, "breathes the right spirit." On the eve of the Civil War another paper claimed that northern depictions of southern white women as disdainful of work only revealed northern ignorance about the South.[14]

It was particularly easy to conclude, as Benson Lossing did, that working in a textile mill was "a usual occupation" for girls and women. Historically, preparing cloth and clothing has been almost universally women's work. This was true in all of the English colonies, north and south. William Byrd II observed in the late seventeenth century that women in the Virginia and Carolina frontier "all Spin, weave, and knit, whereby they make good Shift to cloath the whole Family; and to their credit be it recorded, many of them do it very completely." Some Piedmont women were still spending long laborious hours spinning, weaving, and knitting, and presumably did so very completely, over a hundred years later. It was so common for females on North Carolina's self-sufficient farms to provide clothing for their families that as late as 1810 the state produced more cloth than all of New England.[15]

But the mechanization of the textile industry, first in England in the eighteenth century and subsequently in the northeastern United States, made it increasingly easier for women to buy the yarn or the cloth they needed. The impact on their lives was profound. Thomas Dublin, in his study of Lowell, explains that "on the one hand, the new mills undermined the primary economic activities of farmers' daughters—the spinning of yarn and weaving of cloth. On the other hand, the mills offered employment to these young women and tempted them to leave their rural homes to work in the growing fac-

13. Ann Firor Scott, *The Southern Lady: From Pedestal to Politics, 1830–1930* (Chicago, 1970), 28.
14. *Hillsborough Recorder,* May 29, 1845; *Fayetteville Observer,* January 2, 1860.
15. Julia Cherry Spruill, *Women's Life and Work in the Southern Colonies* (Chapel Hill, 1938), 82–83; Griffin and Standard, "Cotton Textile Industry in Antebellum North Carolina: Part I," 15.

tory towns."[16] Through the nineteenth century the shift from a producer society to a consumer society was replicated in the southern Piedmont.

Of course, the conversion of Alamance to a consumer economy lagged considerably behind the process in the Northeast. Well into the nineteenth century most white families in Alamance survived by quasi-subsistence agriculture. By practicing "safety first" farming, giving priority to the food their families and livestock would consume, many were able to survive largely unconnected to the market economy developing on both sides of the Atlantic. Frank Owsley exaggerated the degree of yeoman democracy in this part of the South, but he did accurately describe many Alamance farm families as engaged in "a diversified self-sufficient type of agriculture where the money crops were subordinated to food crops, and where the labor was performed by the family or the family aided by a few slaves." As Owsley explained, this type of agriculture did save many Piedmont farm families from falling into the ranks of those "poor, ignorant, degraded white people."[17]

Farming for self-sufficiency did not, however, save them all. In 1845 a North Carolina representative to the General Assembly observed that "hard is the lot of these poor men who have large families to support and pay debt besides, with a small portion of what they can raise by their own hands from a barren soil." A century later historian Guion Griffiths Johnson described these antebellum poor as farm tenants, day laborers, and ne'er-do-wells, "those unfortunates who from sickness, desire for drink, or inertia either were unable to acquire land or had lost their holdings through severe reverses in fortune."[18] Both observers recognized the limits to yeoman self-sufficiency, but both missed the gendered nature of poverty, the category of poor that included women and their children independent of male support in a society that demanded female dependence.

It was a common assumption that the poor should be independent and would have no incentive to improve if assistance was too easily attainable. Reformers, therefore, directed their efforts at facilitating and even compelling the poor to pay their own way. Early in the nineteenth century, North Carolina began appointing overseers or wardens of the poor. After 1831 a number of poorhouses were built to house those legally classified as poor, most of them aged or

16. Thomas Dublin, *Women at Work: The Transformation of Work and Community in Lowell, Massachusetts, 1826–1860* (New York, 1979), 5.
17. Frank Owsley, *Plain Folk of the Old South* (Baton Rouge, 1949), 135.
18. Johnson, *Ante-Bellum North Carolina*, 67–69.

diagnosed as mentally or physically afflicted. Occasionally people determined by the wardens to be incapable of earning their own living were given direct assistance, but most were assigned to poorhouses or to the homes of people paid to provide for them. Orphans were commonly apprenticed; sometimes the decision was made when they were still infants. Private philanthropists, who often supplemented the scant public aid, were more likely than government officials to subdivide the poor by sex. Aiding the "worthy poor," particularly indigent women and children, was a major activity of elite women's groups, but for the most part this meant finding ways for poor women to support themselves.[19]

Poor women who had been widowed or deserted by their husbands had few options for sustaining their families. They were expected to support themselves in a society that trained them to be dependent and provided them limited opportunity to work. Laws blind to gender as a category for public assistance while mandating it as a category for legal and civil rights created a type of poverty often overlooked.[20] Advocates of industrialization exploited society's demand that women and children be dependent on men but independent of the state to justify what was to some traditionalists the frightening specter of a working class.

Lack of a male breadwinner was a major cause of poverty for women, but many male-headed households were also at risk. Yeomen farm families proved to be vulnerable to changes in the larger political and economic order, which was dominated by the planter class. Even before the Civil War changed southern lives so profoundly, upcountry self-sufficiency was challenged by the commercialization of agriculture and encroachment of the market economy. Self-sufficient farm folk who fell victim to this transformation were likely candidates for tending the machines of industry.

Edwin Holt may have thought a lot or very little about the impact of his industrial success on gender and class. In his pursuit of profit, he focused primarily on technology, investment, and marketing; his diary and surviving letters reveal almost no interest in theories about labor. His slaves helped construct the mill buildings and mill houses and they may have worked in the dye house, but there is no evidence that they ever tended the spindles and looms. Both Fries and Humphreys offered examples of a mixed-race work force, but

19. Robert Bremner, *The Public Good: Philanthropy and Welfare in the Civil War Era* (New York, 1980), 33; Powell, *North Carolina Through Four Centuries,* 293–94.
20. Johnson, *Ante-Bellum North Carolina,* 67–68.

Holt preferred to use white workers almost exclusively. Probably this was the result of neither opposition to industrial slave labor nor advocacy of employing poor whites, but simply because he needed all of his slaves to perform myriad agricultural and construction tasks. During harvest and other busy times, Holt and Carrigan shared slave labor and Holt occasionally hired additional slaves for agricultural tasks as well. There is no evidence that he ever bought or sold slaves. Because their numbers grew only by natural increase, a majority of the slaves on his plantation at any given time were children.[21] It would not have been economically sound to buy new slaves or to hire them on an annual basis to work in a mill that operated sporadically. White workers, however, could be dismissed when freshets, low water, or a flooded market halted work.

Clearly, for practical reasons, the first Alamance Factory workers were white. The paucity of records means that knowing much more about them will remain elusive. A surviving time book for the Cedar Falls Factory in Randolph County, just south of Alamance, reveals detail about a mill similar to the Alamance Factory and is useful for speculating about it. When Holt visited Cedar Falls in 1846 to consider buying it, he certainly saw the people tending the machinery. The work force he observed there was probably not very different from his own Alamance force. Three-fourths of the laborers were female; approximately three-fourths of these girls and women lived with at least one parent and worked with at least one sibling. Those who came to the village alone were the least likely to remain as long as a year. Thirty-six percent of workers quit every year. The company bookkeeper sometimes recorded why people left, leaving an intriguing glimpse at how the first generation of female textile workers in the North Carolina Piedmont reacted to their work. Clearly many of them had difficulty adjusting to an industrial order, but their responses reveal neither desperation nor docility. Approximately one-fourth of the women who left did so because they married. Another fifth were fired for reasons including "leaving the mill without leaf to visit," "because she could not doe as she was told," "roales violated," "want work," and "cannot spin." Another fifth quit to go to another mill. A slightly smaller number quit because of a specific grievance; one, for example, was quoted as leaving "because I can't get my bored on them old loomes." Sophia Trogden made the most dramatic exit from Cedar Falls. She worked in the mills along with several of her siblings when in the spring of 1856

21. Edwin Michael Holt Diary, January 7, 1847, July 21–28, 1848.

she was fired for cutting the belts in the spinning room. Her story is an indication of the frustration first-generation workers felt when confronted with a technology and work discipline so unfamiliar to them. But Sophia Trogden's story also reveals the measure of power workers could command. Less than a year after she was fired, Cedar Falls management determined that her skills were valuable enough to risk their spinning belts; Trogden was rehired.[22]

Few workers matched Trogden's belligerence. Most likely Elizabeth Carrigan was more typical in her response to the emerging industrial order. When her husband, James, a brother of William Carrigan, died in 1843, Elizabeth was left with several children to support. Apparently some members of the Carrigan family had never approved of James's second marriage to a barely literate woman who owned no property. Although Elizabeth maintained good relationships with some of her stepchildren, including William A. Carrigan, the stepson who taught some of the Holt children and their cousins, she was estranged from her brother-in-law, William Carrigan, whom she blamed, as an executor of her husband's will, for her financial plight. In 1853, shortly after he sold his share in the Alamance Factory, Carrigan assured one of Elizabeth's sons, "I have not defrauded your Father, or his Estate, as has been believed by some of my near kin and others that had no interest in it."[23]

Whether defrauded or not, Elizabeth Carrigan joined the ranks of poor widows, women trained to be dependent but forced to be independent. Within two years after her husband's death, she took her two daughters to work in a Gaston County textile mill. In 1855 she reported that "I though Mary and Cornelia cood make more to worke in the factory. Mary is weeving and Cornelia is a seter[.] we [have] a pleasant place to live in[.] it is brick house we live in[.] the factory belong to Thomas Tate[.] Mr Tate provide for his hands[.] we have preaching hear every third Sabath[.] he is a methidois but he is a good minister." Tate did not, however, provide enough for the three women to live independently of their male relatives. On at least one occasion Elizabeth was forced to ask a stepson to loan her money for essentials because "I have to pay rite smarte for movening heer . . . and every thing is sow deer thate takes all thate one can make to support them."[24]

---

22. Cedar Falls Manufacturing Company Day Book, North Carolina Division of Archives and History, Raleigh [hereinafter cited as NCDAH]. The quotations are presented verbatim from the original.

23. William Carrigan to nephew, June 27, 1853, Carrigan Papers.

24. Elizabeth Carrigan to William A. Carrigan, May 2, 1855, Carrigan Papers.

Elizabeth Carrigan's letters include a brief description of an early southern mill village as a place where people not only worked but developed a community. In Alamance the neat log houses Lossing described were also the center of an evolving village. Some of the sixty-one workers employed by the Alamance Factory in 1850 continued to live on farms nearby, but their numbers in the village steadily increased as more houses were built. In the fall of 1846 "Mrs. Daily moved to the Factory." The following summer "Mr Robertson and family came up," and in September, 1853, "Mrs Hinton came up and Mrs Reeves children." Single men were more likely to come as skilled workers or supervisors. In June 1847, "Mr. Robinson a weaver came here" and in December "Nimrod Moser commenced tending the mill." Although Holt recruited families, single women occasionally moved to the village as well. On February 5, 1849, Elizabeth Robertson, possibly a relative of the Robertsons who had come eighteen months before, "commenced boarding."[25]

At least by the 1850s religious services were provided in the village. Creating distinct religious facilities for workers was part of the process whereby class replaced ethnicity as the primary determinant of religious affiliation among white Protestants. As the Holts moved away from their rural Lutheran roots and emotional revivalism into the more staid First Presbyterian and Episcopal churches, their workers listened to preachers provided for them exclusively. At least by the 1850s, church services and then church buildings for factory workers began to appear in Alamance. On August 8, 1852, Edwin Holt recorded that he "went to preaching at Factory." He occasionally allowed work to stop so that the mill folk could attend revivals. The factory revival John Carrigan described as "all the hollering I ever herd," and as "a frolic to me" was far more than a frolic to the workers. All but three of the factory girls John observed and laughed at professed religion on the night he attended.[26]

There is at least a hint that as early as 1844 Edwin Holt provided schooling for children in the village. On a Monday in September he noted in his diary that "school commenced at Factory after Camp meeting."[27] There are other scattered references in the diary to schools, but apparently they were for the Holt and Carrigan chil-

25. Edwin Michael Holt Diary, November 15, 1846, August 17, 1847, September 13, 1853, June 19, December 3, 1847, February 5, 1849.
26. Ibid., August 8, September 13, 1852; John Carrigan to Dear Cousin, February 19, 1853, Carrigan Papers.
27. Edwin Michael Holt Diary, September 9, 1844.

dren. Their education was carefully attended; if there was any education provided for the mill children, it was starkly separate.

Housing, religious facilities, and other basic necessities provided by owners were early manifestations of the paternalism typically associated with southern mills in the nineteenth century. Theoretically mills offered the poor a means to the financial independence that society demanded of them, but wage work also created a new kind of dependency. Moreover, mill families, especially widows like Mrs. Hamilton and Mrs. Reeves and their children, became dependent on Holt not only for their wages but also for housing, firewood, and some of their food. Each year a small portion of the wheat Holt and Carrigan grew was sent to the factory. In 1848, for example, Holt sent 6 of the 666 bushels he harvested. He also hauled wood for the mill families to use.[28] Numerous workers, however, did retain skills from their agrarian pasts. Typically mill families had their own gardens, as well as a cow and perhaps other animals.

Around the same time they built the factory, Holt and Carrigan opened a store nearby. Many early-nineteenth-century mill owners, North and South, were also merchants and often they paid their workers in store credit or a combination of store credit and cash. The scanty records available indicate that Holt followed this practice. Most accounts at his store were in the name of a male head of household, but several widows and at least one teenage girl, Lettitia Edds, had their own accounts. In 1844 Pena Mangum, whose household included two daughters, Anna and Betsy, bought over twenty-six dollars worth of goods, primarily sewing material, which left her nearly five dollars in debt to Holt's store. Most likely Mangum's account was financed by wages she or her daughters earned in the Alamance Factory. Sometime in the 1840s Mangum also began to take in boarders in order to supplement her income. The two teenage girls and one teenage boy who lived with her in 1850 possibly worked in Holt's mill as well.[29]

Separate housing, religious services, and village stores that sold on credit fostered an impression of cotton mill families as a people apart, but this was an impression that emerged only slowly. Douglas Flamming's observation about mill people in Georgia in the late nineteenth century—"that friends and family were not severed by farm-to-mill migration but instead were bound together by increas-

28. Ibid., August 9, 1848, 1848 addendum.
29. Prude, *Coming of Industrial Order*, 99, 89–90; Alamance Factory Store Ledger, Alamance Cotton Mill Records.

ingly complicated networks of labor"—was true in this time and place as well. Class formation was minimized by the close ties many maintained to agriculture long after they became factory workers and by high turnover in the mills. Mill families often moved back and forth between mill work and farm work or they divided the family between the two. Laborers frequently changed mills or quit altogether, boys and girls grew old enough to choose other options, young women married, mill hands rejected industrial dangers and discipline. Owners and managers frequently found workers unaccustomed to industrial discipline wanting and fired them. When one worker gave up the Alamance Factory, Holt responded "Miller left & glad of it." There is abundant evidence that early southern mill workers displayed as much hostility as docility. Those who came to work in the Alamance Factory were no exception. In 1846 there was a spontaneous protest of workers there against what they considered excessive supervision. A Carrigan cousin wrote Alfred Holt, "I do knot know as I can tell you all the cause but Kimball and some of the hands blown up at Boon for his being to tight and thought that he would get the hands to blow up Boon and then get the whole management of the Factory but uncle [William Carrigan] and your Father [Edwin Holt] told him out of that I expect they have a general clean up there amongst them."[30]

The tag of docility has clung tenaciously to white mill workers, especially those of the South. Jonathan Prude was describing antebellum New England workers when he wrote "industrialization in this country was from the outset marked by significant tension."[31] His observation holds true for the South as well. Flamming, challenging what he calls "one of the most tenacious myths in the history of southern textiles," persuasively argues that "in reality the harmony between wealthy whites and poor whites in the New South broke down almost at the start."[32] The disharmony began in the Old South as men, women, and children found ways to challenge industrial authority. Perhaps scholars interested in the South's first industrial work force have paid too much attention to regional differences and not enough to gender differences. The limited evidence from these two North Carolina mills hints that challenges to harmony came in distinctly male and female ways.

30. Flamming, *Creating the Modern South*, 34; Edwin Michael Holt Diary, January 12, 1847; William A. Carrigan to Alfred Holt, October 17, 1846, Carrigan Papers.
31. Prude, *Coming of Industrial Order*, xiii.
32. Flamming, *Creating the Modern South*, 56–57.

The majority of workers in the antebellum Alamance Factory were female and they were young. In 1860, approximately 184 workers, 47 of them male and 137 female, representing 63 mill families, worked in Alamance County mills. Men had a variety of occupational options, but mill work was one of the few ways girls and women could support themselves or supplement their families' incomes. The ideal of female domesticity, so pervasive in the decades before the Civil War, mandated the home as the only proper sphere for wives and mothers. But the ideal was far more elusive for poor women and their daughters than it was for Emily Holt and hers. Mill owners wanted female laborers because they were cheaper than males. For poor females, however meager the wage, it was an alternative to destitution. The high female-to-male ratio remained a distinguishing characteristic of mill families in the Piedmont throughout the nineteenth century.[33]

In 1860 women headed twenty-three (38 percent) of the Alamance mill families, a much higher percentage than there were female-headed households in the county's population overall. May Ashley, a forty-five-year-old single mother in 1860, kept house with the help of her eleven-year-old daughter; four older daughters, ranging in age from seventeen to twenty-one, supported the family with their mill wages. Ana Woods, either widowed or separated, had no sons of working age. She kept house while her four teenage daughters—Milly, Sallie, Margaret, and Martha—worked in the mill. Her two sons, both under ten years of age, attended school while their five-year-old sister remained at home. Isabella Boggs, who could claim one hundred dollars worth of property in 1860, depended on the wages of two daughters, both in their twenties, but was able to keep a seventeen-year-old daughter at home. In the 1850s Stephen Dickey supported his wife, Charlotte, and their five children, working as a blacksmith. By 1860 Charlotte had died; none of the Dickey's three daughters, then in their late twenties and thirties, had married; they still lived with their father and helped support the family by working in the mill. The Ashley, Woods, Boggs, and

33. Most of the following information on antebellum mill workers presented in this chapter was drawn from my analysis of U.S. census data for Alamance County from 1850 and 1860. Questions raised from this data are concerned with such topics as family structure, parent-child relations, changing roles of men and women, working ages, occupational mobility, education, and family wages. An interactive data-entry program allowed materials to be entered directly into computer files from microfilm copies of the censuses. Analyses were undertaken at both the individual and household levels.

Dickey families, all female headed or including mostly daughters, typified those who found it especially difficult to support themselves farming. The mills offered them a viable option.

Occasionally young women came to a mill village alone, although never in numbers large enough to create a boardinghouse community similar to Lowell. After the death of her parents, Hariett McAdams went to live with her brother William, a bachelor farmer claiming a thousand dollars worth of property, and supported herself with her mill wages. Barbara and Catherine May had been provided for by their father's work as a cooper until at least their mid-teens. Barbara was still attending school when she was sixteen. But as they approached their twenties still unmarried, the two May daughters left home to board in the village and work in the Alamance Factory.

In 1860 married women and women with young children were more likely to work and their young children under the age of fourteen less likely to do so than would be the case in the years of rapid industrial expansion and growth after the war. Ten-year-old Fanny Pleasants, who worked in a mill with her eighty-year-old grandfather as well as an aunt and a cousin, was the only child under the age of fourteen listed as a mill worker in 1860. Fourteen women with children ten and under remained at home with them, while twelve mothers with children in that age group worked in an Alamance mill. In 1860 Margaret Mitchell was married to a farmer who owned five hundred dollars worth of property and had two daughters, aged sixteen and fourteen. Sometime in the 1850s, although her teenage daughters remained at home, Mitchell began working in a mill; she was one of fifteen married female workers. Nine of the twenty-three female heads of household in a mill village, most of them mothers whose husbands were dead or living elsewhere, worked in a mill. At age forty, Fanny Willis, for example, was the sole support of her eight-year-old son.

In Willis's case stark necessity may have dictated that she work, but some women with husbands who could support them also chose mill work, leaving the primary responsibility for housework to a daughter or another female relative. It was not yet necessarily considered a mark of failure to work in a mill. A few families with considerable property had one or more members working in the Alamance Factory. Nancy Murray was married to Eli Murray, a farmer who could claim over thirty thousand dollars worth of property in 1860, making him one of the richest men in Alamance County. Clearly Murray did not view factories as the domain of poor girls who would otherwise be wretched; despite her family's wealth, in her fifties she chose to tend machinery while a daughter and granddaughter remained at home. Nancy Murray was atypical, but other women whose families had at least average means were also willing to give the machines a try. Sometime in the 1850s Celia Crawford's husband died; with the help of her two sons, she continued running a farm that by 1860 was worth four thousand dollars. Although among the wealthier landholders in Alamance County, she sent her eighteen-year-old daughter, Nancy, to work in a mill. Nancy Cook also identified herself as a farmer through the fifties and claimed one thousand dollars worth of property in 1860. But twenty-one-year-old Nehemiah, her only son at home, worked in the mill, along with his two sisters. Susan Barnwell and her husband William were both mill workers, although the couple claimed several thousand dollars worth of property and had an infant son at home.

Unfortunately, it is impossible to know why these people of some means chose mill work. Certainly they were exceptional in working at a task increasingly associated with poor whites. Although Lossing described it as an alternative for "poor girls who might otherwise be wretched," clearly some women found mill work no more than a reordering of their traditional responsibilities for spinning and weaving.

The mill villages, however, were never exclusively female. Despite Makepeace's admonition to recruit widow-headed families, the majority of mill families were always headed by men. They were particularly likely to relocate near the Alamance Factory or send some of their children there if a majority of those children were female. But boys also became mill workers. Sometimes all members of a family who were old enough worked in a mill. Josiah and Libby Bracon worked together along with their twenty-year-old son, James, and teenage daughter, Martha. Although the family listed only forty dollars worth of property, their wage income was adequate to allow thirteen-year-old Ed to remain at home. Mattie Ward and her husband, Jacob, both in their forties, worked in the mill with their four daughters, whose ages ranged from sixteen to twenty-five, as well as their twenty-year-old son. Four younger daughters, twelve and under, stayed at home with their infant brother. Joshua Ward, seventy, and his wife, Mary, six years younger, lived nearby and were probably relatives; they also worked together in the mill with all of their grown children who still lived at home. Two young grandchildren were the only members of the household not listed in the census as workers. In farmer William Noble's extended household, all of the adults worked; his three sisters as well as a woman who boarded there along with her artisan husband were mill workers. Perhaps the Wards and Nobles had working hours varied enough to provide for the young children in their households or perhaps other child-care arrangements were made. In several families there was a grandparent in the home who possibly provided child care. Martha Burch worked in a mill with her three teenage daughters. Most likely her father, who was the retired head of the household, looked after the three younger children, the youngest only one year old. Sixty-five-year-old Patience Mason kept house and took care of a ten-year-old granddaughter while her husband, although in his seventies, worked in the mill with his two middle-aged daughters; three grown sons were artisans.

Mill workers from these sixty-nine Alamance mill families were creating the county's first industrial work force in a place still overwhelmingly agrarian. Over one-third of the family heads, including nine women, farmed. For them, mill work was a means of supplementing the precarious rewards of agriculture. The extra income that mill wages provided was particularly significant for families without many members suited for farm labor. Although farming had enabled James Turner to accumulate fifteen hundred dollars worth of property, his wife, Mary, worked in the mill while their only child, an eleven-year-old daughter, remained at home. Possibly Turner was able to hire farm laborers, but he could not exploit the more tractable labor of sons. Even a female farm head as successful as Celia Crawford found it necessary to send a teenage daughter to the mill. Sarah Hicks, who claimed almost as much property as Crawford, was able to continue farming even though there were no males in her family. Most likely she also hired men to help run her farm, but the wage of her seventeen-year-old daughter was also necessary to supplement their agricultural production.

Unskilled workers made up a majority of the work force. These men, women, and children who exchanged farm work for factory work fairly easily learned the repetitive tasks required of them. But several key skilled individuals were necessary if even a small spinning mill was going to succeed. They were not easy to find in a state almost exclusively agrarian. A northern expert came to Alamance in 1837 along with the machinery Holt bought. After he left eighteen months later, Holt trained a local man to serve as overseer, but he continued to seek the expertise of northerners or Europeans on a fairly regular basis. By the 1840s a small trickle of these skilled individuals were migrating into the South, a few of them into Alamance. Their status varied in correlation with their skill. Although Sidney Holman became owner of his own mill in Alamance, most immigrants remained supervisors or skilled mechanics. In time northern textile men learned the ways of the South sufficiently to promote themselves as particularly qualified in managing southern help.

The southern work force they found at the Alamance Factory during its first quarter century was small, transient, and largely female. Women and their daughters, sometimes along with their husbands and sons, were willing to give the novelty of wage work a try. Some rejected it immediately and most remained for no more than a few years. A small number, however, assumed spinning, weaving, and the other tasks necessary to produce yarn and cloth as their life work and, most significantly, determined that it would be taken up by their children as well. Even before the Civil War, a second generation of workers was coming into the Holt mills. These were the pioneers of a working class.

4

The Rich Man's War

OWNERS AND WORKERS DURING THE CIVIL WAR

"During the middle third of the nineteenth century," Emory M. Thomas has written, "Southerners began to close their minds to alternatives to their 'way of life.' " He describes the South's mind in these years as "Janus-faced: it stood for a distinctive Southern life style and against the Yankee alternative." Thomas also acknowledges that while many southerners were outside the American mainstream, others were "products of the American experience no more peculiar than most other Americans."[1]

Edwin Holt and many industrialists in the North Carolina Piedmont were slave owners and accordingly were in one profound way outside the mainstream and against the Yankee alternative. But they were also products of nineteenth-century America with at least as much in common with their northern bourgeois counterparts as with southern planters. The ties Holt and his sons had developed with the North, and maintained to the eve of the Civil War, also forced a qualification of their commitment to southern nationalism and facilitated their entry into the American mainstream.

Through the 1850s Edwin Holt profited from both farm and factory, but it was the latter that engaged more of his time and ambition. By the 1850s investment in forty slaves assured that he could not escape entirely identifying with the South and its defense of slavery. His commitment to building a family industrial dynasty dictated, however, that he was more detached from questions about southern rights than the many southerners increasingly obsessed with the specter of Yankee interference in their plantation way of life. Years after the Civil War, a grandson claimed that his grandfather advocated gradual abolition of slavery with compensation for

1. Emory Thomas, *The Confederate Nation: 1861–1865* (New York, 1979), 4–5.

owners.[2] Although it is possible that before the war he was willing to consider an eventual end to slavery, it is unlikely that this planter-industrialist was very outspoken on the subject in the fifties; many of the men he knew well, including his brother, took leading roles in defending slavery as a southern right. The priority he placed on industrial development did not require a defense of slavery, but it did demand cooperation with the state's political and economic elite.

No matter how the debate between North and South was framed, the question of slavery was never far from center. During the first fifty years after the American Revolution, abolitionism was generally tolerated in North Carolina and even advocated publicly by some prominent citizens. The Jeffersonian view that slavery was at best a necessary and temporary evil was one Edwin Holt would have heard frequently in his youth. In the 1830s, however, toleration of such views waned in the upper South. Although the strident rhetoric of the fire-eaters, centered in Charleston and the newer cotton states, remained far from Alamance County, by the mid-fifties the sectional conflict dominated public discourse as well as private conversation there. During their frequent trips north in the fifties, Edwin Holt and his sons undoubtedly confronted northern abolitionists demanding an end to the South's peculiar institution. In 1852, on the day Holt returned home from a nine-day trip to Philadelphia, Harriet Beecher Stowe published *Uncle Tom's Cabin*, an emotionally gripping fictional account of slavery. It sold five thousand copies within two days and invigorated opposition to slavery all over the North. Philadelphia, the northern city the Holts were most familiar with, was the cradle of American abolitionism. Not all Philadelphians, however, demanded an end to slavery; businessmen tended to oppose a cause they feared threatened national stability. It is unlikely that the Holts were very often forced to defend their involvement in the horrors Stowe described to the northern businessmen they visited.

On the other hand, there is no evidence that they ever had to defend their northern ties to fellow southerners either. After 1850 newspapers in Alamance and the adjacent counties frequently promoted the idea that northern abolitionists were a threat and that southerners should fight back. But southern nationalism in the North Carolina Piedmont, a place where the importance of industrial development had been acknowledged for several decades, was of a different stripe from that articulated in the Deep South; in coun-

2. Eugene Holt, *Edwin Holt and His Descendants*, 9, 40.

ties like Alamance it was less a defense of slavery than a promotion of southern independence that would include industrial independence. In the spring of 1850 the *Hillsborough Recorder* praised news of cotton factories springing up throughout the southern Piedmont because "these facts show that the South is gradually freeing itself from Northern Bondage." A year later the paper reprinted an article thanking abolitionists for "putting us upon the road of independence." The *Hillsborough Recorder* insisted that it was "consumate folly" to purchase from the North what could be easily produced in the South.[3] This stripe of economic patriotism became increasingly commonplace in Piedmont papers. Edwin Holt and his sons could easily embrace an argument for southern economic development.

Through the early 1850s both major political parties maintained a national unity that challenged sectional divisiveness. Until it shattered under the weight of sectional conflict, the Whig Party served to unite southern industrialists like the Holts with their northern counterparts. Members of both the Whig and Democratic parties and both regions joined in supporting the Compromise of 1850, which attempted to mute the volatile issue of the expansion of slavery. In 1854, however, the facade of unanimity created four years before collapsed when a proposal by Illinois Senator Stephen Douglas to organize Nebraska and Kansas prompted heated exchange as to the fate of slavery there.

The subsequent conflict exacerbated southern defensiveness and destroyed the last vestiges of begrudged tolerance in the North Carolina Piedmont for abolitionism. In 1856, a professor at the University of North Carolina was fired for opposing the expansion of slavery, an event undoubtedly observed by William Edwin Holt, a student there that year. The following year the publication of Hinton Rowan Helper's antislavery tract, *The Impending Crisis of the South: How to Meet It*, particularly galled proslavery North Carolinians because it was the handiwork of a state native. The harassment in 1859 of the Reverend Daniel Worth of Guilford County, whose antislavery sentiments had previously been tolerated, further underscored the growing opposition to antislavery sentiment in the North Carolina Piedmont. In the wake of John Brown's strike against slavery at Harpers Ferry, Virginia, there were demands that Worth be silenced; when he continued to speak out, officials issued warrants for his arrest in a number of counties, including Alamance.

3. *Hillsborough Recorder*, May 14, 1850, August 6, 1851, quoted in *Fayetteville Observer.*

Worth was apprehended and found guilty of disturbing the peace but escaped to New York.[4]

The late 1850s, years in which sectional conflict escalated into disunion and finally war, was also a time of transition and tragedy for Edwin Holt's family. The marriages of his three oldest sons and the births of their first children assured family continuity. This easy progression of the family into the next generation was shattered, however, by the death of his oldest son. Through 1857 and 1858 a typhoid epidemic ravaged the Piedmont, deflecting attention from the growing conflict between North and South. Near hysteria resulted from rumors that the deaths of some of Alamance County's most prominent citizens were the result of drinking water poisoned by mining. One of these prominent citizens was Alfred Augustus Holt, who died at the age of twenty-eight, survived by his wife, Bettie, and three young sons.[5]

Despite Alfred's death, as well as growing concern about Alexander, the one son who seemed unable to conform to his expectations, Edwin Holt had every reason to remain confident that the family dynasty he planned would succeed. In 1858 Thomas became the first son to acquire his own mill. After he finished school, James first trained as a banker. William attended the University of North Carolina for a short time and then became general manager of the Alamance Factory around 1857. Banks, the sixth son, was just completing his formal education when the war broke out. Most likely he would have followed a path similar to his older brothers if he had not instead put on a Confederate uniform. After the four-year hiatus of war, his career developed much as his father had planned.

Banks fought an enemy he had been taught little reason to oppose. Edwin Holt encouraged his sons from boyhood to view northerners not as rivals but as professional friends and models to emulate, a perspective they may have put aside during the war, but one they quickly resumed when it ended. Through the late fifties the Holts retained their ties with businessmen in the North. Because Holt's diary ends in 1854, it is impossible to document that biannual trips to Philadelphia continued after that year, but most likely they did. Francis Fries, Holt's close friend and business associate, continued to travel north until the eve of the war. In April 1860 he consulted with Holt before departing for Philadelphia. When Fries became

4. Powell, *North Carolina Through Four Centuries*, 334–39.

5. H. B. Elliott to Calvin Wiley, April 14, 1858, Calvin Wiley Papers, SHC; Edwin Holt to Thomas Ruffin, [n.d.], Thomas Ruffin Papers; Ashe, *Biographical History of North Carolina*, vol. 7, 174.

ill there, he remained for two months with a Philadelphia industrialist who assured the sick man's wife, "Your good husband will return home better at least than he left."[6]

Not all of Holt's North Carolina friends, however, found the North so hospitable. In 1856 Paul Cameron wrote home from Massachusetts that "very few of the Southern people North—they have staid away and for a purpose." Thomas Ruffin's son John, a student in Philadelphia in the fifties, reported that northerners had come to think of southerners "more as enemies and rivals than as brothers."[7]

The demise of the Whig Party further strained unity among business elites. The party remained active in some states, including North Carolina, until 1860 but nationally was destroyed by conflict over the Kansas-Nebraska Bill. Thomas Holt continued to support the state party but like many southern Whigs was searching for a new national political home by the late 1850s. In May 1860 he represented North Carolina at a Whig convention held in Alabama and also served as a delegate to Whig district meetings that endorsed the Constitutional Union Party, formed in an effort to effect a compromise between the North and South. He also briefly took an active part in the American Party, popularly known as the Know-Nothing Party. Formed in opposition to Catholic immigration, in the 1850s the Know-Nothings capitalized on the disintegration of the Whigs to briefly serve as a viable alternative. To the eve of the war, Edwin Holt remained loyal to the Whigs, but by 1859 his son James and his close friend Francis Fries had both declared themselves Democrats, anticipating a course that most southern Whigs would follow during Reconstruction.[8]

In 1860 the Democratic Party, unable to agree on a candidate at its convention in Charleston, splintered; the northern wing chose Stephen Douglas and the southern one John C. Breckinridge. The Republican Party, formed in the North in the mid-fifties to replace the Whigs and exploit free-soil sentiment, nominated Abraham Lincoln as its second presidential candidate. Lincoln's name did not appear on the ballot in most southern states. North Carolina voters could choose among Breckinridge, Douglas, and John Bell, the Con-

6. Mother to Carrie, April 10, 1860; W. E. Albright to Mrs. L. M. Fries, April 20, 1860, Francis Fries Papers, SHC.
7. Blackwell P. Robinson, "Thomas Ruffin," unpublished manuscript, North Carolina Collection, University of North Carolina in Chapel Hill, 1992, 230.
8. *Hillsborough Recorder*, May 23, 1860, March 23, 1859; Michael Shirley, *From Congregation Town to Industrial City: Culture and Social Change in a Southern Community* (New York, 1994), 111.

stitutional Union Party's candidate. The state's electoral votes went to Breckinridge, the favored candidate of William Rainey Holt.[9] For industrialists in the upper South like Edwin Holt and his sons there was no completely satisfactory choice; most likely they voted for Bell.

Lincoln's election in November 1860 prompted South Carolina to secede the following month and invigorated secessionists in all of the slave states. The Holts, like many southern families, included both secessionists and Unionists. John Carrigan, a twenty-five-year-old farmer in Arkansas in 1860, upon hearing of Lincoln's apparent victory proclaimed that it was a "sad sad calamity indeed if he is elected" and that "it is an overt act sufficient to justify the South to secede." Most likely his uncle, William Rainey Holt, agreed; he was friends with John W. Ellis, North Carolina's secessionist-leaning governor who farmed land adjacent to Linwood; the marriage of his daughter into the Ellis family also bound the families. Less than a month after Lincoln's election, William Holt dined with Governor Ellis and other political leaders at the Executive Mansion along with a visitor from Alabama there to persuade the North Carolinians that Lincoln's election was sufficient grounds to leave the Union. Ellis reported that while only one or two of the North Carolinians agreed with secession, "all were strongly for Southern rights."[10]

Edwin Holt and many of his closest associates remained adamantly opposed to secession in the first months after Lincoln's election. Although for at least a decade ardent secessionist Edmund Ruffin had tried to persuade his kinsman of the merits of his cause, Thomas Ruffin continued to deny that any state had the right to withdraw from the Union. He joined John Morehead as a North Carolina delegate to the Washington Peace Conference, dubbed the "Old Gentlemen's Convention" because most attending were leaders from the past who hoped that political compromise could work yet again.[11]

The peace conference failed, but in early 1861 a majority of North Carolinians remained committed to the Union. Support for secession proved strongest in the eastern part of the state, but its advocates had gained ground in the Piedmont after Lincoln's election

9. Jacob C. Leonard, *Centennial History of Davidson County, North Carolina* (Raleigh, 1927), 166.

10. John Carrigan to William A. Carrigan, November 17, 1860, Carrigan Papers; Norbert J. Tolbert, ed., *The Papers of John W. Ellis*, vol. 2 (Raleigh, 1964), 474.

11. David F. Allmendinger, *Ruffin: Family and Reform in the Old South* (New York, 1990), 133; James M. McPherson, *Battle Cry of Freedom: The Civil War Era* (New York, 1988), 257.

and led a hard fight against the pro-Union majority. When some of them challenged Judge Ruffin for his efforts to maintain the Union, Holt wrote his close friend, "I have not language to express my mortification at the conduct of 'some' of the citizens of Alamance county. I was not aware that we had in our midst men so destitute of principle and who could stoop so low as to be guilty of so base falsehood. I have charity enough yet to believe that our people would act right if left to think for themselves."[12]

All over the South people were acting in a manner Edwin Holt probably did not consider right. In late February 1861, as delegates from six southern states met in Montgomery, Alabama, to form the Confederate States of America, a statewide referendum for a secessionist convention in North Carolina was narrowly defeated. Unionism, however, continued to dominate in Alamance County. During the first week in March, the week Lincoln was inaugurated in Washington, Holt presided over a convention at the Alamance County Courthouse in Graham; he was one of 1,116 delegates who voted to stay in the Union, defeating only 284 who voted to join the Confederacy.[13]

But the tide was turning. In late March, after a visit to Alamance County, Edmund Ruffin could report that Judge Ruffin was a secessionist "& so is every member of his family." The Virginia Ruffin was on his way to Charleston; from a Confederate position in Charleston harbor, this most fanatical defender of southern rights fired the first Confederate shot against Fort Sumter and the United States. In response to this show of southern militance, President Lincoln requested that Governor Ellis send two regiments of North Carolina troops to the United States Army. Ellis responded by sending supplies to the Confederate army instead and by preparing the state militia. On May 20 a convention in Raleigh resolved that North Carolina leave the Union. A great celebration held after the ordinance passed revealed the widespread support for secession that Lincoln's call for troops had fostered among white North Carolinians.[14] Temporarily Unionism nearly vanished. Edwin Holt joined other former Unionists in endorsing the Confederate States of America.

12. Edwin Holt to Thomas Ruffin, March 30, 1861, Thomas Ruffin Papers.
13. William R. Trotter, *Silk Flags and Cold Steel: The Civil War in North Carolina: The Piedmont* (Winston-Salem, N.C., 1988), 22; Whitaker, *Centennial History of Alamance County*, 113–14.
14. Allmendinger, *Ruffin*, 133; Powell, *North Carolina Through Four Centuries*, 346; Trotter, *Silk Flags*, 25.

Historian Jonathan Wiener claims that the support industrialists such as Edwin Holt gave secession was "the ultimate test of their subservience" to the planter class.[15] Even as reluctant a secessionist as Holt, however, quickly found reasons to endorse the new southern nation, reasons not the result of subservience to the planter class. During the early months of this civil war emotional ties dictated not only acceptance but enthusiastic endorsement of a new southern nation. Although ties to the North were genuine and strong, Holt's roots, family, and property were all in the South, and he shared with many southerners a sense of loyalty to place that was exacerbated by the threat of Union invasion. Five of his sons were of military age. Thomas and William enjoyed exemptions from conscription throughout the war and James for most of it, but Alexander and Banks took part in some of the heaviest fighting; both were captured and Banks was seriously wounded. The fact that two sons, a son-in-law, and numerous nephews risked their lives assured Edwin Holt's support of a cause he had initially opposed. In every year of the war the Holt family received news of a casualty; although Alexander and Banks survived, the son-in-law and several nephews did not.

But Edwin Holt and his oldest sons did not endorse the Confederacy merely out of patriotism or concern for the young men in their family. Early in the war they realized that although separation from the North would sever professional ties, close markets, and cut off vital supplies, it would also create tremendous new opportunities for profit. Initially Thomas Holt feared secession and war might be detrimental to his business. When he heard that the nearby Orange Factory had more orders than it could fill Thomas asked for referrals for the number-fourteen yarn he ordinarily sold in Philadelphia "which of course is cut off." Curiously, for a short time Thomas feared being left idle by the disruption of war, prompting him to ask several other mill men if they needed his assistance, because, "as my factory gives me but little employment, I would like to have something to do."[16] But Thomas Holt soon learned that furnishing both the North Carolina government and the Confederate government with the cloth they needed to outfit soldiers would more than compensate for lost northern markets and would give him more than enough to keep busy. As northern supplies were cut off and imports

15. Jonathan M. Wiener, *Social Origins of the New South: Alabama, 1860–1885* (Baton Rouge, 1978), 145–46.
16. Thomas Holt to J. Webb, July 11, 1861, Webb Papers; Thomas Holt to F. V. Fries, April 25, 1862, Fries Papers, SHC.

from abroad became increasingly difficult to obtain, any yarn or cloth available in the South was at a premium.

Although Thomas Holt was slow to recognize it, new markets for Alamance mill products were emerging even before North Carolina joined the Confederacy. James Newlin wrote Holt early in 1861 that the price of his yarn rose weekly. Twelve days before his state seceded, Charles Fisher paid Holt $28.20 for 227 yards of osnaburg and a few days later returned to pay $280.32 more for cloth to equip his new regiment. Thomas Ruffin, who responded to North Carolina's secession by becoming as ardent a Confederate as he had been a Unionist, also bought cloth from Holt, which the women in his household made into clothing for the Alamance Regulators, the historically (and ironically) named regiment led by one of his sons.[17]

These small orders were indicators of the opportunity secession and war offered southern mill men. Early in the conflict Holt confided to his former partner that although mills would suffer from the loss of oil and dye imports "manufacturing will do well if we can keep running." By the fall of 1862, acknowledging that prices had gone from "reasonable to fabulous," Thomas Holt reported receiving $5.50 for a bunch of yarn that had previously sold for $1.30. A year later his father wrote, "I am getting fine prices for my coloured goods" and complained that he could not furnish one-tenth of the demand. Even Thomas Ruffin, early benefactor of the Alamance Factory, was sometimes turned down when he requested cloth.[18] For most people in Alamance a protracted war meant increasing privation; for the Holts it meant increasing profit.

Many mills in the state operated day and night in an effort to meet the demand. But the wartime profits of mill owners did not come unchallenged or unchecked. A four-way struggle developed as the Confederate government, the North Carolina government, and the state's civilian population all claimed a share of the goods mill owners produced. Ironically, although many southerners defined the conflict as a fight for states' rights, industrialists faced greater con-

17. Newlin quoted in Richard W. Griffin, "The Civil War and Cotton Manufacturing in North Carolina," *Cotton History Review* 2 (1961): 153; Richard Iobst and Louis Manarin, *The Bloody Sixth: The Sixth North Carolina Regiment, Confederate States of America* (Raleigh, 1965), 6; Robinson, "Thomas Ruffin," 312–13.
18. Edwin Holt to William Carrigan, September 29, 1861, White Papers; Thomas Holt to C. W. Garrett, November 21, 1862, Pittman Collection, NCDAH; Edwin Holt to Thomas Ruffin, January 6, 1863, Thomas Ruffin Papers.

trol by the Confederacy than they had ever known in the Union. As Emory Thomas has pointed out, southerners soon realized "that Confederate national survival and rigid adherence to ante-bellum Southern ideology were mutually exclusive." Italian historian Raimondo Luraghi has concluded, with some exaggeration when applied to North Carolina, that Confederate authorities "were able to intervene effectively" to assure that the industrialists cooperated. Officials had a number of weapons at their disposal. Although a high percentage of southern mill workers were women and children, the success of textile mills depended on the skills of a small number of men, many of them of conscription age. There is no evidence that either the mill owners or the government considered replacing these men by training women. James Newlin did allow a war-bound weave room worker to turn over his looms to his sister but later concluded that "the work he done is too hard for a girl and his sister is unable now to keep it up."[19] For the most part, rather than replacing soldiers with women, mill owners successfully argued that their skilled male workers were too valuable to be conscripted. Both the Confederate and state governments often agreed to exemptions, but politicians also tried to use their power to threaten denying requests as a means of controlling the mill owners.

Eventually the Confederate government passed stringent laws regulating textile manufacturers; getting state authorities as well as individual mill owners to comply proved a constant struggle. Mill men easily supported the first Confederate industrial laws because they exempted superintendents and operatives from military service and authorized the duty-free importation of textile machinery. In time, however, these laws were superseded by a more restrictive one penalizing profiteering and allowing exemptions only if profits did not exceed 75 percent of production cost.[20]

This law was difficult to enforce, particularly in North Carolina where three war governors were determined to assume almost total control of textile factories. In the summer of 1861 Governor Ellis died; he was replaced by speaker of the senate Henry T. Clark until an election could be held a year later. Clark tried flattering the "Pro-

19. See, for example, Henry Fries, "Reminiscences of Confederate Days," 11, Fries Papers, NCDAH; C. Phifer to H. A. Dowd, May 1, 1864, Pittman Collection; Thomas, *Confederate Nation*, 143; Raimondo Luraghi, *The Rise and Fall of the Plantation South* (New York, 1978), 124; James Newlin to C. W. Garnett, December 17, 1862, Military Collection, NCDAH.

20. Elizabeth Yates Webb, "Cotton Manufacturing and State Regulation in North Carolina, 1861–65," *North Carolina Historical Review* 9 (1932): 117–37.

prietors of Cotton Factories in N.C.," writing them "I may rely, with the most confident expectations, on your patriotism and your zeal in the good cause against our common foe." Adding a stick to his carrot, he also warned that if they did not cooperate the State would "resort to more stringent measures to obtain that supply without which our troops cannot be prepared for the field."[21]

In August 1862 Zebulon Vance, a former college classmate and longtime friend of Thomas Holt, was elected North Carolina's third wartime governor. The close friendship of William Rainey Holt's daughter with Vance's wife—she often stayed in the governor's mansion when Vance was away—also assured the Holt family contact with the new governor. Vance, who represented the Conservative Party that was composed largely of former Whigs and Unionists like the Holts, supported southern independence from the United States but also demanded North Carolina's independence from the Confederate government. He was determined, it was said, to "fight the Yankees and fuss with the Confederacy." Vance's determination to stymie Confederate efforts to control the state's thirty-nine cotton mills and seven woolen mills resulted in an ongoing struggle with the Confederate quartermaster. On at least one occasion, Thomas Holt wrote Vance encouraging him to protest the Confederate government's demands.[22]

While blocking Confederate efforts to control the state's mills with threats of conscription, Vance tried to assume power over them himself. Despite his friendship with several Holts, Vance's ambition resulted in another ongoing struggle between himself and a number of North Carolina mill owners who were determined to thwart efforts of both governments to control them. The state quartermaster received numerous letters from mill owners requesting exemptions from the draft for key male workers. In September 1863 Edwin Holt asked that eleven men, including his son William, be allowed to avoid military service on the grounds that their loss would force him to shut down. Another Alamance mill owner requested that the superintendent in his spinning department be exempted unless the county was invaded by the enemy. Gaston County mill owner Thomas Tate likewise warned the quartermaster that if even one of his skilled workers was conscripted "the work will be stopped as I

21. Buck W. Yearns and John G. Barrett, eds., *North Carolina Civil War Documentary* (Chapel Hill, 1980), xii, 102.
22. Frontis W. Johnston, ed., *The Papers of Zebulon Baird Vance*, vol. 1 (Raleigh, 1963), 66n; Powell, *North Carolina Through Four Centuries*, 370; Thomas Holt to C. A. Dowd, September 30, 1864, Pittman Collection.

know of no other to take the place." Often owners publicly claimed patriotism as grounds for keeping key skilled workers at work, but one more candidly acknowledged privately that his upcoming trip to Raleigh was "to arrange about saving my hands, if possible, from the clutches of the conscript law."[23]

Although the Confederacy protested his leniency, Vance often advised granting exemption requests because of the military demand for the products the mills produced. Not infrequently, however, the exemptions approved were accompanied with a threat. When the quartermaster sent specific instructions to the Webbs, mill owners in Orange County, he also warned that "only on those conditions can your operatives be exempt from conscription if you have any who are liable."[24]

It was difficult for either government to enforce laws regulating the textile industry because opportunities for speculation were manifold. Elizabeth Yates Webb has suggested that "the matter of keeping prices of cotton products down was a rather impossible one, with the mills wanting to take advantage of their first real opportunity to make their business pay and the State putting one weight after another upon them trying to delay the inevitable rise in prices." Edwin Holt acknowledged that many "unprincipled men" pushed prices to "fabulous heights" but always insisted that he and his sons were not among them. Thomas Holt assured North Carolina officials of his determination to support the Confederacy "with great cheerfulness." Their wealth and contacts, however, made it easier for the Holts than for most mill men to mandate the terms of their support. A year after the war began, Thomas Ruffin learned that although Francis Fries would not sell him or anyone cloth without an order from the governor he could usually get what he wanted from Edwin Holt if he was willing to pay the inflated price.[25]

Initially genuine enthusiasm for a southern victory did prompt

23. Edwin Holt to H. A. Dowd, September 16, 1863, Gray and Wilson to Governor Vance, November 7, 1864, T. R. Tate to C. W. Garrett, October 30, 1862, Military Collection, NCDAH; Rufus Patterson to Mother, June 30, 1862, Patterson Papers.

24. Trotter, *Silk Flags,* 88; C. W. Garrett to J. and J. H. Webb, November 18, 1862, Webb Papers.

25. Webb, "Cotton Manufacturing and State Regulation," 134; Edwin M. Holt to C. W. Garrett, November 7, 1862; Thomas Holt to H. A. Dowd, January 13, September 15, 1863, Pittman Collection; Thomas Ruffin to Thomas Ruffin Jr., May 21, 1862, quoted in Yearns and Barrett, eds., *North Carolina Civil War Documentary,* 165. As noted earlier, Ruffin's request was turned down at least once by the Holts but apparently this was due to limited supplies, not government regulation.

the Holts like most mill men to favor the North Carolina and Confederate governments. By the end of second year of war Edwin Holt
was furnishing 80 percent of his sheetings and osnaburgs to the
state. As patriotic zeal for the southern cause waned, however, a
number of textile mill owners, including the Holts, were tempted to
seek higher prices in the private market. One wrote the quartermaster that "the demand for goods is so pressing that it is almost impossible so far to resist the importunity of buyers as to give the State the
amount we have promised." In the summer of 1862, another North
Carolina manufacturer hinted that the Holts were profiteering when
he referred to the seventy-five cents a yard they received for their
checks as "extraordinary." William Holden, editor of the *Raleigh
Standard*, was a particularly acerbic critic of wartime entrepreneurs.
In early 1862 he published his criticism, claiming that while it was
true that some costs had risen, the two basic costs, cotton and labor,
remained low. Accordingly, he demanded that mill owners accept a
maximum of 40 percent profit rather than the more than 100 percent he claimed they were enjoying. The Holts responded directly to
Holden, accusing him of unfairly attacking cotton manufacturers.
They did not, however, deny their great profits.[26]

Fear of government regulation, as well as uneasiness about profiteering at the expense of the Confederate cause, did inspire some
enthusiasm for self-regulation. Edwin Holt joined other mill men
from around the state in assuring Governor Vance that they would
abide by the terms of the Confederate exemption law, which allowed
only 75 percent profit. In December 1862, perhaps alarmed at the degree of state regulation in Georgia, North Carolina producers meeting in Greensboro resolved "to discourage speculation" by selling
only to state agents at set prices that would be published monthly by
the state quartermaster. Manufacturers not in attendance were requested to comply. Holt, attending the meeting with his sons
Thomas and William, was chosen along with George Makepeace to
convey the resolutions to the governor.[27]

Correspondence with the state quartermaster reveals, however,
that mill men never very rigorously policed their own resolutions.
As optimistic expectations of a quick southern victory waned, they
increasingly interpreted the resolutions in a manner calculated to
serve their own best interest. The unanimity mill owners expressed

26. Edwin M. Holt to C. W. Garrett, November 7, 1862, Military Collection; Webb, "Cotton Manufacturers and State Regulation," 131, 128; S. F.
Patterson to Caroline, August 29, 1862, Patterson Papers.
27. *Hillsborough Recorder*, December 10, 1862.

in Greensboro also broke down as some complained of sacrificing more than others. In the spring of 1864 John Murray, another Alamance mill owner, complained that he could no longer sell yarn to the state at twelve dollars a bunch not only because it did not allow him to replace his raw material but also because "we are of the opinion it is less than any other factory in Alamance Co is furnishing your yarns at. Mr. T. M. Holt and Mr. E. M. Holt told us they had been receiving $14 for sometime for theirs."[28]

Mill men also had to defend their profits to the poorer members of their communities including their own workers. The composition of the small working class in Alamance and the surrounding counties varied little during the war years. The majority of textile laborers were children and young women who remained available for work. Some adult male hands quit their jobs when they were conscripted or volunteered to fight, but many of them were exempted. Extant records, not available for the Alamance Factory, reveal that at Cedar Rapids the work force included eleven more women and children (a 14 percent increase) and six fewer men (a nearly 50 percent decrease) after four years of war. It is reasonable to assume that the war had a similar impact on the Alamance work force. As long as they could retain a few key skilled workers, mill owners had no reason to be much concerned about the war disrupting their labor. During the first years the war rarely caused any mill in the state to close except for an occasional day off to support a call for volunteers or so workers could wave the troops off to battle.[29]

Owners had little reason to fear the disruption of their work force, but they did need to fear disruption of class harmony among whites. Bill Cecil-Fronsman has described "the growing sense of class consciousness that the war generated among certain elements of North Carolina's common whites" and explains that for many of them "events of the war seemed to violate the terms of their implicit understanding with their society's status quo."[30]

As they experienced a second year of war, poorer whites changed their attitude toward the war from one of initial widespread enthusiasm for the Confederate cause to anger over sacrifices demanded by a wartime economy. Constant dread of tragic news also eroded initial support. The absence of a large number of men between the ages

28. Murray and Brothers to H. A. Dowd, May 9, 1864, Military Collection.
29. Cedar Falls Manufacturing Company Day Book, 1861–65, NCDAH.
30. Bill Cecil-Fronsman, *Common Whites: Class and Culture in Antebellum North Carolina* (Lexington, 1992), 209.

of eighteen and forty often had dire repercussions for those left behind. An Alamance school teacher noted that "the laboring class of men is scarce, and the farms, in a great measure, have to be cultivated by women and children."[31]

By the winter of 1862–1863, war-related poverty was widespread; many of these women and children bereft of male breadwinners were its major victims. Although most of the men leaving Alamance as soldiers were young and unmarried, some did leave behind wives who had to find alternative means of support for themselves and their children. The government encouraged them to make cloth and garments for the soldiers, work many eagerly sought. In the spring of 1863, a soldier wrote home that "I heard that the women had been preparing thread and cloth in Alamance from all the factorys." It was not easy, however, for poor women to acquire the necessary cards and yarn to clothe their families and have enough left to barter. A Graham man reported to state officials that he knew many women "who make their living entirely by the needle" and requested government aid in helping them.[32] The North Carolina government did make some effort on behalf of indigent women, providing them with cards and requisitioning cloth so that they could make clothing for soldiers and civilians alike.

Government aid, however, never adequately alleviated the enormous war-created misery. In the fall of 1862, Thomas Holt reported that all but one of his mill families were widow headed; he requested a delay in providing for the state so he could exchange his goods for bacon, corn, wheat, and wood to give these indigent families. James Newlin also procured provision for his Alamance County workers, reporting to the state that it required all of his mill's resources after he had met the state's quota.[33] Mill work offered some poor women a means to support themselves, but in the last years of the war the financial crisis of the Confederacy threatened that alternative as well.

Workers in Alamance County were more fortunate than their counterparts in other mills around the state. In 1864 one mill owner in another county complained that he could not pay his hand "a copper." Early in the war another asked if he could pay women who sewed for the troops before he supplied the state, as "they are very

31. C. V. Ferguson, "Educational Growth in Alamance County" (M.A. thesis, University of North Carolina, 1931) 48.

32. Webb, "Cotton Manufacturing and State Regulation," 126, 118; W. H. Moore to Captain Garrett, July 10, 1862, Military Collection.

33. Thomas Holt to H. A. Dowd, November 21, 1862, Pittman Collection; John Newlin to H. A. Dowd, August 25, 1864, Military Collection.

clamorous for their pay and justly too, great many of them being very poor and needy." Clamorous was the word chosen by at least one other manufacturer to describe women unable to obtain even basic necessities. In 1864 a mill man complained that if the state did not soon pay him "my hands say they will have to quit us and go at somethng else."[34]

Leaving and going elsewhere, however, was generally not an option for poor women accustomed to depending on a male provider. Some indigent women apologized to powerful men when forced to seek relief, reflecting their society's arch-conservative tenets concerning proper female behavior. Frances E. Huske, although the daughter of Henry A. Donaldson, builder of a pioneer textile mill in North Carolina, typified many southern women whose already difficult circumstances became worse during a protracted war. Producing cloth had made Donaldson money, but it was not money his daughter inherited. In 1860, a poor widow with six children, she moved her family from North Carolina to Alabama "hoping to find more work and better wages." Her oldest son, described as "all the help I had," died after being wounded at the Battle of Seven Pines. She appealed to Governor Vance for help in light of both her father's accomplishments and her son's death fighting in a North Carolina regiment. Apologizing for troubling him, she asked the governor "who have we poor women to apply to if not to those who are strong in good and generous deeds." Frances Huske was nearly desperate yet retained her faith in paternal benevolence. Sarah F. Goodridge revealed a similar deferential trust in elite men when she asked William Holt to send her cloth on credit since her two brothers had received no military pay for over a year. Although desperate to clothe her family, Goodridge assured Holt that she would assume him right if he refused her request and "feel not the *slightest* vexation." The letter, signed "with lasting gratitude your obliged friend," was marked "answ *no*."[35]

It became a commonplace of southern rhetoric after the war to praise white women as pillars of the Confederacy. A history of Alamance County extolled those women who "endured the hardships of the war years with quiet courage." In reality many women were not quiet at all but complained bitterly about the sacrifices they

34. H. H. Tate to H. A. Dowd, J. C. Moore to J. Devereaux, October [no day], 1861, Gerry [?] Winston to H. A. Dowd, May 31, 1864, T. R. Tate to H. A. Dowd, May 31, 1864, Military Collection.
35. Frances E. Huskee to Governor Vance, March 9, 1864, Military Collection; Sarah F. Goodridge to William Holt, November 16, 1864, Alamance Cotton Mill Records.

made for a war they had no voice in making. War undermined female deference. Some women, rather than trusting in the benevolence of powerful men, responded to war-created misery in ways
that belied images of southern white female gentility. "Poverty,"
historian Victoria Bynum explains in her study of social and sexual
control in three North Carolina Piedmont counties, was "the most
compelling catalyst for unruly behavior during the Civil War." Because yarn and cloth were necessities hard for civilians to acquire,
poor women often made textile manufacturers the targets of their
unruly behavior. Less than a year after the war began, the *North Carolina Standard* claimed that the "great mass of people are indignant
at the conduct of the cotton manufacturers."[36] Women swelled the
ranks of those willing to express their indignation.

Revealing the limits of patriarchy, some women publicly challenged elite men like Edwin Holt for violating their rights. More
than a year after the war erupted, Holt acknowledged that "my refusal to furnish individuals with the goods for their families has created great prejudice and has brought down an immense amount of
abuse on me." In 1864 his son Thomas concurred that "manufacturers are looked upon by a great many persons as the greatest extor-
tioners our country affords, whether or not they are." He appealed to
the state to lower his quota "in order to let out as much as possible
to the old women (for I assure you they are indescribable)." Some
days several hundred women sought yarn at the Granite Factory. A
record of the anger poor women felt has been preserved by the few
who wrote to their governor. Nancy Mangum complained to Vance
that although poor people had difficulty getting necessities, the
Holts "are speculating every day. Their is old Ed. Holt where has a
factory on Alamance he has maid his brages [brags] is this war holds
on 2 years longer he would own all of Allamance County he has
cloth and thread and wont let no body have it without wheat or corn
or meet." In the last years of the war this sense of injustice, shared
by many poor women, prompted food riots including at least two in
the North Carolina Piedmont.[37]

36. Whitaker, *Centennial History of Alamance County,* 117; Victoria
Bynum, *Unruly Women: The Politics of Social and Sexual Control in the
Old South* (Chapel Hill, 1992), 125; Griffin, "Civil War and Cotton Manufac-
turing in North Carolina," 153.
37. Edwin Holt to C. W. Garrett, November 7, 1862, Military Collection;
Thomas Holt to H. A. Dowd, January 13, 1864, Pittman Collection; Thomas
Holt to H. A. Dowd, September 15, 18, 1863, Military Collection; Nancy
Mangum to Governor Vance, April 9, 1863, Zebulon Baird Vance Papers,
SHC; Bynum, *Unruly Women,* 128–29; Thomas, *Confederate Nation,* 204.

Men sometimes complained on behalf of wives who found it increasingly difficult to clothe their families. Shortly before the war ended, soldier James T. Pugh wrote his wife in Haw River of his dismay that she had been charged seventy-five dollars for a bunch of thread that in Virginia cost only forty dollars. Most likely with the Holts in mind, he concluded, "I do think that any body that would charge a soldier's wife seventy five dollars a bunch ought to be damned. But all right I hope all such will get this reward if not from the yankees our own soldiers for no good will ever come of such people."[38]

The Holts tried to defend themselves before a demanding government and the angry poor while at the same time protecting their property and profits. Thomas assured the state quartermaster that he had given hundreds of bunches of yarn to poor families and that he often sold to consumers at a lower rate than traders offered him. Members of the family could also claim contributions to hospitals and to ladies aid societies, but as the refusal of Goodridge's request for credit reveals, there were clearly limits to their benevolence.[39]

Another defense was to point out their own difficulties acquiring necessities. The Union blockade underscored how dependent southern mill men were on northern machinery, supplies, and expertise. Early in the war, Edwin Holt had realized that acquiring oil and dyestuff would be a major problem and appealed to the North Carolina government for help. The state responded to numerous such appeals by outfitting a blockade runner, which included "large quantities of machinery supplies" in its inventories after eleven trips to Europe. But supplying through blockade running was haphazard at best. In the summer of 1864, Thomas Holt complained that the oil he received "is but little better than peanut," not the "good lard oil that is the next best to sperm," and questioned "Would it not be a good idea to bring in some *genuine sperm*?" Disappointed by the state, Thomas tried turning to private suppliers. Around the time he was complaining about the poor quality of the state-supplied oil he also canceled a request for card clothing after acquiring what he needed from a private blockade runner.[40]

The endemic problems that plagued nineteenth-century mills

38. James T. Pugh to wife, February 6, 1865, James Pugh Papers, SHC.
39. Thomas Holt to H. A. Dowd, January 15, 1864, Edwin Holt to C. W. Garrett, November 7, 1862, Military Collection.
40. Edwin Holt to William Carrigan, August [no day], 1861, December 1, 1861, Carrigan Papers; Webb, "Cotton Manufacturing and State Regulation," 125; Thomas Holt to H. A. Dowd, June 4, 1864, Military Collection.

compounded those created by the war. In the winter of 1861–1862, a measles epidemic prevented Holt's workers from fulfilling his quota. A year later several cases of smallpox threatened the mill villages with an even more serious epidemic. Estrangement from northern machine companies made it more difficult than usual to repair broken machinery. In the winter of 1864 Thomas reported that he could not send his weekly quota "on account of a *serious* break." Although the master machinist at the railroad shops had "kindly offered to mend it" he could not do so for some time. Every war year both flooding and drought forced a work stoppage for at least a few days. In July and then again in August 1862 severe freshets tore out the headgates at the Granite Factory and did slight damage to the dam as well. In January 1865 a major flood submerged Edwin Holt's machinery in water, destroying his warps and damaging the looms he used for making his famous checked cloth.[41]

As frustrating as making do with damaged and aging machinery and second-rate supplies could be, the Holts also benefited from the blockade because it stymied the creation of new mills in competition with theirs. Although a few new ones were founded—Rufus Patterson built a mill in Salem and George Brandt one in Fayetteville—more closed for want of new machinery and supplies. Men less well connected with government officials than Edwin Holt and his sons found it especially difficult to replace machinery and acquire supplies; some had to close their mills. In the last year of the war, as Union troops moved throughout much of North Carolina, some of the mills that had survived the blockade were destroyed by the armies.[42]

The warring armies were not a presence in the North Carolina Piedmont until late 1864, but initial enthusiasm for the Confederacy had waned well before that time. North Carolina experienced the highest desertion rate of any state in the Confederacy. By late 1862 Unionism had revived in the state's "Quaker Belt," which centered in Randolph and Guilford Counties but also included parts of Alamance. The Heroes of America, an antiwar organization with per-

41. Thomas Holt to Grasty-Rison, February 5, 1862, Grasty-Rison Papers, Manuscripts Division, Perkins Library, Duke University; Ferguson, "Educational Growth in Alamance County," 47; Thomas Holt to H. A. Dowd, February 11, April 12, 1864, Edwin Holt to H. A. Dowd, January 12, 19, 1865, Military Collection.

42. Richard W. Griffin, "Reconstruction of the North Carolina Textile Industry, 1865–1885," *North Carolina Historical Review* 41 (1957): 34.

haps as many as ten thousand members, was especially active in promoting peace and North Carolina's return to the Union. Once they realized that defeat of the Confederacy was inevitable, wealthy men like the Holts had reason to advocate a quick restoration of the Union as well. They did not, however, condone a group that fostered class division more than national unity. There was no place for them in an organization made up largely of lower-class whites whose sense of grievance had been exacerbated by war. According to historians of the Heroes, its support for the military defeat of the Confederacy was an "expression of antipathy to the political and social elite who ruled the state and the Confederacy," and accordingly anathema to "many of the Whiggish politicians who favored the peace movement." Furthermore, in light of the profits they enjoyed in a wartime economy, textile producers had reason to feel ambivalent about peace and Union activism. Mill owner Rufus Patterson, a former college classmate of Thomas Holt, complained that "every man who is pursuing an honest calling & realizing *profit* is renounced by these people—and they are crying out 'oh! for the old union that Luciver [?] might confiscate the property of the *rich* & give it to the [illegible] poor.' "[43]

Most likely Edwin Holt and his sons agreed with Patterson and joined in condemning members of the Heroes of America as traitors despite sharing with them a growing disillusionment with the Confederacy. Although the Holts continued to express at least tepid support of the southern cause, their activities increasingly revealed something less than enthusiasm. By the fall of 1862 Holt's initial optimism waned as he acknowledged the dim prospect of a southern victory, although he continued to hope that something, perhaps recognition from England and France, could turn the tide. The Holts recognized that they profited handsomely from this experiment in southern independence, but spiraling inflation and growing pessimism about the possibility of Confederate victory prompted them to join in the chorus of mill owners complaining about what they perceived as excessive sacrifice. In the fall of 1864, Edwin Holt received a lengthy letter from Gaston County mill owner Jasper Stowe

43. Richard Reid, "A Test Case of the 'Crying Evil': Desertion Among North Carolina Troops During the Civil War," *North Carolina Historical Review* 58 (1981): 237; William T. Auman and David D. Scarboro, "The Heroes of America in Civil War North Carolina," *North Carolina Historical Review* 58 (1981): 345–47; Rufus Patterson to father, February 6, 1862, Patterson Papers.

detailing his grievances with the Quartermaster Department, which he branded as "infamously corrupt," and calling on mill owners to unite in resistance.[44]

There is no evidence that the Holts joined Stowe in collective protest, but they often complained individually to the quartermaster that they were at best inconvenienced and even unfairly treated. In the winter of 1863–1864 Thomas Holt was singled out for charging the government exorbitant prices and thus profiting from the war while soldiers were paid in almost worthless Confederate money. He responded with a lengthy and indignant letter introduced with his regret "that after the cheerful manner in which I have always complied with the requisition of the state that she should become dissatisfied with me." Thomas rebutted the charge that he received a six-dollar profit on each bunch of yarn by claiming that expenses and taxes consumed half of that amount, leaving him "$3.00 (worth in coin about 15c) out of which I am to support my family, educate my children & give $175.00 for a pt. of boots, $2.00 for port, ect. ect." Holt also insisted that he was forced to raise his prices due to the sharp rise in the cost of cotton. He threatened the quartermaster department that if forced to drop prices to the level suggested "the result will be one of two things. I will either become bankrupt or will have to starve my hands." While still a loyal enough Confederate to proclaim "myself & all I have is at the disposal of my country," Thomas added that he could not "see any just cause why I should work for nothing." A few months later Thomas's father defended himself for raising the price of goods because what "I have charged you heretofore does not more than pay cost . . . the cotton in a bunch of yarn now cost $10.50 and it cost me all of $4.50 to spin it, which leaves me no profit and a heavy tax to pay." The son echoed this defense, writing:

> I do not think the state ought to complain as I am *confident* that the nett profit on it (after paying my taxes which with various other incidentals, are not counted in the cost), will not exceed 20 pct in Confederate currency which when reduced to old prices is very little. The state of Va. has offered me $30. which their manufacturers say is within the 75 pr ct. I refused their offer, as I prefer to furnish my own state, as long as they want,

44. Edwin Holt to William Carrigan, November 5, 1862, Carrigan Papers; Jasper Stowe to Edwin Holt, November 15, 1864, Archibald Smith Papers, SHC.

even at the difference in price, if I can replace my cotton, pay all expenses & receive fair wages for my time & ware and tare of machinery, in my transactions with the state. I will be satisfied & think that she ought not to ask more.[45]

The day Thomas Holt wrote at length to defend his considerable profits, his younger brother Banks wrote in the small diary he kept through the war that he was in "a hot & bloody conflict." In July 1861 Banks and Alexander Holt joined Company F of the North Carolina Sixth Infantry, organized by Charles Fisher before his state left the Union. In early June Fisher moved the Sixth from Charlotte to Company Shops, where he held drills all month. He continued buying supplies out of pocket (he was later reimbursed five thousand dollars) because, according to the historians of his regiment, he wanted to go to war "like a wealthy gentleman." On July 3, the day Alexander and Banks joined, the Sixth Regiment was officially transferred to the Confederate States of America. Most of the soldiers enrolled were young, unmarried sons of farm families in Alamance and surrounding counties. There were only three men in the Sixth who can be documented as from mill families. A few weeks after joining, Alexander and Banks marched with their regiment day and night, occasionally finding relief by train, to Virginia where they were assigned to General Barnard Bee's brigade shortly before the First Battle of Manassas (Bull Run), the first major battle of the war. During that battle, Colonel Fisher and fifteen of his soldiers were killed; Edwin Holt's sons took part in some of the worst fighting but survived unharmed. This early decisive Confederate victory created a brief moment of widespread optimism and exuberant Confederate nationalism that even captured Edwin Holt, only a few months before firmly committed to national unity. He described the battle as "a terrible affair," but also as "a most glorious victory on our part" and "a perfect rout of the Yankeys," who were "driven back panick stricken." Banks wrote his father of seeing twenty-seven dead horses and forty-three dead men within one acre, of seeing a man on one side of him killed and one on the other side seriously wounded. A ball passed so close to Alexander that it scorched his hair, but he was not injured. Holt knew only one of the men killed and few of those who were seriously wounded. Responding to this victory and a subsequent one at Leesburg, he wrote, "God be praised for his goodness. . . . I hope and pray

45. Thomas Holt to H. A. Dowd, January 13, May 20, 1864, Edwin Holt to H. A. Dowd, May 4, 1864, Pittman Collection.

that his protection will continue not only over my own sons but over the whole Confederate army to the end."[46]

Despite this enthusiastic response to the South's first major victory, Edwin Holt ultimately proved far more pragmatic about the Confederacy than his brother. Through the 1850s, as his brother and nephews cultivated industrial ties with the North, William Holt advocated southern nationalism. When the war came, while Edwin stressed the safety of his sons and the other soldiers, William stressed the rightness of a glorious cause. Early in the war he enthused, "I feel highly honored and much gratification that I have had 4 nephews and one son in the ranks battling for the rights and honor of our country, a Confederacy when a peace can be conquered, unequalled in solid advantage, for young and old, by any country on the face of the earth."[47]

Both this son and one who joined later, as well as William Carrigan's two youngest sons, would die in the war. For them as for thousands of young men, the adventure of becoming a soldier gave way to the horror of being a soldier. The Sixth Regiment took part in so much heavy fighting that it became known as the "Bloody Sixth." One of its soldiers wrote a brother at home in Alamance County, "I will advise you not to come here if there is any other chance in the world, because you dont know the hardships you have no idea. And I dont believe that you could stand it here, by no means."[48]

Both Banks and Alexander continued to be involved in their regiment's bloody fighting. Six months after they enlisted, their father wrote wistfully about his one disappointing son, "Alexander they say is in fine health and makes an excelent soldier." Through much of 1862 Alexander remained in Virginia, fighting at Williamsburg, Seven Pines, Chickahominy, and Malvern Hill. According to his father, he "came out clean," but he "sank under the excesive fatigue of a weeks fighting" and was granted a furlough to come home. In November 1863 Alexander was captured at Rappahannock Station, Virginia, and imprisoned in Maryland. Six months later he was paroled through exchange and in December 1864 received a furlough.[49]

46. Banks Holt Diary, May 20, 1864 (in the possession of the Mary Stalter Family); Iobst and Manarin, *Bloody Sixth*, 12; Eighth Census of the United States, 1860, Alamance County, North Carolina; Weymouth T. Jordan, comp., *North Carolina Troops, 1861–1865* (Raleigh, 1973); Edwin Holt to William Carrigan, August [no day] 1861, White Papers.

47. William R. Holt to William Carrigan, September 29, 1861, White Papers.

48. Iobst and Manarin, *Bloody Sixth*, 145.

49. Edwin Holt to William Carrigan, December 1, 1861, November 5, 1862, White Papers; Jordan, *North Carolina Troops*, 337.

In the fall of 1861 Banks also returned home "weak and feeble" but recovered sufficiently to rejoin the army by the end of the year. After being promoted to first lieutenant in the Eighth Regiment, he was captured early in 1862 and held prisoner until paroled. When he rejoined his regiment he again took part in some of the heaviest fighting and was wounded during the Confederate defense of Charleston. In the spring of 1864 he marched with the Eighth through North Carolina to join Confederate forces fighting around Petersburg, Virginia. In early June his brother-in-law Thomas Slade was killed nearby at Cold Harbor, leaving Frances a widow at the age of twenty-seven.[50]

Most of his diary entries were in a lighthearted vein, but after several years observing war firsthand, Banks wrote "should I be slain on the battlefield or die in a hospital for the sake of humanity inform Mrs. Emily Holt of Graham Alamance Co NC of the fact." Fortunately Emily and her husband were only informed that Banks had received a serious leg wound at Fort Harrison, Virginia, and had been imprisoned at Fortress Monroe. According to family legend, he successfully persuaded the doctors there that his wealthy father would compensate them if they saved his leg. When sufficiently recovered, Banks was imprisoned at Fort Delaware. Through the intervention of a northern contact, his father was able to send him clothing, although it took two months to arrive.[51]

While in prison, Banks continued by mail his courtship with Catherine Mebane, the daughter of Giles Mebane, a prominent North Carolina politician. Although he married Catherine shortly after the war ended, while a captive of the North he amused himself copying or writing doggerel expressing his distaste for women and marriage. "A female to my mind I ne'er expect to find," and "to take to me a wife would grieve my very life," are examples of his prison musings. In June 1865 Banks Holt was released from Fort Delaware.[52]

James Holt, twenty-eight years old and the father of three children when North Carolina joined the Confederacy, claimed an exemption for the first three years of the war. Then in the spring of

50. Edwin Holt to William Carrigan, December 1, 1861, White Papers; Jordan, *North Carolina Troops*, vol. 7, 67.

51. Banks Holt Diary; W. E. Holt to H. A. Dowd, February 20, 1864, Pittman Collection; Walter Clark, ed., *Histories of the Several Regiments and Battalions from North Carolina in the Great War, 1861–65*, vol. 4 (Goldsboro, N.C., 1901), 497.

52. Banks Holt Diary; Interview with Mary Stalter, August 10, 1992; Louis H. Manarin, *North Carolina Troops 1861–1865: A Roster* (Raleigh, 1971).

1864 he resigned his position as a bank cashier in Thomasville and volunteered in the Tenth North Carolina Artillery. James was stationed at Fort Fisher until Governor Vance commissioned him captain and named him commandant of a military academy in Fayetteville.[53] His older brother Thomas and younger brother William enjoyed exemptions throughout the war justified by their claims that they could better serve the Confederacy as textile manufacturers.

Edwin Holt's sons survived, but four of his nephews and his only son-in-law did not. John Carrigan was an early casualty. In the spring of 1861 John and his youngest brother joined the cavalry in Arkansas and were sent to fight in northwestern Missouri. On August 9 John Carrigan died at the Battle of Oakhill, the only member of his company even seriously wounded. His father mourned "thus has pass'd away a favorite son in the 25th year of his age, he was not a member of any Church, but a good moral and orderly member of society, respected & lov'd by all that knew him." James, his father wrote North Carolina relatives, "carried the flag manfully through the whole battle." Three years later James visited the Holts in Alamance County while on furlough. Thomas Holt requested jacket cloth from the state quartermaster for his cousin as well as for his brother-in-law, promising to pay by deducting the price from the state's bill. While in North Carolina James Carrigan married Cora Moore, a sister-in-law of Thomas and James Holt. He returned to the army and was killed in the fighting around Atlanta several months before the birth of a son.[54]

Shortly after his Carrigan nephew was killed, William Rainey Holt reassured the boy's father that "the steadiness and bravery displayed there by our noble soldiery in which he took so high a part has stricken our enemies with terror and made them to feel and see that to conquer us, is vain." This ability to rationalize served him again when his own two sons died. William Michael was a victim of typhoid fever in 1862; his father passed by Locust Grove as he carried his son's remains home from Richmond. His youngest son, Eugene, died while a prisoner in 1865.[55]

Concern about sons and relatives made war a daily reality for

53. Ashe, *Biographical History of North Carolina*, vol. 7, 196.
54. William Carrigan to Edwin Holt, December 7, 1861, White Papers; Thomas Holt to H. A. Dowd, April 5, 1864, Military Collection; Interview with Joanne Carrigan, January 3, 1996.
55. William Rainey Holt to William Carrigan, September 29, 1861, White Papers; Thomas Holt to Thomas Ruffin, [n.d.], Ruffin Papers.

members of Edwin Holt's immediate family. War meant profit, but it also brought constant news of casualties among family and friends. After the death of his nephew as well as the sons of several neighbors, Holt wrote, "We have truly troublesome times but I hope the day is not far distant when we shale emerge from the gloom now hanging over us." Extraordinary inflation as well as the failure of European countries to recognize the Confederate states added to Holt's growing pessimism; his family, however, never experienced the desperation of the poor or the dislocation of the planters. Although Holt continued to cultivate the soil with slave labor, by 1860 he and his oldest sons were financially independent as manufacturers. Industrial capital enabled them to survive the war with far less dislocation than most southerners suffered. In September 1863, as most around them struggled to procure necessities, Edwin Holt turned down an offer of four thousand dollars worth of lard, peanut oil, corn, and bacon for his textiles, explaining that he had enough of all four commodities. Thomas complained that high prices made it difficult to buy boots or port, but in reality he profited handsomely. Neither Thomas nor his brother James suffered much wartime disruption in their lives. Two daughters were born to Thomas and his wife during the first two years of the war. In the fall of 1862 he hired men to plaster his new house and bought furniture for the space needed to accommodate his growing family. Nine days before North Carolina seceded from the Union, James's second son, named Edwin, was born. In the winter of 1861 his two oldest children caught diphtheria and four-year-old Ida died after what her grandfather described as "8 days of great suffering."[56] Two more sons were born during the war.

Emily Holt and her daughters experienced the war from the restricted perspective of elite southern white women. Not much can be known about their specific experiences since almost nothing that they wrote or was written about them during these years survives. George Rable, in his study of gender and the Civil War, concludes that while "many women wavered in their support for the Southern cause . . . they seldom questioned the racial, class, and sexual dogmas of their society." Certainly the Holt women shared with many southern white women their constant concern about the fate of sons and brothers fighting for a country women had little part in creating.

56. Edwin Holt to William Carrigan, November 5, 1862, December 1, 1861, White Papers; G. Y. Thomas to Mr. Fuller, September 18, 1863, Fuller-Thomas Papers, Manuscripts Division, Perkins Library, Duke University; Thomas Holt to Grasty-Rison, October 23, 1862, Grasty-Rison Papers.

Frances Holt shared the fate of young war widows. She knew her first husband only as a soldier. Thomas Slade was a forty-year-old widower with two children when he married her in 1862. Slade owned property worth approximately fifteen thousand dollars, modest compared to his new father-in-law's wealth but adequate to place him in the same economic class. According to Rable, the war meant "lessened parental influence" in the courtship and marital decisions of southern women. This may have been true for Frances Holt, but her parents probably approved of her marriage which, like those of her older brothers, was within the family's social and kinship network. Members of the Slade family were intermarried with and lived close to Emily's relatives in Caswell County. Slade enlisted sometime shortly after his marriage; he was killed at Cold Harbor in the summer of 1864.[57]

Mary and Emma Holt were sixteen and fourteen respectively when the war began. Mary most likely finished her formal education around 1863. Emma may have been among the young women whose educations were disrupted by the loss of teachers and the threat of approaching armies, although male academies closed more frequently than those for females as their students became soldiers. Rable concludes that "adolescent girls who had known only conflict and war seemed even more adrift and alone." One adolescent girl from North Carolina, Emma LeConte, who was about the same age as Emma Holt, wrote that for four years she knew "no pleasure, no enjoyment . . . nothing but the stern realities of life." Holt's two youngest daughters may have found their adolescence less carefree than girls of their class traditionally enjoyed in peacetime, but it is unlikely that they experienced the war in quite so grim a fashion. A party that took place in the Piedmont late in the war was described as an occasion where the "pretty young ladies in their beautiful homespun dresses" and "the young men . . . all dressed up in new fresh looking uniforms all resplendent in gold lace and shiny buttons" spent the evening dancing, singing, and playing games. Although they undoubtedly had to make some sacrifices, the war also gave elite women like Emily Holt and her daughters an unusual opportunity to contribute to a cause. Extant sources reveal that women in the families of Paul Cameron, Thomas Ruffin, and William Graham, all close friends of the Holts, took an active part in the Ladies

57. George C. Rable, *Civil Wars: Women and the Crisis of Southern Nationalism* (Urbana, 1989), x, 51; Eighth Manuscript Census of the United States, 1860, Rockingham County, North Carolina; Jordan, *North Carolina Troops*, vol. 7, 67.

Aid Society of Hillsborough; most likely the Holt women were involved in similar activities in Alamance County as well.[58]

Elite white women were far better prepared to survive wartime deprivation and slaughter than poor women, but they also had to find ways to make do in light of war-created scarcities. Cornelia Phillips Spencer, reminiscing about wartime life in Orange County, praised the civilians of central North Carolina because "many families of the highest respectability and refinement lived for months on corn-bread, sorghum, and peas . . . and ladies made their own shoes, and wove their own homespuns," all with "an energy and a cheerfulness that may well be called heroic." Whether Emily Holt and her daughters made their own shoes or not, they undoubtedly made some sacrifices. Almost everyone got by with reduced quantities of sugar, salt, coffee, and tea, and many did without commodities once considered necessities altogether. Clearly at least sometimes the Holt women had to make do—on one occasion a shipment of salt Thomas Holt ordered was lost and another arrived covered with corn—but more than most women they benefited from the barter economy that emerged in the wartime South. Edwin Holt condemned "many unprincipled men who are making efforts to run almost every article to fabulous prices," a charge that would increasingly be directed at his family. But at least through 1862, in light of his considerable profits, he found that "all seems to average about equal."[59]

Planter families with most of their wealth in land and slaves had much more difficulty maintaining their prewar life-style. William Rainey Holt had neither the economic security of a textile mill nor the good fortune of seeing his sons survive the war that Edwin enjoyed; at the end of the war he was bankrupt. In the beginning William called on family members to make sacrifices out of patriotism, but as the fighting continued they were increasingly made out of necessity. In the fall of 1861 he reported that "providence has favored us with fine & bountiful crops of all kinds . . . so that we have the greatest abundance of the means of living." But he also found coffee so expensive that he decided to do without and purchased

58. Farnham, *Education of the Southern Belle*, 182–83; La Conte quoted in Rable, *Civil Wars*, 222; Trotter, *Silk Flags*, 15; Lucy London Anderson, *North Carolina Women of the Confederacy* (Fayetteville, N.C., 1926), 29.

59. Cornelia Phillips Spencer, *The Last Ninety Days of the War in North Carolina* (New York, 1866), 30; Thomas Holt to Grasty-Rison, August 2, September 23, 1862, Grasty-Rison Papers; Edwin Holt to William Carrigan, December [no day], 1861, November 5, 1862, Carrigan Papers.

only a small quantity of salt. Even when stores in Lexington remained full of goods, William Holt asked his family to wear only old clothes so they could give the soldiers their newer ones. Louisa and her three daughters were frequently alone in their Lexington home because William stayed at the Linwood plantation, hoping to protect it from raiders. According to local legend, when Union troops under General Judson Kilpatrick entered Lexington, women in the town poured out all the whiskey they could find. A story passed down in the Holt family, possibly embellished with each retelling, claims that Louisa cleverly protected her home from these Union soldiers by persuading their general and his staff to be her guests. Her three daughters, less willing to accommodate Yankees, remained in their rooms even for meals while their mother presided at table. General Kilpatrick provided sugar, coffee, and other scarce items and ordered his chef to join the Holts' slaves in preparing meals. Upon his departure the general left Louisa some gold and a pony, which she named Kilpatrick. The gold and the generosity of Edwin Holt were about all that enabled William Holt's family to survive the collapse of the Confederacy. By the end of the war they were so destitute that this once wealthy planter was forced to sell most of his property to his brother and his nephew Thomas.[60]

The Civil War has been called a rich man's war and a poor man's fight. The hard military experiences of two of Edwin Holt's sons and the deaths of four nephews and a son-in-law are testimony that the wealthy fought and died alongside the poor. Yet in significant ways rich and poor did experience the war differently. The sons of wealthy men like Edwin Holt were often exuberant volunteers for military service but also assumed that, like Charles Fisher, they would go to war as gentlemen. The son of a Piedmont mill owner encouraged his brother to buy a horse and join the cavalry as "Pa will gladly send you any amount you may need. He is making about one thousand dollars a day and surely you can afford a horse."[61] William Carrigan's sons also chose the cavalry, but their Holt cousins, perhaps reflecting that they had spent less time riding and hunting, joined the army. Even in the more egalitarian army they enjoyed certain privileges. Both Banks and Alexander occasionally returned to the haven

60. William Rainey Holt to William Carrigan, September 29, 1861, Carrigan Papers; Anderson, *North Carolina Women of the Confederacy*, 99–101; Thomas Holt to William Carrigan, January 12, 1867, White Papers.

61. George Phifer to Will, September 9, 1863, George Phifer Papers, SHC.

of their parents' home to recuperate. Edwin and Thomas Holt had the means to supply the soldiers in their family with clothing during the last desperate days of the Confederacy when many southern soldiers were dressed in rags. Banks may have used his father's wealth to avoid becoming a victim of the wholesale amputation common in army hospitals.

Although it has not been documented that poorer whites bore a disproportionate share of the fighting, clearly class did play a major role in determining how service was avoided. The "Twenty-Negro Law," which exempted some men from large slaveholding families or offered them the option of buying a substitute, was frequently condemned as class biased. The elite were also privileged to enjoy other specified exemptions. William Edwin Holt, twenty-two and unmarried when the war began, successfully used his position in his father's mill to avoid service for the duration of the war. Men from poorer families and those without valued skills were often forced to evade the conscription officers or desert if they wanted to avoid the slaughter. Many of them joined with the Heroes of America to express their discontent with a war not of their making.[62]

The families who sent men to war and those who saw them die also experienced the war differently as rich or as poor. Thomas Slade's death was an emotional tragedy for Edwin Holt's oldest daughter, but it was not a financial tragedy; she continued living with her family whose wealth, combined with what she inherited from her husband, assured her security.[63] In sharp contrast, for poor women like Henry Donaldson's daughter Frances Huske, even the temporary loss of a husband, brother, or for her, a son, "all the help I had," to the Confederate army could mean economic catastrophe.

There were all too many war widows and orphans. An image of the Civil War creating almost as many destitute women and children as dead soldiers, however, distorts the reality of this young man's war. A majority of its casualties were young men not yet married. The roster of troops for Company E of the Thirteenth Regiment, made up largely of men from Alamance County, includes the ages of 124 of the 150 men enrolled. Thirty-four (27 percent) of them were nineteen or younger and another thirty-three were between

62. McPherson, *Battle Cry of Freedom*, 611–12.
63. Rockingham County Wills, Will of Thomas T. Slade. Slade wrote in his will that "I will to my beloved wife Fannie A. Slade that all be sold and money turned over to her unless she wants to run plantation herself but advise against it."

twenty and twenty-two. Only one man was over forty; he was discouraged from joining on the grounds that he was too old.[64] By the end of the war, as the Confederate government grew desperate for replacements, it raised the maximum age for conscription; the average soldier, however, remained a young man under the age of twenty-five who was not married and had no children.

Most soldiers from Alamance County left their families' farms. Only twenty-eight males between the ages of thirteen and thirty worked in Alamance County mills in 1860, a small minority of the labor force. Records indicate that only four of them left to join the army. Robert Evans had been brought from Virginia by his widowed mother so he and his sister could support her and two younger children with mill wages. In 1861 he enlisted; three years later he was killed at Strasburg. Eighteen-year-old James Hatchett boarded with a widow while he was a factory worker. Only four months after joining the army in July 1862 he was killed. Elmore Shanklin also boarded, with Jacob and Mattie Ward, and worked in a mill along with five of their ten children. In June 1861 he entered the army and, like Hatchett, died four months later. Both Shanklin and Hatchett were under twenty-one and single when they died; they were typical war casualties but for the fact that before the war they had worked in a factory rather than on a farm. James Keck was discharged from the army late in the war for a permanent disability. Perhaps because of this injury, he did not return to work in an Alamance mill.[65]

Like Evans, Shanklin, and Hatchett, the majority of men who died in this bloody war did not leave behind widows; they did, however, leave behind a generation of young women who would find it hard to marry in a society that offered them few economic options. For them, as well as for the war's widows and orphans, textile mills could be an alternative means of support.

Poorer whites had less to lose with the arrival of Union troops, but they also had far fewer resources to survive the casualties and deprivations of war. Although North Carolina was spared the widespread destruction of battles fought in Virginia and elsewhere, it had the highest casualty rate of any southern state. Until late in the war most of the fighting there took place along the coast; some coastal planters looked to Alamance County as a safe place to shelter slaves they feared would be freed by Union troops. Until the last year Ala-

64. [No author] *Confederate Memoirs: Alamance County Troops of the War Between the States, 1861–1865* (Centennial edition; N.p., n.d.), 24–28.
65. Eighth Census of the United States, 1860, Alamance County, North Carolina; *Confederate Memoirs*, 14–28.

mance was spared battles, but virtually no one in the county remained unaffected. According to a county historian, the twelve companies raised included more men than the county had voters. In one company sixty-nine men, approximately a third of the total, died. Only some families were devastated by the death of kin, but virtually all citizens and slaves in Alamance suffered the miseries of uncontrolled spiraling inflation; prices reached heights well beyond the means of most. Between 1862 and 1865 the cost of sugar rose from seventy-five cents to thirty dollars a pound, corn from a dollar and ten cents to thirty dollars a bushel, and flour from eighteen to five hundred dollars a barrel. Furthermore, although spared warring armies, Alamance was not spared violence. The high desertion rate in the upper Piedmont resulted in near guerrilla warfare between local officials and men who refused to fight for the Confederacy.[66]

The people of Alamance grew accustomed to men going off to war, but not until the fall of 1864, when over a thirty-six-hour period thousands of Confederate soldiers passed through Swepsonville on their way to reinforce Lee's army in Virginia, did they see the armies firsthand. County civilians, many themselves impoverished by the war, came to feed and clothe soldiers described years later as marching by "tired, hungry, half-naked . . . barefoot and listlessly." Some of these men returned several months later to fight as the war spread into the North Carolina Piedmont. In February 1865 General William T. Sherman's troops marched into North Carolina from the south and General George Stoneman's from the west. Sherman's goal was to join the fighting in Virginia, but he was met at Bentonville, in a county adjacent to Alamance, by General Joseph E. Johnston. The result was a fight that produced more than four thousand casualties, making it the bloodiest battle fought in North Carolina. Sherman's entry into Raleigh and Stoneman's march toward Greensboro left Alamance County surrounded by the war. The county's railroad assured a steady stream of soldiers, supplies, and wounded. Assuming that it was at least safer than Raleigh, Governor Vance sent the state archives to Graham. But Alamance was not safe enough to protect planters from Union soldiers. Yankees camped on Thomas Ruffin's plantation, stole all but three horses, used fences for firewood, and turned livestock into his wheat fields. Paul Cameron's plantation was also visited by enemy troops; a relative claimed the northern sol-

66. Wayne K. Durrill, *War of Another Kind: A Southern Community in the Great Rebellion* (New York, 1990), 83; Whitaker, *Centennial History of Alamance County,* 116–17; Iobst and Manarin, *Bloody Sixth,* 368–84; Trotter, *Silk Flags,* 142.

diers "played the wild." Although Union soldiers also visited the adjacent Albright farm, Locust Grove was spared.[67]

Edwin Holt did, however, dramatically confront the reality of war during the last days of the conflict. Returning from business in Company Shops, he met a desperately sick soldier, just released from a hospital, who was trying to get to his family's home near the Alamance Factory. Holt offered to transport him there in his carriage; the soldier, however, died en route. Holt then ordered the driver to arrange for a coffin and sent the remains to one more bereaved Alamance County family.[68]

The Holts confronted the defeat of the Confederacy with their mills still running; not all of the state's mill men, however, were as fortunate. Some of the mills that had survived four years of wear and tear on machinery did not survive the arrival of Union troops. Stoneman's soldiers destroyed Rufus Patterson's plant and then opened the Fries mill to a local crowd. People the Frieses had thought "friendly neighbors" helped themselves, cutting goods right off the looms. Some later returned what they took, claiming they were saving it from the Yankees, but others kept what may have been the only cloth they had been able to obtain for several years.[69]

Long after the war a rumor survived in Alamance that Edwin Holt and his sons actually benefited from the arrival of Union troops in the county. Several variations of the story that Holt "borrowed" or "stole" cotton from the Union army or perhaps from the South circulated as local political gossip. A history of Alamance County presented a version described by the author as the "humorous story" of Holt getting friends and neighbors together late at night to "borrow" cotton that Sherman had seized in South Carolina and was sending north. Whether true or not, it is clear that in contrast to most mill men, the Holts had sufficient cotton to run their mills in the months after defeat.[70]

Stanley Lebergott has convincingly argued that Confederate defeat "proved inevitable because the South was not prepared to forego

67. Whitaker, *Centennial History of Alamance County,* 119–21; Trotter, *Silk Flags,* 321–34; Robinson, "Thomas Ruffin," 344–45; *Alamance County: The Legacy of Its People and Places,* 29.

68. *Alamance County,* 336–37.

69. Henry Fries, "Reminiscences of Confederate Days," 15, Fries Papers, NCDAH; Adelaide Fries, "One Hundred Years of Textiles in Salem," *North Carolina Historical Review* 27 (January 1950): 15.

70. Stockard, "Daughter of the Piedmont: Chapel Hill's First Co-ed Graduate" unpublished paper, copy in the North Carolina Collection, University of North Carolina at Chapel Hill, n.d., 55–56.

short-term monetary goals." Lebergott referred to cotton planters, but his thesis is applicable to manufacturers, men like Edwin Holt and his sons, as well. Their textiles, vital to the Confederacy, were furnished begrudgingly with personal monetary goals clearly taking precedence over national survival. One exasperated member of the Confederate Congress wrote near the end of the war that "the love of money had been the greatest difficulty on our way to independence—it is now our chiefest obstacle."[71]

Edwin Holt was ambitious to make money and exploited wartime demand to do so. Clearly Holt's wealth was a symbol of his industrial success. He lost nephews and a son-in-law and risked sons to the southern effort for independence. He also gained profit from the losing cause, profit that carried him and his family securely into the "New South."

71. Stanley Lebergott, "Why the South Lost: Commercial Purpose in the Confederacy, 1861–1865," *Journal of American History* 70 (1983): 74, 63.

5

A Sort of Resurrection

THE HOLT MILLS DURING
RECONSTRUCTION

In his study of postbellum textile mills, historian Richard Griffin concluded that "the final few months of the Civil War dealt a serious blow to the North Carolina textile industry" and that "chaos reigned in the first few months after the War, and the usual routines of life came to a standstill." He described mill owners as "faced with a bleak outlook in 1865." However grim for most, the outlook was far less bleak for the Holts; their mills had survived the war and they had a supply of cotton to run them. To many impoverished whites in Alamance as well as from the surrounding counties, the two Holt mills offered a rare opportunity to earn a wage. According to Dover Heritage, whose parents moved there after the war, "Everyone was talking about Alamance County because its cotton mills had more work than any other place in the state. People wanted to go to Alamance."[1]

Not everyone already living there was as optimistic. For many whites in Alamance the future did indeed appear bleak in the aftermath of defeat. Sallie Stockard remembered the Reconstruction years as a time when everyone was poor. B. L. Rike was so distraught by the disarray he perceived that he considered moving to Arkansas because, he wrote his brother, "this county has got so that it is too hard for me to stay in. Also the people in Alamance have all lost their [?] kindness and principles. Every man for hisself."[2]

Rike's despair was shared by at least some of the county's white

1. Griffin, "Reconstruction of the North Carolina Textile Industry," 34–35; Dover G. Heritage, Corinne E. Bivins, and Gail Cox Bolden, *When Shoeshines Were a Nickel: An Oral History of Alamance County, North Carolina* (Burlington, N.C., 1986), 28.
2. Sallie Stockard, "Daughter of the Piedmont: Chapel Hill's First Co-ed," unpublished paper, n.d., 16; B. L. Rike to brother, November 28, 1869, Andrew Rike Papers, SHC.

elite. Thomas Ruffin's daughter described him as having "almost given up looking after things"; she concluded "it is down right *ridiculous* to be so poor, so dead poor." Ruffin, who estimated that he lost $250,000 as a result of the war, was forced to sell some of his property to George Swepson at a sheriff's auction. Although one of the state's most prominent citizens, Ruffin considered leaving North Carolina because he concluded that "anyplace is to be preferred to one which exposes us to the equality and savage rule of the colored race." Ruffin's wealthy son-in-law, Paul Cameron, quickly recovered from war-related financial losses; he proved less able to recover psychologically from the destruction of his antebellum way of life. In 1867 he wrote his wife "as for me my life is one long dark night," describing a depression that hardly lifted until his death nearly twenty-five years later.[3]

William Rainey Holt lost two sons to the war; he also lost the plantation he had spent a lifetime making into an agrarian showcase. A year before the war ended he remained so convinced that his plantation way of life would survive that he attempted to buy more land, offering a neighbor payment in corn. By the end of 1866, William Holt's debts were so great that he was forced to sell all he owned even "down to his family Bible and Prayer Book." When a creditor sued Holt the court reported that whereas ten years earlier he had been worth $100,000 "now he is worse than nothing." His wife and three daughters, who knew nothing of his financial problems until his property was sold, were described by Thomas Holt as embarrassed and depressed by the loss although "Uncle William seems pretty cheerful under it." Thomas paid twenty thousand dollars for over eight hundred acres of the Linwood plantation; his father bought another two hundred acres, the house in Lexington, some animals, carriages, and most of the family's household goods. The rest of William's property, including his stock, "one of his great hobbys," was sold at auction. Perhaps the hardest blow for this proud southern planter was selling his stallion Medley for three hundred dollars; a few years before he had refused General Kilpatrick's offer to buy the horse for two thousand dollars. Edwin allowed his brother, so often his creditor in the past, to keep his family in their Lexington home, where, according to Thomas, they were "as comfortable as ever they were." William Holt remained dependent on his younger brother until his death in 1868; Edwin continued to sup-

3. Robinson, "Thomas Ruffin," 342, 388; Jean Bradley Anderson, *Piedmont Plantation: The Bennehan-Cameron Family and Lands in North Carolina* (Durham, N.C., 1985), 119, 125.

port Louisa Holt and her daughters for years afterward. In the spring of 1870 Thomas wrote William Carrigan "as to Aunt Lou's business I can only say that Pa has the bills to foot. I do not know how they get along."[4]

William Rainey Holt remained confident that he could restore his plantation until he was forced to sell it. William Carrigan had determined by 1850 that staple crop agriculture would be more lucrative than manufacturing but had grown disillusioned even before the war began. A few years after moving to Arkansas he concluded, "I will never see myself as comfortably fix'd again as it was there [in North Carolina]"; in 1860 he reiterated, "I am making nothing." Eight years after the war Carrigan wrote his former mill partner of suffering "a very fatal want of crops both in corn & cotton" and added "I am very much in need at this time."[5]

In contrast to his brother and brother-in-law, Edwin Holt survived the war still a wealthy man. Only a year after the war he was estimated to be worth around $200,000.[6]

War, defeat, and emancipation brought much less dramatic change to Edwin Holt than it did his brother and most other southern elites; he could not, however, simply resume his antebellum life. Politics, in particular, demanded reevaluation; ironically, Edwin was compelled by the exigencies of defeat to more closely conform to the political views of his older brother. The two had long disagreed politically; perhaps William found some small degree of satisfaction that Edwin was now forced to became a Democrat.

Political alignments that had dominated North Carolina for years unraveled during the war and its aftermath. The possibility of black political participation made any simple return to the antebellum status quo impossible. The demise of the Whig Party was virtually complete when the war began; when the fighting stopped the Republican Party had not firmly established itself in North Carolina or any southern state. It was not immediately clear to many former Whigs, Unionists to the eve of the war and longtime advocates of industrial development, how their interests could best be served politically. Only in time would the Democrats, who often assumed the

4. William R. Holt to R. L. Beall, April 26, 1864, Beall-Harper Papers, SHC; John Dorsett to Jonathan Worth, September 25, 1867, Jonathan Worth Papers, NCDAH; Thomas Holt to William Carrigan, January 12, 1867, March 8, 1870, White Papers.

5. William Carrigan to Edwin Holt, June 1, 1855, February 4, 1869, Carrigan Papers; William Carrigan to Edwin Holt, January 10, 1874, typed copy, Battle Family Papers, SHC.

6. Dun and Bradstreet Credit Ratings, Alamance County, 1865, 1866.

name "Conservative" in an effort to entice former Whigs, convince them that their party was the only acceptable choice for the majority of whites.

In May 1865 President Andrew Johnson appointed William Holden provisional governor of North Carolina. Seven months later an election pitted the recently converted Republican Holden against longtime Democrat Jonathan Worth. Edwin Holt voted for Holden, a man his son Thomas had a year before described as an "arch traitor" whom he hoped was "politically *dead.*" Probably Holt voted for the Republican Party because he considered it the party most likely to facilitate the smooth reentry of North Carolina into the Union and to foster its economic development. The war had proven financially advantageous to the Holts, but after Confederate defeat the quick return of North Carolina to the Union made good business sense. Probably few southerners were as quick to shed their Confederate mantle as the Holts. First Thomas and then other members of the family traveled north again within months of the war's end. There is very little evidence that they often joined in nostalgia for the lost cause. In 1871 Thomas predicted "our political skys are brightning" and expressed confidence that "ere long, we will be back on the Old Constitution of our fathers."[7] But the circumstances of Reconstruction made it impossible for the Holts to renew allegiance to the Old Constitution as Whigs become Republicans.

Worth, not Holden, won the election, a victory not pleasing to radical Republicans who increasingly took control of Reconstruction away from President Johnson. Once out of office, Holden began organizing the Republican Party in the state; as all over the South, Republican success depended on the political empowerment of black men. In March 1867 Congress placed all of the former Confederate states except Tennessee, rewarded for ratifying the Fourteenth Amendment, into five military districts. Sixteen months later, after North Carolina ratified the amendment guaranteeing equal rights to all of its adult male citizens, it was restored to the Union. After voting for Holden, Edwin Holt never again voted for a Republican; his political realignment quickly became so complete that by 1870 a neighbor could describe him as "a dyed-in-the-wool Democrat."[8]

There were two major reasons for Holt's political transforma-

7. Testimony of E. M. Holt, U.S. Congress, Senate Reports, 42d Cong., 1st sess., no. 1, 253 ; Thomas Holt to Zebulon Vance, August 13, 1864, January 25, 1871, Vance Papers.

8. Testimony of Jacob Long, U.S. Congress, Senate Reports, 42d Cong., 1st sess., no. 1, 17.

tion: Republican support of black political rights and the association of North Carolina Republicans with corruption. For the Holts the most serious corruption included the financial schemes of George Swepson, the man who had emerged as their only serious rival to achieving near total domination of the textile industry in Alamance County. It was less financially and emotionally difficult for Edwin Holt to free his slaves than it was for most southern planters. Although he would complain in the years after emancipation about the difficulty of hiring black farm laborers and compelling them to work, the stability of his all-white factory work force was more important to him.[9] Slave labor was expendable but a hierarchy of control was not. Order—the deference of subordinates to superiors, women to men, children to parents, workers to capitalists, and blacks to whites—was fundamental to Edwin Holt's sense of a proper and prosperous society. War and emancipation, however, seriously undermined deferential behavior; postwar Alamance County was a most disorderly place.

Blacks, most of them freed from slavery in 1865, made up approximately 25 percent of the total population of Alamance County in 1870. Free black men had a realistic chance of achieving political success only if they had strong white allies. A few white men in Alamance County, notably George Swepson, were willing to ally politically with blacks if it served their own ambitions. The majority of whites, however, adamantly opposed black political participation. The specter of black political equality prompted the organization of a number of terrorist groups, commonly referred to generically as the Ku Klux Klan. By 1870 approximately seven hundred men belonged to one of these organizations in Alamance County, described as "where the worst of the crimes occurred." Support for Klan-style groups was widespread among all classes of whites, but there was also opposition. Thomas Ruffin, despite his own arch-racist views, condemned Klan groups as "highly immoral and wrong."[10] Edwin Holt and his sons remained aloof, but there is no evidence that they were outspoken in opposition. Dolph Moore, Thomas Holt's brother-in-law and business partner, was openly a Klan leader, a position that apparently caused him no friction with the Holts.

Historian Eric Foner, writing about Holden's fight against the Klan in Alamance and Caswell Counties, suggests that "the suspension of constitutional rights in the interest of law enforcement car-

9. Edwin Holt to James White, November 10, 1873, White Papers.
10. Horace W. Raper, *William W. Holden: North Carolina's Political Enigma* (Chapel Hill, 1985), 161; Robinson, "Thomas Ruffin," 406.

ries its own risks, especially the possibility of transforming perpetrators of violence from criminals into victims in the eyes of citizens who sympathized with the motives, if not the methods, of those arrested." Foner's insight serves as an accurate description of the Holts' response to Dolph Moore and other Klansmen. Moore was described by one of the officers stationed in Alamance as "a ruffian" who "goes boldly about town, and no one dares to interfere with him," and by a witness before a U.S. Senate investigating committee as among the "desperate men belonging to the organization who would commit any crime to carry out their purposes and designs." Despite reservations the Holts may have had about the Klan, Thomas's partner and brother-in-law openly boasted about his Klan activity without fear of retaliation from his wealthy in-laws.[11]

Most Alamance County victims of Klan violence were whipped or beaten, but several people, including an infant, were killed. The most widely publicized murder in the county was the lynching of Wyatt Outlaw, a black leader of the Union League, which promoted black participation in the Republican Party. Late one night in February 1870, a crowd estimated as close to one hundred men seized him from his home and hung him from an elm thirty yards from the Graham County Courthouse; his body remained hanging until eleven o'clock the next morning. A note pinned to the dead man warned "beware ye guilty black and white." Authorities never officially accused anyone of the crime, but it was rumored that Dolph Moore had placed the noose around Outlaw's neck. When Moore heard another black man talking about the Outlaw lynching, he beat him, breaking his leg.[12]

Moore boasted that he was not afraid of either Holden or the Yankees, but for at least a short time he had reason to fear. When no charges were brought in the Outlaw case in Alamance County or for the murder of a white Republican leader in Caswell County, Governor Holden declared both counties to be in a state of insurrection and sent in militia from eastern Tennessee commanded by General George Kirk. In the resulting struggle for power known as the Holden-Kirk War, Kirk tried to control Klan groups by rounding up and imprisoning known leaders. Edwin Holt was in Graham visiting his daughter when he witnessed the arrest of a lawyer in a manner he described as "exceedingly rude." He then rode to Thomas's home

11. Eric Foner, *Reconstruction: America's Unfinished Revolution, 1863–1877* (New York, 1988), 440; "Conditions of Affairs in the Southern States," U.S. Congress, Senate Reports, xci, cxiii, 8.
12. Raper, *William W. Holden*, 174.

in Haw River in time to see Dolph Moore's arrest, which he likewise described as "a very rude one indeed." Emma Holt was also visiting in Haw River that day and shared her father's sense of outrage, recalling later "I never felt so indignant & angry as I did when I saw their proceedings." She described the men who arrested Moore as "cowards" who were "of the *very lowest* out castes from the mountains in the western part of the state & commanded by that *horrible desperado* 'Kirk' [and]—the *conservative, radicals negroes.*"[13]

Officials also briefly arrested Thomas Holt but he was soon released. Thomas then wrote his relatives in Arkansas a lengthy description of his perspective concerning events in Alamance County. The letter is worth quoting in full because it is especially insightful as to how this white elite man rationalized opposition to a more racially egalitarian society:

> On the 26th of last Feby. there was a negroe hung in Graham. An inquest was held, but no clue could be found to it. A little after a man was killed in Yanceyville, no clue could be found to that. Some few weeks before these things Holden had a bill passed [in] the Legislature giving him power to declare any counties in a state of insurrection, whenever in *his* judgment he thought it necessary. About the first of this month, he organized 2 regiments of militia or state troops, mostly from East Tenn. & brought some 400 of them here, having previously declared this & Caswell Counties in a state of insurrection. On the 15th July they commenced arresting our best citizen, gave no reasons, nor authority except it is Gov Holdens orders. Among the first was Dolph, Sid Scott, J. T. Hunter & many others. Subsequently I came in (they however did not detain me long) In Caswell Sam Hill, John Kerr, Dr. Roan & 2 sons, & many others. Giving no cause, reason or authority for anything, he sent out writs before [?] Chief Justice Person, from which he backed down from fear. As Grant had promised Holden to sustain him, & was daily sending U.S. troops to back him. We have all quietly submitted & the arresting kept going on until this morning (have heard of none today) All the best Lawyers & old Judges in the State, voluntarily offered their services & have been doing all they could, but to no effect until the United States District Judge took the matter in hand, & issued writs of habeus corpus & ordered the men to be brought before him to-

13. Testimony of E. M. Holt, U.S. Congress, Senate Reports, 42d Cong., 1st sess., no. 1, 255; Emma Holt to James White, July 11, 18, 1870, White Papers.

morrow in Salisbury which will be done & there it will end. The whole object was to carry the election which thank the good Lord has failed. We carry the state by 20,000 & will have a 2/3 majority in both houses & 5 out of the 7 congressmen & a U.S. Senator to elect this winter. The first programm was to try by military commission [?] the prisoners, for the murder of these men had some negroes to do the swearing but backed down from that. Could not get any person to sit on it. They now say they will turn them over to the Civil Courts all that have not been released. they have released 100 or more of us. One man who they treated very badly has sued the Gov. for $10,000 Dr. Mebane & Col Wm Bingham will sue as soon as they are released & hundreds of others, Holden on yesterday made his property over to his wife & has left, no one seems to know where he has gone. His Adj. Genl has gone. So I think the farce will now close. It can be proven (so it is said) the th Pool Settle & Holden concocted the thing in Washington & will be sued for conspiracy. Joe Turner is a prisoner. The [illegible] of it are certainly badly scared. I write under excitement & very hurridly. Will go to Salisbury to night. Have no fears about Dolph all is right he is guilty of nothing. Will write Cousin Alfred in a few days & give more particularlers. Tongue cannot describe the indignation of our *whole* people. Old men, yes the children all to the oldest men are terribly arroused but all determined to make no resistance by which we have beat them at their own game & now will beat them at the law. Holden is done forever. The negroes curse him.[14]

A few days after the arrests Thomas described, Kirk rejected a court-issued writ of habeas corpus. Moore and a number of other Klan leaders remained imprisoned for over a month; the two counties remained officially in a state of insurrection until November 1870.[15]

The following year a United States Senate investigation into Klanlike activity in the South identified Alamance County as a particularly violent place. Because he had served as a county magistrate, federal officials invited Edwin Holt to Washington to testify about conditions there. A former Klan leader from Alamance County also called to testify, asked if Edwin Holt sympathized with the Klan, answered "he was in sympathy with the purposes as I understood them, but as much opposed to the commission of crimes as

14. Thomas Holt to William Carrigan, August 9, 1870, White Papers.
15. Raper, *William W. Holden*, 174–98.

any man in the world." Holt's testimony was a model of evasiveness, the response of a man who wished to neither condone nor expose Klan violence. He did not deny that there had been some destruction of property in Alamance and the surrounding counties but insisted that law-abiding citizens had nothing to fear. While admitting that some people—he referred to them as "several notorious characters"—had been punished, he insisted that "they were persons of very bad character." Holt first identified Outlaw as a man accused of retailing liquor but when pressed acknowledged that this was not actually the reason given for his murder. He also claimed to have helped plan a meeting to protest Outlaw's murder, which had been canceled only because of the arrival of Kirk's troops.[16]

Edwin Holt knew more about the violence in Alamance and the surrounding counties than he was willing to tell northern senators. John Bason was a night watchman at Thomas Holt's Haw River store when he was seized at work and whipped by Klansmen who accused him of failing to vote. Thomas Siddall, a former employee of Francis Fries subsequently hired as superintendent of the Carolina mill, was also a victim; he was taken from his bed and whipped, probably because Klansmen found this outspoken Englishman who had lived for some time in the North generally obnoxious. Edwin Holt probably knew something about how the Klan treated these two mill workers. He definitely knew a great deal about what they did to Caswell Holt.

Caswell Holt was born around 1835 and for the first thirty years of his life was enslaved by Edwin Holt. Edwin mentioned Caswell several times in his diary, once noting that he was used as a half-hand when he was sixteen and on another occasion that he was too sick to work. Most likely Caswell helped build the Alamance Factory and houses for its white workers; he occasionally worked in the dye house. Caswell married Amy, also a slave of the Holts; by 1870 they had nine children. After emancipation Amy and Caswell left the plantation and supported their family by cropping for Jeremiah Holt, their former master's cousin, in Graham. Edwin Holt maintained a paternalistic relationship with Caswell and Amy Holt even after they left his land. For a few years Caswell was deferential enough to avoid conflict with his former master. His cropping arrangement was adequate to feed the family of eleven. Sometimes

16. "Conditions of Affairs in the Southern States," U.S. Congress, Senate Reports; Testimony of Jacob Long, Testimony of E.M. Holt, U.S. Congress, Senate Reports, 42d Cong., 1st sess., no 1, 17, 252.

his sons stayed at night to serve Jeremiah Holt's family; on at least one occasion they were rewarded with a pair of chickens.[17]

The paternalistic relationship that both Edwin and Jeremiah Holt demanded assumed deferential behavior on the part of recently freed men and women who were grappling with new concepts of equality offered by the Radical Republicans. Caswell Holt, however, was determined to enjoy rights, including the right to vote and to vote for the party that he chose, that most whites including his former master were equally determined to deny him. The Klan, which some elite white men overtly rejected, nevertheless served as an important instrument of coercion against recalcitrant former slaves.

Late one night approximately sixteen men adorned in long white robes and hoods complete with three horns sewn on top appeared unexpectedly, seized Caswell from his bed, took him to the woods, and threatened to kill him. After stringing him from a tree with his feet barely reaching the ground they asked him repeatedly about the chickens. When he refused to confess that he had stolen anything, they beat him again, warned him to tell no one about what had happened and to leave Alamance County within ten days. But Caswell Holt did report what had happened, first to Jeremiah Holt, who tried to persuade the aggrieved black man that he had been beaten by people coming from a thousand miles away. Once recovered, Caswell rode four miles to Locust Grove seeking a sympathetic hearing from his former master. Edwin Holt's response revealed the stark limits to the paternalistic and deferential relationship he had always presumed and that Caswell Holt had more or less conformed to. After this meeting Caswell became so disgusted with the deceit of his former master that he willingly exposed "Squire Holt" before United States senators. He described his beating and Holt's response:

> Yes sir. I talked with him about it. He asked me some questions about it, and told me that the less I said about it the better; that I would find out more by saying nothing about it, and not trying to have them arrested, than I would be undertaking to have them arrested. It was a new thing there; about the first outrage that was committed in Alamance. He said to me, "Cas, these things have been raging in the Northern States for years; they are something mysterious; something that we people can't

17. Edwin Michael Holt Diary, October 22, 1847, September 28, 30, 1848; U.S. Manuscript Census, 1870, Alamance County, North Carolina; Testimony of Caswell Holt, U.S. Congress, Senate Reports, 42d Cong., 1st sess., no. 1, 341.

understand; it is a sort of resurrection; that's what it is, Cas." I said "Yes sir, but look here, master, you have been my master; you raised me from a child." He said "Yes I raised you, Cas, and I respect you as one of my own children." I said "Well, do you suppose that the Almighty has given the dead power to rise now and go about beating people, and mummucking them all up in that way?" He said "It is something we can't understand, Cas; something that has been existing for some time, and we can't understand it." I said, "Well, I can tell you this: you read the Bible, and I can't; but I tell you, if the Almighty has given the dead power to rise at this day and beat people who are living, the next time they come to my house there will be two of us there in the morning; for I will kill one if I can, and if I do he will not come there any more till God does raise him right." He said, "Good evening," and that is the last he and I said about it.

Caswell Holt also reported that Klansmen visited him again a year later and shot him, whipped his little girls when they cried, and broke many of the family's household goods, including their looking glass, crockery, and spinning wheel. They warned Caswell Holt that this time they were punishing him for claiming he was not afraid of the Klan; he assumed the real reason was that despite Jeremiah Holt's commanding him to vote for the Democratic Party, he voted Republican. The Democrats in the county, he reported (and according to the transcript, he laughed as he reported it), claimed no Klan existed, that those doing the beating came out of graves.[18] The Senate hearings attended by Edwin Holt and Caswell Holt questioned the racial order in the postbellum South. Probably Caswell Holt rarely talked to white mill workers but he could have taught them quite a lot about paternalism, Holt style.

To Edwin Holt the beating and shooting of a black man, even one to whom he could say "I respect you as I respect my own children," was not a crime. But fleecing the public till was. He identified George Swepson and his ring, not Dolph Moore and his Klansmen, as the real criminals in post–Civil War Alamance County. Sometime in the 1850s Swepson, a native of Virginia, had moved first to Caswell County and then to Alamance. In 1860 he owned property worth approximately seventy thousand dollars. By then he was well acquainted with the Holts. For a short period before the war Alexander Holt lived in Swepson's home and worked for him as a merchant. Swepson's effort during the war to buy a mill in or near Alamance

18. Testimony of Caswell Holt, 341–45.

may have fueled the animosity between him and the county's leading mill family. A confidential letter Swepson wrote to a fellow Republican hints at the growing estrangement. Detailing a clandestine scheme to get his own railroad bonds paid, he concluded "let Mordecai and the Holts wait."[19]

Swepson joined the Holts in the ranks of the minority of southerners who survived the war with their wealth intact. Swepson and his wife even bettered the Holts in the conspicuous display of their wealth. An acquaintance observed that the Swepsons "have the most eloquent home . . . the very best servants and most eloquent table, splendid [illegible] of horses & fine carriage . . . in a word any luxury that wealth can gain."[20]

But George Swepson was ambitious for more than luxury and conspicuous display. During the Civil War rumors circulated that he was attempting to buy John Trolinger's mill; he definitely made inquiries about buying the Orange Factory from the Webbs. A few years later he bought Big Falls Mill, which he renamed Falls of the Neuse. Control of railroads rather than textile mills, however, seemed to this ambitious man the surest route to success and power. After the war, Governor Holden appointed him president of the Western North Carolina Railroad, a position he used to cultivate business and political connections. In the summer of 1868 Swepson launched a complicated scheme to take control of at least seven railroads in the state (as well as some in Florida) which he attempted to facilitate by bribing key legislators. His eventual failure resulted in considerable financial loss.[21]

Edwin Holt considered Swepson and his allies the villains responsible for the chaos that gripped Alamance County after the war. Testifying before the United States Senate, he responded to one senator's leading question—"Was it believed generally that Governor Holden and his radical legislature had brought the State to the brink of ruin and bankruptcy?"—by answering "Yes sir, that was the opinion," and adding, "The state is bankrupt beyond all redemption. I am a large tax-payer myself."[22]

19. U.S. Manuscript Census, 1860, Alamance County, North Carolina; [No author] "State v. Josiah Turner," North Carolina Collection, 58.

20. Mrs. Graves to husband, April 2, 1876, Graves Family Papers, SHC.

21. R. T. Nutt to F. and H. Fries, December 22, 1862, Fries Papers, SHC; George Swepson to Webbs, December 30, 1862, Webb Papers; Charles L. Price, "The Railroad Schemes of George W. Swepson," *Essays in American History*, vol. 1 (1964), 32–50.

22. Testimony of E. M. Holt, U.S. Congress, Senate Reports, 42d Cong., 1st sess., no 1, 255.

Swepson evaded criminal charges, but the state's Republican governor did not. While Holt testified in Washington, William Holden faced eight charges of impeachment in Raleigh, including the charge that he refused to obey the writ of habeas corpus in Dolph Moore's case. When the impeachment trial began Thomas Holt confidently predicted Holden's conviction because "in fact I cannot see how it could be otherwise."[23] His prediction proved accurate; Holden was convicted because resurgent Democrats agreed it could not be otherwise and removed him from office. The Republican Party of North Carolina, which he had played a key role in creating, steadily declined, although it did retain control of the executive branch until 1877 when Zebulon Vance was reelected.

Thwarted in his scheme to control the state's railroads, Swepson refocused his attention on his Alamance County mill. In 1874 he claimed wealth of around $100,000, although it is possible he exaggerated his financial success. The following year Dun and Bradstreet reported that Swepson was by some "said to be very wealthy & by others to be [worth] very little."[24]

Although the Holts had maintained good relations with a number of small mill owners in Alamance, conflict with Swepson was probably inevitable. To these newly dyed-in-the-wool Democrats George Swepson was a scalawag of the worst order: a Republican who offered at least a modicum of support for black men who asserted their right to vote and who also exploited the upheaval of Reconstruction for his own personal gain. It must have been particularly galling when he acquired land that Thomas Ruffin had once offered Edwin Holt for his first mill and had subsequently been forced to sell at auction after the war. According to a county historian, this kind of property exchange especially outraged "aristocrats of Alamance and Caswell like Holt and Moore." Furthermore, Swepson's home, within twenty-five yards of Holt and Moore's store and near their factory, occupied land they particularly coveted. Perhaps most galling of all was that the zone of safety provided by Swepson's grounds emboldened blacks to hurl insults at passing whites.[25]

Political and economic conflict was also exacerbated by the deep-seated hatred George Swepson and Dolph Moore had developed for one another. The origin of their feud is not known. Swepson had

23. Raper, *William W. Holden*, 207; Thomas Holt to William Carrigan, January 25, 1871, Carrigan Papers.
24. Dun and Bradstreet Credit Ratings, Alamance County, 1874, 1875.
25. Hughes, *Development of the Textile Industry in Alamance*, 47; *Alamance Gleaner*, February 8, 1876.

lived next to the Moores in Caswell County when Dolph was a boy. Their conflict may have begun then or possibly in the early years of Reconstruction when Moore advocated violence to restore the old racial order while Swepson represented the scalawags willing at a minimum to modify that order. Even after the collapse of his railroad scheme in 1868, Swepson maintained civil relations with some of the Holts although not with Dolph Moore. Swepson chided Alexander Holt for being the one son left out of his father's mill dynasty and suggested that his father should create a partnership for him with Banks. He also publicized through Alexander that if Dolph Moore was not involved, his brother Thomas could acquire any of the Swepson land around his store and factory that he wanted.[26]

Swepson's efforts to recruit allies among the Holts, whatever the intended purpose, failed. His return to textile manufacturing only exacerbated the conflict with them and Moore. By the early seventies Swepson's factory was producing so much cloth that it glutted the market, forcing the Granite Factory to temporarily discontinue production of the famous Alamance plaids. Swepson also successfully lured away workers from the Holt mills. On one occasion Dolph Moore accused him of not only trying to entice his factory girls away but also of trying to seduce them. Moore became enraged when Swepson retaliated by reversing the charges. During the 1874 Christmas season cards circulated throughout the Piedmont insinuating that Moore sought improper relations with factory girls. These cards also questioned the virtue of Moore's sisters; two of his sisters were married to Thomas and James Holt. When a detective concluded that the accusations were the work of Swepson, Moore tried to kill his rival and enemy. He was convicted of assault and for a year was under a restraining order. It did not restrain his hatred, which reached a fever pitch as he frequently cursed Swepson and swore they could not both live under the same sun.[27]

On January 25, 1876, Moore asked Sam Oliver, a fourteen-year-old worker in the Granite Factory, to accompany him duck hunting in the morning; he asked Sam and another boy to go with him again after dinner. Both times they took an unusual route by Swepson's house; on each trip Moore carried his two guns cocked. Although the boys testified that Moore was sober, they both agreed that he did drink some and that when not cursing Swepson, he sang loudly and made a noise like a bugle. People in the factory store, where he spent

26. *Alamance Gleaner*, February 8, 1876.
27. Ibid.

most of his time between outings, were left with the strong impression that a fight was imminent. It was. The second time Moore passed Swepson's home he spotted the owner and demanded that he come out and shoot in the open. Swepson responded by shooting first, from the safety of his house. His second shot lodged in Moore's spinal cord, leaving him paralyzed. The two boys were sent to tell Moore's partner and his wife that he was a dead man. By the time Thomas and Louisa arrived a large crowd of mill workers gathered around were praying for the dying man; he died two days later. Most workers from the Granite Factory and store attended Moore's funeral. One described Thomas as "completely broken down," and the killing as "cold blooded cruel murder." Swepson's workers responded by defending their employer as having acted out of self-defense.[28]

The murder divided not only Alamance County workers but sentiment all over the state. The wife of a prominent Democrat in Raleigh expressed widespread concern that "the law will not do anything to Swep." The tremendous publicity in Alamance County promoted the prosecutor to conclude "the case has been very much canvassed and talked about by all classes of people in the said county, greatly to the prejudice of the interests of the State and many men of position and influence in the said county have been actively engaged in manufacturing public sentiment favorable to the accused and adverse to the State." He reported that people employed by Swepson had "taken a deep interest in behalf of the accused and been active in getting up a sympathy for the accused." The actions of "his agents, employees and friends," the prosecutor concluded, had done much "to prejudice the minds of the public in the said county against the interests of the State," which of course were also the interests of the Holts. The prosecutor successfully moved the trial to Wake County where Swepson was found not guilty on the grounds that he had acted out of self-defense.[29]

He was acquitted, but Swepson never again seriously threatened the Holts' domination of textile manufacturing in Alamance County. A year after his trial, credit raters were "unable to give his wo[rth]" but reported "there are large judgments . . . against him."[30] Swepson's failure was one chapter in the inability of southern Re-

28. A. T. Benton to J. M. Pugh, January 30, 1876, Pugh Papers, SHC; *Alamance Gleaner*, February 8, 1876.
29. Mother to Daughter, February 1, 1876, Scales Papers; *Alamance Gleaner*, February 8, July 11, 1876.
30. Dun and Bradstreet Credit Ratings, Alamance County, 1877.

publicans to maintain power. The disputed presidential election occurring the same year Moore was killed was resolved by the Compromise of 1877, which mandated withdrawal of the last federal troops from the South. For black southerners it was aptly called "a revolution gone backward." For many white southerners the compromise was the symbolic end to a failed rebellion and the beginning of a New South modeled after the North they had so recently tried to defeat.

The Holts had fought for the Confederacy and against the new political and racial order briefly promised by Republican ascendancy. But they had no fundamental quarrel with the future that Union victory assured. During four years of war and another decade and more of conflict over Reconstruction, years that left most southern whites impoverished, the Holt family prospered. During war and Reconstruction Edwin Holt successfully established his sons and sons-in-law as textile manufacturers in Alamance County. In the last decades of the nineteenth century the Holt family would dominate the industry in Alamance County and establish itself as the most successful textile mill family in the state.

They used their wealth and success to facilitate reestablishing the racial order assumed in the past. Former slave Caswell Holt was among those who could not tolerate that order; he was spared the fate of Wyatt Outlaw but was forced to leave the county. Other former slaves remained deferential enough to assure the Holts' protection. When "Aunt Dorcas" Holt died in 1891, the *Alamance Gleaner* praised her as a woman who "thought a great deal of the white family to which she belonged" and one who "took a delight in honoring them and in doing anything she could for them." When Stephen Holt died the following year he was likewise praised as "a faithful and obedient servent" as well as one who "always voted the Democratic ticket." The Holts provided burials for both of these "faithful servants."[31]

The paternalistic racial dominance that Edwin Holt had imbibed as a child facilitated his assumption of paternalistic class dominance. There is no record that Squire Holt ever tried to control his white workers with the kind of ghost story told Caswell Holt. The incident, however, is revealing as to his assumptions about the acceptable behavior of all subordinates. A worker could be respected as one of Holt's own children as long as it was understood that he or she was permanently a deferential child. The metaphor of family ap-

---

31. *Alamance Gleaner*, August 3, 1891, January 7, 1892.

plied to slave plantations was increasingly applied to mill villages in the decades after the war. To those looking behind the facade of paternalism, however, it was always abundantly clear that as on southern plantations, these mill families were ones of profoundly unequal relations.

Edwin Michael Holt at age fifty, January 14, 1857

Emily Farish Holt

Postcard of the Alamance Factory

Locust Grove, built by Edwin Michael Holt in 1849

Lynn Banks Holt in the uniform of the Sixth North Carolina Infantry

Capt. James N. Williamson and his wife,
Mary Elizabeth Holt Williamson

Governor Thomas Michael Holt

The Alamance Factory as rebuilt after the fire of 1871

Workers at the Granite Factory in Haw River, 1885

Home of Lynn Banks Holt, constructed in Graham, N.C., in 1885

James Holt Sr. and his seven sons ca. the early 1890s

Caswell Holt, former slave of Edwin Michael Holt.
This photograph was made in 1912,
when Caswell Holt was about seventy-eight years old.

6

Truly a Manufacturing Section

THE HOLT MILLS,
1865–1900

Although politics could threaten to be all consuming through the tumultuous years of Reconstruction, the Holts never lost their focus on building textile mills. They were remarkably resilient. Within a year of the Confederacy's collapse, Edwin Holt and his sons were not only expanding their businesses but also restoring their ties in the North. In April 1865, as all over the South Confederate soldiers, including his brother Banks, left their defeated armies and returned home, Thomas Holt was busy making bricks to enlarge his factory. In November he returned to the North, apparently the first southern textile manufacturer to do so. Northern markets soon replaced Confederate markets. In the summer of 1866, James S. Woodward and Sons Commission House in Philadelphia reported to Edwin Holt, "We sold all the coarse yarn and mixed bales you sent per last invoice at 50c . . . this was the best price our market affords at present & we were able to make prompt sales of it because it was 'Holt-yarn.' " When Dun and Bradstreet resumed rating southern businesses in 1866, they described Holt as having "good character" and as "perfectly safe." Repeatedly Edwin Holt and his sons were described as "men of large means."[1]

At the age of fifty-nine, with his northern contacts and markets restored, Edwin Holt decided to retire from active control of the Alamance Factory. He created E. M. Holt and Sons, a partnership that included James, William, and Banks, as well as his nephew and son-in-law, James Williamson, with a fifth partnership reserved for Lawrence when he turned twenty-one in 1872, to run the mill he

---

1. C. B. Denson, *An Address in Memory of Thomas M. Holt* (Raleigh: Bynum and Christopher, 1899), 7, NCDAH; James S. Woodward and Sons to E. M. Holt, July 23, 1866, Alamance Cotton Mills Records; Dun and Company Credit Ratings for Alamance County, 1860s, 1870s.

had successfully operated for three decades. Edwin Holt officially retired in 1866, but he remained actively involved in his family's expanding textile dynasty—advising sons, whom he continued calling
"the boys" even when they were middle-aged, closely supervising
his sons-in-law, and launching the textile careers of his grandsons—
until his death nearly twenty years later. Rather than joining his
brothers, in the late sixties Thomas made his brother-in-law, Dolph
Moore, a partner in the Granite Factory. Moore bought one-third interest in both the cotton mill and a profitable flouring mill.

In 1869 E. M. Holt and Sons built the Carolina Mill; its three
thousand spindles and sixty looms allowed the partnership to more
than double production.[2] Two years later Edwin Holt bought interest
in the Saxapahaw Factory from James Newlin and for four years
maintained a partnership with him. In 1875 he bought Newlin's
share and created a new partnership, Holt, White, and Williamson;
he required the two sons-in-law involved to contribute one-third of
the necessary capital and allowed them to divide the profits but
maintained ownership in trust for his daughters Frances and Emma.
The patriarch was never entirely confident that their husbands
would become first-rate mill men, so he always maintained a role in
providing for his daughters. In return he virtually mandated that
they live nearby rather than on their husbands' farms.

All of the new mills the Holts built or bought proved successful.
A year after Appomattox, Dun and Bradstreet described Edwin Holt
as "very good," as "wealthy" with wealth estimated to be around
$200,000. In 1872 a manufacturer from a nearby county noted "Mr.
Holt has the reputation of making money." The following year Dun
and Bradstreet reconfirmed that the Holts "are making money
rapidly." It was a reputation sustained by sons who became successful textile manufacturers from the time they took control of their
own mills. In 1875 Thomas and his partner were described as "men
of large means" with "high char. reliable and making move up."[3]

There were those in the county who wanted to block the move
up, to prevent the near total domination of the textile industry in
Alamance County and even statewide by the Holts. In 1869 Thomas
wrote Henry Fries "I have learned *confidentially* that Morehead,

2. Pierpont, "Development of the Textile Industry in Alamance
County," 44.
3. Dun and Bradstreet Credit Ratings, Alamance County, 1866, 1873,
1874; C. Phifer to George Phifer, March 10, 1872, Edward W. Phifer Jr. Collection, NCDAH.

Webb and R. S. Tucker had formed a combination to best us next summer." If the three men, two of them old family friends, tried to combine against the Holts, they failed. In 1870, a year in which Carolinians were preoccupied with the violence Reconstruction wrought, Thomas could report that "cotton spinning has been paying very well this year" and that he had "a magnificent mill & I expect making money fast *on checks*" because "there is more money in checks than anything else & no end to the demand." Three years later it was rumored that Holt and Moore made $300,000 clear profit.[4]

George Swepson was a more serious rival than this Piedmont triumvirate. In 1876 his overproduction of plaids at Falls of the Neuse glutted the market to the point that Holt and Moore had to temporarily suspend production of their own famous Alamance plaids.[5] It was at the height of his success, however, that Swepson was tried and acquitted of murdering Dolph Moore; publicity surrounding the case forced him to leave Alamance County, removing him as a serious threat to the Holt's textile dynasty. Although the Holts naturally pointed the finger at Swepson, in reality a glutted market resulted as much from their own singular focus on plaids as from rival competition.

Thomas's younger brothers became almost as successful as he was in the seventies by concentrating on the production of Alamance plaids. Two months after Thomas boasted of the money he was going to make, William reported "cotton manufacturing is dull now." Nonetheless William remained confident of "a heavy trade this fall" and began investigating facilities for marketing his "beautiful goods" in New Orleans. A few years later his father reported, "We are having a good trade, I never knew it better at this season of the year but [it] has required an active effort to keep it up."[6]

Success demanded not only an active effort but also capital sufficient to withstand recessions and various catastrophes that ruined many small mills. On April 24, 1872, as the family prepared to celebrate the marriages of William and Emma, fire destroyed the Alamance Factory, a $60,000 loss covered by only $25,000 worth of insurance. In the wake of the disaster Edwin Holt wrote his former

4. Thomas Holt to H. W. Fries, November 15, 1869, Fries Papers, SHC; Thomas Holt to William Carrigan, March 8, 1870, White Papers; Dun and Bradstreet Credit Ratings, Alamance County, 1874.

5. Hughes, *Development of the Textile Industry in Alamance*, 15.

6. William E. Holt to William Carrigan, May 17, 1870, Carrigan Papers; E. M. Holt to James W. White, December 19, 1873, White Papers.

partner, "The loss is a very heavy one" and "there is a small boy missing and I have no doubt was burnt. There is great distress amongst the hand[s] and realy I don't see how they are to get along—I take [?] it calmly knowing I shall have the simpathy of many while [?] others may be glade." Holt could confront the destruction of his first mill calmly because years of success assured his family resources to rebuild almost immediately. The new Alamance Factory was larger than the original mill and equipped with the most modern machinery.[7] After rebuilding the Alamance Factory, the Holts did not add any new mills until 1879.

Broadus Mitchell's 1920s publication, *The Rise of Cotton Mills in the South*, enshrined 1880 as the year the southern textile industry took off. Although Edwin Holt began building his textile dynasty in Alamance County much earlier, the rapid expansion of family mills in the last two decades of the nineteenth century largely reinforces Mitchell's thesis. The number of Holt mills increased from three in the late 1870s to over twenty-five by the end of the century. In 1879, during a nationwide recession, James and William built Glencoe. They originally planned to install eight thousand spindles and two hundred looms, which would have made it the largest mill in the county, but by 1884 they still had less than half the projected number of spindles in place. Banks and Lawrence also formed a new partnership in 1879 and invested forty thousand dollars in a mill they named Bellemont.[8]

In 1872 Holt and Moore completed a large addition to their mill. Between 1879 and 1883 Thomas, who assumed sole ownership after his partner's death, nearly doubled the Granite Factory's capacity, increasing the number of spindles to 8,424 and looms to 220, making it among North Carolina mills second in yarn production only to a Gaston County spinning mill. In 1881 the *Alamance Gleaner* claimed that "the capacity of the Granite Mills is ahead of anything in Alamance County and it is our opinion the largest or the equal of any in the state." The same year, James Williamson, breaking the family pattern of partnerships, built Ossipee, which he owned alone until his sons were old enough to join him. In 1883 Banks and Lawrence created E. M. Holt Plaids, their second partnership, which also included William and Locke Erwin, Lawrence's brothers-in-law,

7. Edwin M. Holt to William Carrigan, April 25, 1871, White Papers; Pierpont, "Development of the Textile Industry in Alamance County," 45.
8. Pierpont, "Development of the Textile Industry in Alamance County," 46; Dun and Bradstreet Credit Ratings, Alamance County, 1879

both grandsons of William Rainey Holt. The two youngest Holt sons also formed a partnership with another in-law to build the Altamahaw Mill. In 1885 Lawrence bought the bankrupt Lafayette Mill, renamed it Aurora, and hired Lafayette Holt, the distant cousin who had founded it, as his manager. Thomas built a second mill, designed after ones he had visited in New England, which he named Cora for his oldest daughter. In 1893 he founded his third mill, the Thomas M. Holt Manufacturing Company, financed in part with a twenty-five-thousand-dollar loan from Benjamin Duke, member of a family whose fortune in tobacco manufacturing would surpass what the Holts made in textiles.[9]

Edwin Holt's sons continued their father's practice of establishing retail stores throughout Alamance and even beyond as centers where they could sell their yarn and cloth as well as a variety of other goods. It was from the one he owned in partnership with Thomas Holt in Graham that Dolph Moore set off on his ill-fated hunting trip. Through the early eighties, Holt, Erwin, and Holt advertised groceries, notions, buggies, and ladies clothes. Banks Holt also frequently advertised the variety of goods he had to sell.[10]

Although generally the Holts continued the tradition of creating family partnerships within Alamance County, they did occasionally invest elsewhere and outside of the family. Shortly after the war, Edwin Holt founded E. M. Holt and Company Commission Merchants in Charlotte; by 1869, under his close supervision it had become the most successful commission house there. At the time of his death in 1884, he also owned both a store and a small tobacco factory in Lexington. In the mid-seventies, Lawrence initiated his family's investment in the National Bank of Charlotte, increasing their interest in the state's largest city. Thomas also invested in a drugstore and several newspapers, the latter, he explained, "to establish a good Democratic paper" rather "than to make money." By 1884 Banks held shares in several mills outside of Alamance County. In 1893 he and Lawrence joined the Dukes, Moses and Cae-

9. Dun and Bradstreet Credit Ratings, Alamance County, 1872; *Alamance Gleaner,* June 22, 1882; Pierpont, "Development of the Textile Industry in Alamance County," 79–80; Hughes, *Development of the Textile Industry in Alamance,* 18; A. W. Haywood to B. N. Duke, July 24, 1895, Washington Duke Papers, Manuscripts Division, Perkins Library, Duke University. Before Lawrence Holt bought Lafayette Mill, it was briefly owned by R. J. Reynolds and a son of Francis Fries.

10. See, for example, *Alamance Gleaner,* May 5, 1880 and numerous other issues of the *Gleaner.*

sar Cone, who had recently moved to Greensboro from Baltimore, the Odells of Concord, and "other gentlemen of large means n & s" in founding the Southern Finishing and Warehouse in Greensboro.[11]

Because only fragmentary evidence reveals the quantity of production, location of markets, and magnitude of profits for the Holt mills, it is impossible to establish a complete profile of their business activities. Most of the mills the Holt family built were small, and through the late nineteenth century, despite steady expansion, most of them lost ground in numbers of spindles and looms to other North Carolina mills. The exception was the Granite Factory. A businessman as astute as his father, Thomas carefully monitored his own enterprise, borrowing money when he needed it and rigorously pursuing monies owed him. When Grasty and Rison, a company his father had done business with since before the war, fell behind in paying off a debt for nearly four hundred dollars, he demanded "as we are needing the money *very badly*," because "our business is heavy & requires a large capital to operate," that they repay at once.[12]

Thomas Holt continued expanding his mill in the early eighties despite a recession that ruined businesses all over the country. He blamed this depression on "Wall Street Shylockers" whom he hoped would eventually be frozen out so "honest business men get the profit they deserve." The flooded market that resulted from the depression forced Thomas to finance the expansion of the Granite Factory on credit. In 1880 he asked the Whitin Machine Company for an additional several months to pay them since he had been unable to sell his goods in the summer and because the cost of improvements to his mill had proven greater than expected. Thomas combined Linwood, valued at $300,000, and his father's wealth as adequate security for the extension. Two years later, after what Thomas Holt described as the dullest year he had known in his career, he owed Whitin more than $22,000. This time he pointed to the value of his mill and machinery, which he had insured for $150,000, as well as his livestock and store, to assure Whitin that the debt would be paid.[13]

11. L. S. Williams [?] to Edwin Holt, July 31, 1869, Archibald Smith Papers; Thomas Holt to Walter Clark, August 11, 1877, September 14, November 7, 1878, January 17, 1879, Walter Clark Papers, NCDAH; Thomas Holt to Captain S. A. Ashe, July 21, 1893, Samuel Ashe Papers; *Alamance Gleaner*, February 23, 1893.

12. Thomas Holt to Grasty-Rison, November 8, 1867, Grasty-Rison Papers.

13. Thomas Holt to George Whitin, December 4, 1882, Whitin Papers, Baker Library, Harvard University.

Plaids continued to be profitable and eventually Thomas paid his debts. In 1883 he reported more orders for his Alamance cloth than he could fill; over the next three years he installed eleven railroad carloads of machinery in the Granite Mills, making a considerable increase in production possible. The new machinery raised the capital invested in the factory to over half a million dollars; 450 workers produced goods worth approximately $300,000 annually.[14]

His brothers and brothers-in-law prospered as well. Holt, White, and Williamson was described as a "good branch of the Holt family," and the partners as men who "do well . . . making money." In the summer of 1886 the *Gleaner* reported that in one day Banks shipped 26,000 yards of plaids, which, the paper enthused, "rings like business."[15]

Through the eighties the Holt mills produced a variety of fabrics, including sheeting, ticking, and coarse gingham, although they continued to concentrate on their famous plaids. In the late nineteenth century the family sold most of its cloth out of state. In the mid-eighties, for example, nine-tenths of the output of the Granite Factory was sent out by rail, primarily throughout the Southeast and into the Midwest where it was marketed by jobbers. The Holts also did business in the West, primarily through jobbers in St. Louis and Galveston. In the spring of 1895 the manager of the Bellemont Mill reported a successful selling trip to Missouri, Iowa, Nebraska, and Minnesota as well as some far western states.[16]

By the 1880s they joined other southern textile men in seeking international markets. The Holts inquired about selling in Africa although there is no evidence that they ever successfully expanded there. They did make some sales in Brazil and China. In 1883 the *Manufacturers' Record* reported that "southern mills are beginning to compete quite strongly for the China trade." By the 1890s the Holt mills were among those sending cloth there, a trade that Lawrence described as "extraordinarily prosperous."[17]

The sale of yarn and cloth made all of Edwin Holt's sons rich men. They had been trained from boyhood to heed their father's two

14. U.S. Treasury Department to Thomas M. Holt, April 4, 1886, Wiley Papers.

15. Dun and Bradstreet Credit Ratings, Alamance County, 1879; *Alamance Gleaner*, July 8, 1886.

16. Thomas M. Holt to Calvin Wiley, April 4, 1886, Wiley Papers; *Alamance Gleaner*, April 18, 1895.

17. *Manufacturers' Record*, May 3, 1883, quoted in Patrick Hearden, *Independence and Empire: The New South's Cotton Mill Campaign, 1865–1901* (DeKalb, 1982), 56; Greensboro *Patriot*, December 26, 1900.

favorite maxims: "You will have your good years and your bad years; stick to business," and "Put your profits into your business." They followed his advice and they prospered. His sons-in-law, although also successful, required more frequent coaching. Extant letters Holt wrote to James White in the early seventies, when he was success-fully transforming Emma's husband from a South Carolina planter into a North Carolina mill man, offer rare insight into Holt's busi-ness tactics, rare because, as he explained to White, "I keep my opin-ions to myself and do not publish them to others that are not interested."[18]

In the fall of 1873 he assured a son-in-law hesitant to leave his plantation that textile manufacturing "if properly managed . . . can be made a good business to all who have capital to run." His formula for success included an assessment of northern mills, which he ex-plained to James White were "stopped or running on short time which will reduce the stock of goods on the market and cause a greater demand." Accordingly, he concluded that although "times look squally for manufacture . . . it can be turned to good account . . . for those who have means," and advised White "not to sell at present prices as prices must go up when there is money to move it." He also advised him to "*mark the prediction* that great change will take place in commercial and financial matters." Holt encouraged his son-in-law to follow his example concerning advertising, pointing out that the circulars he sent out were so effective that he was constantly behind in orders.[19]

Holt's basic business philosophy remained constant to the end of his life. In the summer of 1882, less than two years before he died, the seventy-five-year-old patriarch took time while on vacation in the mountains to write White, "Advise Woodward not to sacrifice our yarns as I am confident they will advance."[20] It was the kind of confidence, the willingness to hold out for the greatest opportunity, that made Edwin Holt one of the most successful manufacturers in the nineteenth-century South.

Yet for all of his success Edwin Holt never really lost what Allen Tullos has described as "the beside-the-old-mill-stream mentality." His sound advice as well as his financial resources made his sons successful, but to compete in the late nineteenth century they had

18. Ashe, *Biographical History of North Carolina*, vol. 7, 185–89; Edwin Holt to James White, October 30, 1873, White Papers.
19. Ibid., November 29, 1873.
20. Edwin Holt to James White and John Williamson, August 2, 1882, White Papers.

to shed loyalty to some of their father's ways and build what Tullos describes as "beside-the-railroad factories relying on coal and, soon, electricity." Once the railroad transected the county in the mid-1850s, it remained the critical means of transporting goods through the rest of the nineteenth century. Water power continued to be used, but first steam and then electricity gradually replaced it. Until Edwin Holt bought it from them in the early seventies, the Newlin family owned what many considered the best water-power site in the county. They were disadvantaged, however, by their location twelve miles from the railroad. George Swepson's mill not only enjoyed good water power but was also the only site in the county that made it possible to ship goods by water. The Granite Factory, which boasted both good water power and a location directly on the railroad, was the one mill that enjoyed a physical setting superior to Swepson's during the water power era. Once steam power became more common, the location of new mills depended primarily on proximity to the railroad.[21]

Edwin Holt had been an enthusiastic booster of railroads from the beginning, but he was not able to embrace so easily the technology that transformed industrial America in the late nineteenth century. Along with many Americans he most vividly confronted the new machinery at the United States Centennial Celebration. In the summer of 1876, accompanied by several members of his family, he made what was most likely his last trip to Philadelphia to see the exhibits. Through the summer most of his sons went as well. Machinery Hall, the main attraction, displayed the wonders of modern technology, all powered by a thirty-foot Corliss Double Walkin-Beam Steam Engine, the "tremendous iron heart" that a popular guidebook advised visitors to see first. Alan Trachtenberg has described this and similar expositions as "pedagogies, teaching the prominence of machines as instruments of a distinctively American progress."[22]

Apparently Edwin Holt was not convinced. Although no record of his response to the Centennial survives, according to a county historian "when a generator was put in at Haw River it looked very frightening to old Mr. Holt. He didn't like it or approve of it at all."

21. Tullos, *Habits of Industry*, 21; *Alamance Gleaner*, March 17, 1880; Pierpont, "Development of the Textile Industry in Alamance County," 52, 84.
22. *Alamance Gleaner*, September 26, 1876; Henderson Monroe Fowler Diary, May 11, September 25, 1976, SHC; John Kasson, *Civilizing the Machine: Technology and Republican Values in America, 1776–1900* (New York, 1976), 164; Alan Trachtenberg, *The Incorporation of America: Culture and Society in the Gilded Age* (New York, 1982), 41.

His sons, however, were more willing to learn the lessons offered by Machinery Hall. Numerous trips north presented them with convincing evidence that technology was the instrument of progress. "I want to rigg up in first class style," Thomas wrote Whitin and Company, the machine company he most often did business with, and reported with obvious pride that a northern observer had found his mill first class in every way.[23]

By the eighties being first class required the technology displayed in Philadelphia and most readily available in the North. Perhaps reflecting a second-generational division, Edwin Holt's two youngest sons led their brothers in technological innovation. In July 1880 Banks and Lawrence purchased a new engine so massive that the effort to install it became a public occasion. Henderson Fowler, foreman in the Alamance Factory, recorded the three-day struggle: "LB & LS Holts Engine was drawn the first day to David Whitsell by 10 mules second day to the big hill in Troxlers lane by 12 mules arrived the 3rd day at race bridge 10 mit to 11 oclock got [illegible] up to store 10 mit to 2 oclock 14 mules & got to Belmont 9 oclock at night."[24]

The wonders of technology also made it possible to replace the dangerous lamps traditionally used to illuminate mills and frequently the cause of their burning down. Around the same time that the Holt brothers bought their engine, their foreman recorded that a gas man came to the factory and "the night of 31est he lit up the weave room in splendor."[25]

Although always interested in the latest technology available for modernizing textile mills, Thomas Holt continued to depend on water power years after his younger brothers had converted to steam. In 1885 he did acquire a three-hundred-horse-power engine, which, according to the *Gleaner,* was the largest in the state, but he planned to use it only when water was low. In 1881 the paper described Ossipee as having the "most modern style," with machinery driven by "two immense turbine water wheels, one of sixty and the other of eighty-five horse power." In 1886 James Williamson became the first member of the family to install a Corliss engine and also the first mill owner in the county to wire his mill for electricity. Three years later he had telephones installed in his offices.[26]

23. Beecher, *Science and Change,* 36; Thomas Holt to C. A. Taft, July 1, 1882, Whitin Papers.
24. Fowler Diary, July 2, 1880.
25. Ibid., July 31, 1880.
26. *Alamance Gleaner,* September 10, 17, 1885, December 19, 1881, November 4, 1886, May 2, 1889.

Lafayette Holt, a distant relative of Edwin Holt's family, bought the first Corliss engine in Alamance County. More than his more-successful cousins, this Holt understood the technology he imported into North Carolina. After studying construction and machinery in Lowell, he designed his own mill in Alamance County. Although he lacked the capital Edwin Holt and his sons could draw on to keep their mills solvent during recessions, Lafayette had the technological expertise so desperately needed if his state was going to become industrially competitive. His efforts proved crucial in persuading mill owners in the Piedmont to switch to steam power, thus freeing them from the vagaries of rivers and streams. He also introduced knitting machines and for a time it appeared that his knitted hosiery would make him successful. Lafayette Holt's ability to design mills and machinery was a step in the direction of freeing southern mill men from dependency on northern expertise. His own need for outside capital, however, ultimately forced him to sell the Lafayette Mill to Lawrence Holt. In the nineties Lafayette designed Elmira, Windsor, and Lakeside Mills, all owned by James Holt's sons; he also owned a machine shop after he sold his own mill.[27]

Lafayette Holt was one of the most skilled technicians in North Carolina. Although trained from earliest boyhood to be mill men, Holt's sons were almost as dependent as he was on northern experts for advice. Like their father they developed close professional relationships and even friendships with northerners, particularly the owners and employees of the companies that sold them machinery. It is Patrick Hearden's (as well as W. J. Cash's) contention that many southerners advocated building textile mills "as a way of defeating the hated Yankees." Little evidence exists, however, that the Holts joined in the hating. Their relations with northerners suggest a sense of common interest far more than animosity. In 1882 Thomas wrote northern business acquaintances complaining about injustices dealt to "honest business men" like themselves. Often they returned the compliment. A Philadelphia businessman described James and William Holt as "men of excellent hab. [habits] high char. [character] & standg . . . of large wealth perfectly solvent and relia [reliable]."[28]

The revival and expansion of the southern textile industry, par-

27. Allison Harris Black, comp., *An Architectural History of Burlington, North Carolina* (Burlington, 1987), 19–20.
28. Hearden, *Independence and Empire*, xiv; Thomas Holt to George Taft, December 4, 1882, Whitin Papers; Dun and Bradstreet Credit Ratings, Alamance County, 1874.

ticularly after 1880, did cause some alarm among northern manufacturers who feared the loss of markets. A sense of common class interest in an era of rising labor unrest, however, mitigated the potential friction. There is no evidence that any of the Holts developed close ties with northern textile manufacturers, although some southern mill men did. Beginning in 1872 several southerners were elected each year to join the New England Manufacturers Association, the major organization for textile mill owners in the country. Although none of the Holts became members, John T. Morehead, a family friend and owner of a factory Banks Holt invested in, was included.[29]

The Holts and most southern textile mill owners developed their closest northern ties with commission houses and, especially, with machine company officials. David Carlton has suggested that for prospective North Carolina industrialists "reliance on outside marketing skills was in some ways even more telling" than that on machine companies, but this does not appear to have been the case for the Holts. They did sell some of their products through commission houses but were not dependent on them. James S. Woodward and Sons, the commission house that had sold antebellum Alamance Factory goods, sold for the Saxapahaw and Granite factories after the war as well. Some time before 1882 the Alamance Factory switched to J. N. Conway and Company in New York. In 1882 the Carolina Mill was working with both of these companies. In contrast to less experienced mill men, the Holts depended more on the services commission houses provided than on their advice. In 1882 the Woodward firm failed, prompting a trip to Philadelphia by James Holt in order to assure that his family's interests were protected, a trip reminiscent of the one his uncle had made over thirty years earlier when the A. W. Adams Commission House failed. Woodward revived within a year and some of the Holts resumed selling their goods through them. Sometimes selling through a commission house was done for the expediency of a quick sale. In 1873 Edwin Holt advised James White to sell sheeting on commission because "the goods may as well be there as at the factory." In 1883 Thomas asked Whitin for an extension of credit to enable him to take time and sell his goods himself for the highest price, but he also assured them that he was willing to pay immediately by selling quickly through an agent. Apparently the Holts worked with commission houses in St. Louis and Galveston for sales in the West; they mar-

---

29. *Proceedings of the Semi-annual Meeting* (Boston, 1872), and other proceedings of the New England Manufacturers Association.

keted at least some of the goods they sold in the South through their own commission house in Charlotte. By the nineties Thomas had stopped working through a commission house even for sales in the Northeast. Several other members of the Holt family, however, signed a contract with Caesar and Moses Cone to sell their Alamance plaids for a 5-percent commission.[30]

Some southern mill men sold their own products, but few of them—in Alamance County perhaps only Lafayette Holt—could operate the increasingly more complex equipment they purchased without the assistance of northern machine companies. These companies and southern mills developed a reciprocal relationship, especially as the southern textile industry began rapid expansion after 1880 and northern companies became increasingly competitive for a share of the South's business. Common interest created close professional ties that sometimes developed into personal relationships as well. According to a machine company historian, "the 'trip North' became a deep-rooted custom of the Southern mill managers, just as the 'trip South' became a seasonal function of the machine-shop treasurers and superintendents." Thomas Holt and C. A. Taft, a Whitin Machine Company official, became especially close friends. They frequently exchanged visits and also entertained while helping train one another's sons.[31]

When Thomas Holt first became a customer of Whitin in 1871 he sent as references the names of the Danforth Machine Company and James S. Woodward Commission House, the firms his father had done business with since before the Civil War. Whitin officials responded that they wanted to merit "the confidence of the best manufacturers in the Old North State," and further assured him of enough confidence in his family's dependability to sell to him on credit. Thomas reciprocated by assuring them "I am a *Geo. E. Taft Whitin Machine Man*," and "I am pleased with you as *men* & your machinery is all I can ask for."[32]

30. David L. Carlton, "The Revolution from Above: The National Market and the Beginnings of Industrialization in North Carolina," *Journal of American History* 77 (1990): 468; Pierpont, "Development of the Textile Industry in Alamance County," 105; Edwin Holt to James White, November 29, 1873, White Papers; Moses H. Cone to William H. Williamson, September 30, 1892, Pilot Cotton Mills Correspondence, Manuscripts Division, Perkins Library, Duke University.

31. Gibbs, *Saco-Lowell Shops*, 242; Correspondence between Thomas Holt and C. A. Taft, Whitin Papers.

32. Thomas Holt to Whitin Machine Company, November 12, 1879. Whitin Papers.

Thomas tried persuading his brothers to give their business to Whitin as well, but he was not always successful. When Banks and Lawrence placed an order for new machinery with the Lowell Machine Company, Thomas wrote his preferred company that although disappointed, he remained optimistic that he could convince them to reconsider. But the Holt brothers also realized that buying from several different companies created competition, thus giving them some leverage to bargain for better terms. On several occasions Thomas complained to Whitin that his brothers received better prices from Lowell and attempted to parlay these complaints into a better arrangement for himself. In the 1870s and 1880s machine companies were often eager to generate southern business and, accordingly, made some concessions. By the nineties, however, Whitin had concluded that business in the North was sufficient for them to give up some of their southern customers; one official explained, "We are not going to do business for fun, not even for old customers in the South—they will soon come around to paying regular prices."[33]

In important ways, however, nineteenth-century southern mill men were not regular customers; compared to their northern counterparts, they had limited firsthand exposure to the technological innovation that was transforming industrial America. When William Holt complained about being charged for the services of a man sent south to assemble his spinning frames, Whitin rejoined that although the frames cost the same in the North and South, northern mill owners knew how to put them up themselves.[34]

Thomas Holt aspired to become a well-rounded mechanic competent to set up his own machines. Toward the end of his career he reminisced, "I always determined to know my business thoroughly. There is nothing there that I have not done with my own hands. I have been at the dye-tubs and the gin, and have worked from the foundation to the roof. If need be, there is no portion of the machinery that I cannot take to pieces and repair, and no man's task which I cannot do myself." Yet however confident he was in his ability to run a textile mill, Thomas generally deferred to northern experts, frequently seeking their assistance even though it could be costly. Apparently the northern experts who knew him well concurred that he sometimes needed their help. In the mid-eighties George Taft

33. Thomas Holt to George Whitin, September 17, 1879, January 26, 1880, C. A. Taft to Stuart Cramer, July 13, 1899, Whitin Papers.
34. George Whitin to William E. Holt, July 12, 1887, Whitin Papers.

wrote that although he was confident Thomas could set up and start his new frames, it was preferable that Whitin send a man down to do it for him. On one occasion Thomas asked that they send one man rather than two to save him the extra expense; for the most part, however, he willingly paid for the expert advice necessary to build a first-class mill. In February 1880 he wrote Taft, "I wish very much you would come to Haw River from Baltimore. I wish your advise about some matters which I cannot explain." As an incentive he offered to pay Taft's expenses and volunteered to help him secure orders from his brothers. Thomas frequently wrote that his work would remain "completely balked" until he could obtain the assistance or the equipment he needed from Whitin. On one occasion he complained that he would be delayed ten days in starting his new machinery because they had sent the wrong man to set it up; another time he reported that Alex Kingsburg, an employee of Whitin who worked in the South in the early eighties as a roving mechanic, had not arrived although "we are ready and waiting for him."[35]

The necessity of getting not only machinery but also a variety of supplies from the North further handicapped southern mill men. When Thomas Holt received the wrong bobbins he offered his standard complaint: "We are completely balked." During the summer of 1880 Kingsburg advised Holt that the company had not delivered enough rawhide belting and then two months later that parts for the spinning frames were broken.[36]

Thomas was only one of the Carolina mill owners eager to obtain the services of Kingsburg. While awaiting a part for the Fries mill in Salem, the talented northern mechanic wrote his company, "I am looking round and fixing anything and everything that I see needs fixing." It was the kind of service southern mechanics, often trained on the job, were less able to provide. When Kingsburg tried to teach Thomas Holt's North Carolina–born superintendent about the machinery he supervised, he was forced to conclude that "from what little I have seen of him he would do better out on a farm." A month later he complained again because he had "taken Lashley and showed him as well as explained to him about all the different parts and different changes but he dont seem to have brains enough to comprehend it." When Kingsburg left Whitin, Thomas expressed re-

35. Denson, *Address in Memory of Thomas M. Holt*, 6; Thomas Holt to C. A. Taft, February 23, 1880, Thomas Holt to gentlemen, September 13, 1879, Thomas Holt to George E. Taft, July 5, August 12, 1880, February 23, 1881, Whitin Papers.

36. Thomas Holt to G. E. Taft, July 24, August 28, 1880, Whitin Papers.

gret that he had not known in time to offer him a position. He concluded that the northern mechanic "was very much pleased with Haw River" and possibly would have considered working there.[37]

Thomas Holt failed to recruit Alex Kingsburg to oversee his mill and had to make do with Lashley. Most of the skilled northerners working in antebellum southern textile mills left when the war broke out, although a few, like Thomas Siddall, remained. In the late sixties Siddall was hired by James and William Holt to oversee the Carolina mill. After his confrontation with the Klan, Siddall may have questioned his decision to remain in the South, but once southern states were restored to an equal place in the Union and Klan-led violence dissipated, more skilled northern textile men willingly joined him there. Their skills proved critical to the success of the southern textile industry, although not all of them performed as satisfactorily as Siddall or Kingsburg. In 1892 Thomas Holt wrote, concerning a man who worked for him only briefly before he was fired, "I do not care to notice the fool. He is no doubt some trifling fellow, brought down here from the North & proved to be a *fraud* & was discharged." In a rare display of southern defensiveness, he continued that "we have many such fellows as, I take this one to be, appling for positions, I have tried several of them, & have invariably been *'burnt.'* *They* think *we* know nothing, but we are generally *smart* enough to find out that they do not *know* it *all.*" The man Thomas discharged must have been particularly obnoxious; usually the Holts and most southern mill men enjoyed good relationships with the northerners they hired. Massachusetts native A. L. Ware, superintendent of Oneida in the nineties, was on such good terms with Banks Holt that his parents were the Holts' guests when they visited their son. When Philadelphian G. Estlow worked as superintendent of weaving at Oneida, his mother and father also visited, and possibly were entertained by the Holts as well.[38]

Because there were never enough skilled northerners to meet the demand, North Carolina mill owners, as well as other southerners, constantly competed to hire them. As need increasingly outstripped supply, a lobby developed for the improvement of technical education in the state. To become competitive for the most skilled

37. Alex Kingsburg to C. A. Taft, July 13, 1881, Alex Kingsburg to G. E. Taft, March 1, 1882, Thomas Holt to G. E. Taft, March 1, 1882, Whitin Papers.
38. Thomas M. Holt to Edward A. Oldham, March 26, 1892, Oldham Papers, Manuscripts Division, Perkins Library, Duke University; *Alamance Gleaner*, March 23, May 11, December 7, 1899.

jobs, southerners needed the technological training that until the nineties was only available in the North. Lafayette Holt and several of Edwin Holt's grandsons were among the young southern men who trained in the famous Lowell mills or elsewhere in the North in order to learn thoroughly the technology of textile production. By 1880 aspirant textile men from North Carolina had become so common in Lowell that their evening meeting place became known as North Carolina Square. Young men from other southern states also studied in the famous textile city and may have had their own meeting places. Northern experience slowly developed southern expertise; when in 1886 Lawrence Holt wrote a prominent manufacturer in South Carolina soliciting information about southerners available who could dress textile machinery, he was informed of several suitable young men from Georgia and South Carolina.[39]

The Holts and most southern mill men rarely questioned the propriety of sending their sons and protégés north to train. To some North Carolina mill men, notably Daniel Tompkins, however, this dependency on Yankees underscored the South's industrial backwardness. None of the Holts were as outspoken as this successful Charlotte mill developer and New South booster in advocating development of technological expertise within the South in order to end dependence on the North. In the mid-1890s his efforts paid off with the creation of a textile school at North Carolina State College in Raleigh where young men from the state could train for the technological and managerial positions traditionally awarded to either northerners or northern-trained southerners.[40]

Although generally more critical of the North than the Holts, Tompkins was more willing to challenge the southern dogma of loyalty to the Democratic Party. Before the Civil War, economic ties between northern and southern industrialists had been reinforced by the national Whig Party. After 1865 some in North Carolina, notably the Dukes and Tompkins, joined the Republican Party rising from the ashes of the Whigs because they considered it the party most likely to serve their class and economic interests. But the circumstances of emancipation and Reconstruction within the South made it impossible for most industrialists there to embrace the party of Lincoln and restore political unity with their northern counterparts. The Holts joined the majority in reacting to the politics of race and em-

39. Ibid., November 21, 1881; H. P. Hammett to Lawrence S. Holt, March 7, 1886. Hammett Papers, South Caroliniana Room, University of South Carolina.

40. Tullos, *Habits of Industry*, 159.

braced the Democratic Party. In the mid-nineties James Henry Holt Jr. did briefly declare himself a Republican because of the party's support for a protective tariff. He left a Republican state convention he attended in 1896 convinced, however, that he had not understood the "dark" days of Reconstruction until he confronted a "crowd of howling negroes." No longer, he assured Alamance Democrats, would he associate with a party that included a "mob of howling savages."[41]

His father and uncles, Whigs as young men, never questioned their allegiance to the Democratic Party in the years after the war. But political disagreement did not preclude ties with northern or southern Republicans based on mutual economic interest. In the early 1890s some of the Holts successfully cultivated close relationships, both personal and professional, with the wealthy and Republican Duke family, whose success in tobacco exceeded their own in textiles. Different members of the Holt family stayed with the Dukes when they visited Durham and reciprocated by entertaining in Alamance County. After one visit Thomas wrote Washington Duke "I *love* an *honest* man (as I *believe you* are) one who makes an honest living & adds to the prosperity of N.C. though he may differ with me in politics. I am a Democrat. You are a Republican yet I believe you would do nothing intentionally to hurt any man in church or state." Several years later Thomas thanked Duke for his hospitality, assuring him "I enjoyed very much our conversation on the state of our country, and feel that if our material men could see more of each other socially, as in the days of yore & interchange opinions on public policy, our government would be stronger, our people happier, & more contented—less envy and jelousy & moare love and patriotism."[42]

The letter to Washington Duke advocating stronger class ties came only a year after Thomas Holt had completed a two-year term as governor of North Carolina. Although Thomas was the only member of his family who sought elective office, his brothers, brothers-in-law, and a number of their sons also took an active part in local Democratic politics; in the summer of 1876, for example, Thomas, William, and Lawrence as well as James Williamson served as delegates from Alamance County to the state Democratic convention and Banks sat on the county executive committee. Thomas's brothers may have declined to run for office at least in part to avoid the

41. *Alamance Gleaner*, May 21, 1896.
42. Thomas Holt to Washington Duke, September 21, 1892, June 18, 1894, Duke Papers.

charge that they were an elite family that profiteered during the war, a charge that always plagued Thomas when he was a candidate. His campaigns generated debate about the social consequences of the industrial transformation of North Carolina, a transformation that his family had played a major role in initiating. When Thomas was nominated to run for the state senate in the summer of 1876, the *Gleaner,* always a loyal Democratic paper, praised him "as one of the most public spirited, enterprising citizens of the state" and "a man of large fortune almost exclusively the accumulation of his own industry, forsight and business capacity."[43]

Not all voters in Alamance agreed that having a large fortune was a political asset; Republican attempts to make Thomas's wealth an issue prompted the *Gleaner* to sarcastically rejoin "Terrible! Tom Holt's house is surrounded by shrubbery. That is one of the charges now being circulated against him and, if it becomes generally known, there is no telling the consequences." During the same campaign, another Holt defender who signed his letter to the *Gleaner* "maimed confederate soldier" chose to defend Thomas Holt's wartime activity rather than his shrubbery. Turning the tables on Holt's critics, he argued that it was really poor women, women who had bought yarn from Holt for much less than he could have commanded from other buyers and then resold it for twice as much, who profiteered during the war.[44]

Holt won a narrow election victory and became a state representative in 1876 but four years later lost to Junius Scales in a close four-way race; he carried Alamance County by only a few votes. Through the eighties several papers endorsed Thomas Holt for either lieutenant governor or governor; the *Gleaner* supported him on the grounds that he was "from the people and one of the people," adding that his wealth should be viewed not as a liability, but as making him especially suited for political leadership. In 1884 the editor proclaimed of this southerner who had enjoyed an exemption during the war, "Col. Holt is a gentleman of large means of various kinds, hence of wide information, and thus his store of knowledge can be used to great advantage in legislating for the people." That year the *Durham Recorder* also endorsed Holt's candidacy by pointing to the success he had enjoyed as a textile manufacturer. After Holt failed to be nominated governor, the *Recorder* promoted him for speaker of the house because

43. *Alamance Gleaner,* June 6, 27, August 22, October 10, 1876.
44. Ibid., October 10, 17, 1876.

aside from politics he has proven to the world by strict attention to his business, that this state is truly a manufacturing section. His wonderful success as a cotton manufacturer has made
his name famous throughout the state, and all manufacturing
circles. We believe that such men deserve the reward of our
people. They by their peculiar ability and enterprise give employment to hundreds of our people and fresh laurels to the reputation of the old North State.[45]

After two years out of office, Thomas was reelected to the North Carolina House of Representatives in 1882 where he served six years, the
last four as speaker. In 1888 he was elected lieutenant governor;
when Governor Daniel Fowle died three years later he served the last
two years of Fowle's unexpired term.

Edwin Holt did not live to see his second son inaugurated governor of North Carolina. In 1882, when Thomas sent his condolences
to executives at Whitin on the death of their president, he also noted
his concern that his father would probably not live much longer. Although feeble and in poor health, Edwin Holt did live two more
years and remained actively involved in supervising his family's
mills. In early 1884 his health again deteriorated. In February a relative noted that "aunt Bet and Jul [Alfred's wife and oldest son] came
out tonight to go up to see old Mr. Holt, he is sick, not expected to
live." A few days later the *Gleaner* could report that the Holt family
patriarch had rallied, but in the spring he again neared death and
family members were summoned once more. On May 14, 1884, at
the age of seventy-seven, Edwin Michael Holt died. On his deathbed
he gathered his sons around him and asked them, "Do you remem-
ber any instance in my life in which I ever took an unfair advantage
of any man or woman or child? If so, tell me, for I want to make it
right." When his sons assured him that they knew of no such instance, he replied, "Then I die contented." At Holt's funeral Paul
Cameron stood by the casket of an old friend he had known most of
his life and said of him, "Thus ends a useful and well-spent life."[46]
Cameron had been the richest man in antebellum North Carolina but lived to see the industrial wealth amassed by Holt surpass
his own. At his death, Edwin Michael Holt's estate of nearly $2 mil-

45. *Durham Recorder* quoted in *Alamance Gleaner,* June 2, 1880, September 4, December 4, 1884.
46. Thomas Holt to George Whitin, April 28, 1882, Whitin Papers;
Mother to Dear Son, February 12, 1884, Mebane Family Papers; Ashe, *Biographical History of North Carolina,* vol. 7, 188–89.

lion made him one of the richest men, perhaps the richest, in North Carolina.

Edwin Holt was a remarkable patriarch who had successfully steered all but one of his ten children, as well as many of their children, along the paths that he chose for them. In his will he attempted to assure his patriarchal control past death, to reward those who met his standards, warn those who threatened not to, and punish the one son who had clearly disappointed him. Holt left Locust Grove and the surrounding land to "my beloved wife Emily" until her death, at which time it would go to Lawrence, the only one of their ten children born there. Banks received his grandfather's home and the adjacent land, William and James additional land in Alamance, and Thomas the portion of Linwood his father owned. The lots and houses in Graham he had given Frances and Emma were their share of real estate. The Alamance Factory reverted to James, William, Banks, and Lawrence with a share also going to Mary, presumably because she had not received real estate in Graham. Holt left no explanation for this bequest, but it is unlikely that he anticipated his daughter becoming actively involved. He had virtually mandated that his daughters live near him and always assumed a role in providing for them, even holding title to the Whites' home until he willed it to Emma. But rather than trusting his daughters to manage their own property, he left control in the hands of trustees. Holt always remained confident that his own sons, and possibly his nephew James Williamson as well, would successfully manage their mills; he remained doubtful that without his direction his other two sons-in-law could do so. He granted them the right to withdraw their working capital from Saxapahaw but instructed the trustees to continue running the factory on behalf of his daughters, advising them to enlarge and improve it. He expressed "great confidence in the success of the work," which "if properly managed must do well," but added that "fearing said sons-in-law may not work harmonious" he wanted "to obviate any difficulty or derangement in operating the factory which requires concert of action."[47]

By the time he wrote his will, Holt had concluded that Alexander, the son he once wistfully reported might make a good soldier, would never make a good mill man. At least by the early seventies Alexander struggled with alcoholism. His father allowed him only a minor role in the family mills, assigning him such tasks as paying

47. Alamance County Wills, Will of Edwin Michael Holt.

and collecting bills. He willed Alexander no property outright but did leave him $25,000, which trustees were to oversee for his "decent support but not for excessive indulgence."[48]

Alfred's three sons threatened to disappoint as well. When their grandfather wrote his will they were young men in their twenties; Junius and Eddy had married and become fathers. But none of them had settled into the pattern of responsible work that Edwin Holt demanded. He left each one ten thousand dollars controlled by trustees and dictated that "in no case shall said trustees furnish said grandsons funds for excessive indulgence a [and] dissipation." Edwin instructed trustees to grant these grandsons control of their property if in time it appeared they were capable of managing it, but if any one of them failed to merit that trust his share was to be held "to prevent idleness and dissipation."[49]

Holt had more confidence in Frances's oldest son, Edwin Holt Williamson, although the boy was only twelve years old when he wrote his will. The grandfather attempted to oversee his namesake's training, writing "I desire his education be with a view of a businessman, and when he comes to years of maturity and is of steady sober habits I desire he shall be taken to the Factory to be trained and to aid in any position he may be fitted for." Although still a minor, this grandson received a share in Saxapahaw and an account to protect his profits. John Williamson and his two sons from his first marriage also received shares, but their right to sell was restricted to within the Holt family.[50]

What was not specifically bequeathed in his will, Holt left to eight of his children (he excluded Alexander) to share equally. His final attempt to control his family and assure their harmony and unity was a declaration that if any legatee dissented, that beneficiary's share would be reduced to one hundred dollars.[51]

When Edwin Holt died his oldest grandsons were already training to become mill men. Mary's son William Holt Williamson, born at Locust Grove and raised nearby, reminisced that "since I was old enough to think of such subjects, I made up my mind to adopt a business career following the work of my father, a cotton goods manufacturer." William Williamson remained in North Carolina to train; in June 1884, a month after his grandfather's death, he began at the age of seventeen working his way up from the most menial jobs

48. Ibid.
49. Ibid.
50. Ibid.
51. Ibid.

at Ossipee. After he trained for three years his father made him a partner. Most of Edwin Holt's grandsons also remained in North Carolina and trained with their fathers or uncles, but several of them went north. In the summer of 1881 James's oldest son, Walter, attended Eastman Business College in Poughkeepsie, New York. The following summer Charles Holt, the elder of Thomas's two sons, worked at Chicopee in western Massachusetts.[52]

After only a few years of training, this generation of Holts began building mills of their own. In 1886 James's sons Walter and Edwin built a new mill in Burlington (formerly Company Shops), the first of a number of mills founded by the grandsons. When two years later James Henry Jr. and Robert built the Windsor mill, the *Alamance Gleaner* enthused that "these young men know the cotton mill business and that they will make a success goes without saying."[53] Charles Holt, whose only brother was thirteen years younger, became a partner with his father and Ben Robertson, a man apparently not related to the Holt family, in the Thomas M. Holt Manufacturing Company. Edwin Holt Williamson, the grandson whom Edwin had singled out in his will, did dutifully train to become a textile manufacturer. He formed a partnership with another of James Holt's sons, but, perhaps finding the field already crowded in Alamance, they left to build a new mill in Fayetteville which they called Holt-Williamson. Lawrence joined a partnership with his three sons; Banks, without sons of his own, formed one with his nephew and namesake, Lynn Banks Williamson. In 1901 Emma Holt White joined her three sons in forming the Travora Mill in Graham. At least nominal involvement of both Mary and Emma in family partnerships suggests some change in the perception of the role of women in this family dynasty. There is no evidence, however, that either was actively involved.

According to one of them, all twenty-six of Edwin Holt's grandsons were involved in the textile industry at some time. Most made it their lifelong profession; they built mills not only in Alamance County but throughout North Carolina. At least several of the grandsons, however, briefly or ultimately resisted the example of their fathers and grandfather. Alfred's sons never founded mills of their own and despite their grandfather's effort to reform them, apparently continued to live lives he would have considered dissipated.

52. Hughes, *Development of the Textile Industry in Alamance County,* 110; *Alamance County: The Legacy of Its People and Places* (Greensboro, 1984), 490; *Alamance Gleaner,* August 22, 1881, March 13, 1882.
53. *Alamance Gleaner,* January 23, 1890.

Frances's son Finley moved to Newport News, Virginia, with the intention of staying and selling real estate there. Six months later he succumbed to family pressure and returned home to work as a bookkeeper for one of his uncles. James's son Samuel made the boldest effort to strike out on his own. At twenty-one, an age when most of his brothers and male cousins were training for textile careers, Sam, "desiring to extend my knowledge of the outside world & to gratify a life long desire," decided to join a voyage to the West Indies. After signing aboard, however, Sam found that "my parents were so much opposed to my going I had to abandon that voyage & wait for another opportunity, which soon presented itself." He succeeded on the second try, perhaps because this time he left without informing his parents. After his return, however, Sam conformed to what they expected of him; he joined a new partnership with his youngest brother, Ernest, who apparently felt no more enthusiastic about a career in textiles than Sam did. Shortly after their father died, the two brothers gave up the textile business for good and went to Paris, Texas, to ranch. In time, Sam returned to sea.[54]

A number of the men who married Edwin Holt's granddaughters also became mill men. All three of Thomas's sons-in-law entered partnerships in his mills. Because he had no sons, Banks was particularly eager to bring the men who married his seven daughters into the textile business. Although Mamie's husband had trained as a physician, he reluctantly gave up medicine to join his father-in law in a mill venture in Asheville, in the North Carolina mountains. Louisa's husband also agreed to become involved in textiles but refused to work in Alamance County.[55]

The third generation closely conformed to the pattern set by their grandfather and followed by their fathers and uncles. Usually two brothers or cousins, sometimes in partnership with their father or an uncle, founded a small mill that produced primarily Alamance plaids. Despite the competition the numerous family mills created, Holt's sons and sons-in-law never relented in their effort to bring all of their boys into the business. But as this third generation came of age, Thomas's optimistic prediction of the 1870s that there was "no end to the demand" for Alamance plaids gave way to concern with

54. Mrs. B. F. Mebane to Daughter, November 14, 1889, March 22, September 6, 1893, Mebane Family Papers; Logbook of Captain Sam. M. Holt, Alamance County Historical Museum; Interview with Bill Vincent, January 3, 1990.
55. Interview with Mary Graves Stalter, August 10, 1992.

overproduction. As a result, although most of them were prominent and successful textile men, no one member of the family dominated the industry; instead they competed with each other for a share of national and increasingly international markets. "As we look at it now," one grandson concluded long after he entered the business, "this was not good economics," because "had they [his family] incorporated one or more large companies and united their efforts they would have dominated the colored goods industry in the South for a good many years."[56]

Overproduction did prompt efforts to organize the production of plaids. In 1884 at least fifteen plaid mills, eight of them from Alamance, organized the Cotton Plaid Manufacturers' Association and elected Thomas Holt president. Such associations were becoming common nationally in the late nineteenth century, but as two economic historians have explained, they "had to depend upon the good will of the members to attain their objectives" and that "proved to be a precarious foundation." Over the next four years, despite efforts of the association to control production, the state's output of plaids increased by over 100 percent. In 1888 the members agreed to cut production by one-third. Within a year the *Gleaner* reported that "the cotton mills in this county are not all running full time now, which is due to the high price of raw material and the difficulty of disposing of the product at remunerative prices."[57] The real cause may have been the Holts' effort to cooperate with the association's roll back. Their steady addition of new plaid mills, however, undermined any long-range effort to reduce the production of plaids.

In 1890 Moses and Caesar Cone, merchants who had moved from Baltimore to Greensboro, founded the Cone Export and Commission Company in another attempt to organize the state's plaid mills. Within a few years the Cones were selling for Altamahaw, the Alamance Factory, Aurora, Bellemont, E. M. Holt and Sons, Glencoe, and for several of the new mills built by the third generation of Holts. For a short time the Cone Company sold for over half of the state's plaid mills, but by 1900 it had lost the business of a number of them. In 1896 some of the Holts joined other southern textile men in founding the Southern Textile Manufacturers Association; Banks Holt was elected a vice president, and George Mebane, his

56. William Plummer Jacobs, *The Pioneer* (Clinton, S.C., 1934), 57.
57. Thomas C. Cochran and William Miller, *The Age of Enterprise: A Social History of Industrial America* (New York, 1942), 141; *Alamance Gleaner*, September 5, 1889.

son-in-law, a director. Mebane also served on the "committee to confer with manufacturing regarding limitation of product" and William Holt Williamson on the "committee to promote membership."[58]

Thomas Holt died the year the manufacturers association was founded and his brother James the following year. The three youngest sons of Edwin Holt remained active textile manufacturers well into the twentieth century. An historian of the Alamance mills has written that William "of all the sons of E. M. Holt, probably exerted the greatest influence on the state at large, and the least upon his native county." After he moved from Alamance, William founded mills in Lexington and then Charlotte before his death in 1917. When Banks passed away three years later he owned five mills, which combined included 30,000 spindles and 1,100 looms, and held investments in several others. Lawrence died in 1937, exactly one hundred years after his father founded the Alamance Factory. Four years before his death, in the midst of the Great Depression, the partnership he had formed with his three sons was liquidated. Thomas Holt's two sons both died at an early age, a few years after their father; their mills were consolidated by Thomas's daughters and their husbands as Holt-Granite Manufacturing, the family's first corporation. It operated successfully into the twentieth century, but after reaching a peak production in 1912 the company declined so rapidly that four years later Holt-Granite fell into receivership. Two of Edwin Holt's grandsons eventually acquired the property once owned by their uncle but, although it temporarily made them wealthy men, they eventually lost everything they owned, including their homes.[59]

Other grandsons were more successful, but not one of them was able to maintain control of a mill in Alamance County through the 1930s. A hundred years after he founded the Alamance Factory, the textile dynasty Edwin Holt built in Alamance County had all but disappeared.

58. Pierpont,"Development of the Textile Industry in Alamance County," 97–98; Carlton, "Revolution from Above," 471; *Alamance Gleaner*, August 1, 1889; Cone Export and Commission Company stationery, Mebane Family Papers; Moses Cone to William H. Williamson, September 30, 1892, Pilot Cotton Mills Correspondence; "Proceedings of the Organizing Convention and Constitution and By-Laws of the Southern Textile Manufacturers Association," 2–3, DeRenne Collection, Special Collections Division, University of Georgia.

59. Pierpont, "Development of the Textile Industry in Alamance County," 183, 172, 178.

When Edwin Holt built the Alamance Factory in 1837, he patterned it on "the traditional American business firm" described by Alfred Chandler as "a single-unit business enterprise," in which "an individual or a small number of owners operated a shop, factory, bank, or transportation." By World War I, Chandler explains, this traditional enterprise had been largely replaced by "the multiunit enterprise administered by a set of salaried middle and top managers," which he describes as "modern."[60] Edwin Holt built a profitable traditional firm. His sons and then his grandsons successfully followed his example; in the twentieth century, however, their small, family-controlled partnerships could not compete. Ultimately they had learned his lessons all too well.

I am suggesting that Edwin Holt was the product of a particular time, the early phase of industrial development that left him and ultimately his sons and grandsons ill prepared to compete in the modern era Chandler describes. The question remains whether his success was inhibited by place as well. Were the Holts "southern" industrialists, different in fundamental ways from their northern counterparts? Ironically this most successful nineteenth-century southern textile family failed in the early decades of the twentieth century, the time when the South surpassed the North in productivity. It would be hard to argue that Edwin Holt or his sons were saddled with a planter mentality that made them peculiarly southern industrialists. But as David Carlton has explained, "If southern industrialists failed to inherit the mentality of their planter predecessors, they nonetheless had to grapple with the structural disabilities bequeathed the region by its plantation past." Although Holt had been one of the few southern textile men to develop northern markets before the war and saw his sons maintain them in the decades after, it was yet true for his family, as Carlton explains, that "integration into a national market placed North Carolina [and the Holts] in direct competition with one of the most dynamic and sophisticated industrial regions on earth, the manufacturing belt of the American Northeast and (increasingly) Midwest." Considering the industrial development of the state as a whole, Carlton describes "the problems distance from customers and support services could pose to merchandising."[61] Although more successful than most, the Holts were always dependent on degrees of northern technological and entrepreneurial skill. Ultimately they were more southern than they wanted to be.

60. Alfred D. Chandler Jr., *The Visible Hand: The Managerial Revolution in American Business* (Cambridge, Mass., 1972), 3.
61. Carlton, "Revolution from Above," 447, 458, 460.

7

Badges of Social Standing

THE HOLT FAMILY,
1865-1900

On October 26, 1865, Edwin and Emily Holt hosted a double wedding for two of their children; Mary married her first cousin, James Nathaniel Williamson, and Banks, four months home from federal prison, married Mary Catherine Mebane. Two months later, on Christmas day, Frances was married for the second time, to John Lea Williamson. The three weddings symbolized the good fortune of Edwin Holt's family; the Holts concluded the war with their wealth intact and continued to prosper socially as well as economically in the next decades. They were the wealthiest family in Alamance County and in the late nineteenth century set the standards for bourgeois respectability and accomplishment.

The three marriages left only Alexander, who never married, and William, who remained single until he was over thirty, along with their adolescent siblings, Emma and Lawrence, at home. The lives of the two youngest Holt children in the years between school and marriage were shaped primarily by the gendered expectations of their class, expectations that had more or less survived the war intact. Emma and Lawrence had seen the impact of war all around them; cousins barely older than they had been killed. Despite the war, however, their lives diverged little from the patterns of their older siblings who came of age in the 1840s and 1850s. Their schooling may have been disrupted, as it was for many southern youth attending academies. Lawrence entered the Horner Military School in Oxford, about fifty miles away from his home, sometime during the war, and remained there until 1868 when he enrolled at Davidson College. In contrast to his oldest brother, Thomas, he left college at his own initiative, despite his father's opposition, and moved to Charlotte to work with merchants his father knew there. Otherwise, his path from schoolboy to successful businessman closely resembled that of his older brother. Thomas had written from Philadel-phia, "I must only go where my business directs"; at about the same age Lawrence worked so hard in Charlotte that Emma complained he had no time to visit home.[1]

As she matured, Emma's life contrasted sharply with the experi-ences of her work-driven brothers. Like her older sisters, she devoted the years after school to finding a suitable husband. After the war frequent visiting again became an important social activity for young women trying to fill up the years between school and mar-riage as well as a means of finding a man to marry. In March 1870 Emma spent four weeks with friends in New Bern, in the eastern part of the state, primarily to attend a friend's wedding. She so en-joyed her "lively time" there that she turned down a chance to travel in the North with her brother Thomas and his wife. In May she spent two weeks in Caswell County, probably staying with her numerous cousins, where she enjoyed "some delightful rides and walks and 1 picnic" where "to my surprise I caught 22 fish just 20 more than I ever caught in my whole life." While on a visit to a fur-niture factory with other young women, Emma successfully drew for a rolling pin, considered a sign that she would be the first among them to marry. Her third lengthy trip away from home in 1870 was to Morganton, where she and a cousin joined other young people from North Carolina gathered to spend the hottest summer months in the cooler western part of the state. She also made short visits with family members, especially with her sisters, who both had sev-eral small children. In January 1870, a cousin from Morganton asked Emma to help solicit money for the widow of a minister, a hint that Emma's activities between school and marriage also involved volun-teer work.[2]

In 1871 Emma's carefree life of visiting and courting came to an end when she married James Wilson White, a war veteran from a South Carolina planter family. She alone among the Holt children married out of their parent's circle of kin and family connections in Alamance and surrounding counties. Despite the close relationships she enjoyed with her parents and siblings, Emma initially kept her courtship with White secret. For some time after they met, Emma and James continued keeping the company of other men and

1. Thomas Holt to William Scott, May 4, 1851, William Scott Papers; Emma Holt to James White, July 18, 1870, White Papers.
2. Emma Holt to James White, April 8, 22, May 15, 30, July 1, Septem-ber 20, 1870, White Papers; Hennie Erwin to Emma Holt, January 20, 1870, White Papers.

women, privately kidding about their ruse. Emma assured James that the New Bern gentleman who visited "is *only* a friend, *nothing more*," but reported without comment on the man from Caswell County who brought her flowers. When Frances asked about her gentlemen, she talked mostly of Mr. Tate but, she assured James, "only for a blind," because she "spoke more seldom of the one I thought of frequently."[3]

Their courtship grew more impassioned—she assured him "there is no person under heaven who could win my heart and hand from you," and he responded "I love you more and more every day"—until finally they were engaged. In January 1871 James wrote Emily Holt asking for permission to marry her youngest daughter. Her reply revealed the close emotional bonds she had with her daughters in a society starkly divided by gender. She wrote her future son-in-law:

> I received your letter yesterday and it is quite a sad task for me to answer it, as it involved the giving away of my last daughter which I have often thought would be almost an utter impossibility to do. Emma had told me of the existing engagement, as she has always bestowed upon me the confidence due a mother. As you have so wholy won the affection, and confidence and I believe you to be worthy of it I will yield to your request and give you a Mother's blessing praying that Gods richest blessing may ever rest upon your union. I feel assured if she makes you as good and amiable a wife as she has me a daughter you will indeed feel that you have won a prize.[4]

For several months after her engagement, Emma stayed home and planned her wedding; she wrote James that although things were dull in Alamance, "I have not the same desire for visiting I formerly had." Emma's choices for attendants, which included young women from the Webb, Fries, and Steele families, reflected the strong social bonds that had developed within North Carolina's industrial class. After naming her attendants, she wrote James, "I think we will have ladies plenty. It is much better to have a few more gentlemen I think than ladies to make a party pleasant."[5]

Both James and Emma entered matrimony with a clear sense of

3. Emma Holt to James White, May 30, June 18, September 25, 1870.
4. James White to Emma Holt, n.d.; Emily Holt to James White, February 22, 1871, White Papers.
5. Emily Holt to James White, January 21, 1871, Edwin Holt to James White, March 27, 1871, Emma Holt to James White, April 15, 1871, White Papers.

their proper gender roles. Emma did occasionally digress from the topic of their impending wedding to that of the tumultuous political climate in Alamance County during Reconstruction but also apologized that "I ought to refrain from talking on this subject." She never mentioned the mills that so consumed her father and brothers. Speculating on her future as a farmer's wife, she queried James, "What can 'poor little me' do with a '*hoe*'?" She also kidded him of her amusement "when I imagine you keeping house for I know tis on the style of all gentlemen's house-keeping."[6]

During the months Emma was preparing for her wedding, her brother William was courting their first cousin, Amelia Holt. On April 25, 1871, the day before Emma and James's wedding, Edwin Holt's son and William Rainey Holt's daughter were married. The two families were again united by marriage a year later when Lawrence married Margaret Locke Erwin, William Rainey Holt's granddaughter. After their wedding in Morganton, Lawrence brought his wife to Locust Grove where his parents held an "infare" to honor the couple. All of their family, including twenty-four grandchildren, as well as numerous friends, attended the celebratory dinner of turkey and macaroni. Years later a little girl who had been present still remembered Maggie Erwin Holt as "the vision of loveliness that every bride would wish to be . . . in her beautiful lavender silk dress, sitting in the center of the room, smiling at all those who crowded around to greet her." The occasion was only slightly marred when some of the grandchildren picked armloads of hyacinths in Emily's garden, leaving her "so angry that she could hardly speak."[7]

Probably her husband took no more than passing notice of the pilfered flower bed. The occasion marked the maturity of his youngest son, who turned twenty-one a month later and became a partner in the Alamance Factory. Edwin Holt had, his son Thomas later recalled, "trained all of his sons in the manufacturing business."[8] Now the youngest had joined his brothers in becoming a mill man.

Edwin Holt was a bourgeois capitalist helping shape a modern order in North Carolina by training his sons to give priority to industrial development. He was also a patriarch who reflected the values of his rural origin as he successfully guided the adult lives of his three daughters. He was determined that they live close by and that

6. Emma Holt to James White, July 11, 1870, January 19, 1871, May 30, 1870.
7. Mary Alves Long, *High Time To Tell It* (Durham, N.C., 1950), 69–70.
8. Ashe, *Biographical History of North Carolina*, vol. 7, 185.

their husbands join him and his sons in building mills in Alamance County. According to a county historian, he insisted that his nephew James Williamson, only twenty-three when he married Mary Holt, leave Caswell County and move to Alamance. It was somewhat more difficult to persuade John Williamson, who at forty-two was already an established planter and physician with several children when he married Frances, or James White, who owned a farm in Fort Mill, South Carolina, when he married Emma. Both men initially took their wives to their own homes.

Neither Emma nor Frances continued to live outside of Alamance County for very long. Although Emma had warned her prospective husband that relatives would not like him taking her so far away, shortly after the wedding she assured him that "you must know that I am *perfectly* happy with you at your home or any you might take me to." But only a month after their wedding she made such a lengthy visit to Locust Grove that he complained. She also returned to her parents' home for the birth of a daughter she named Emily Holt White. On the day of the baby's birth, Edwin wrote James, advising him about arrangements to visit his wife and first child. Emily did spend much of 1872 in Fort Mill but by January 1873 was back at Locust Grove writing James, "Papa says to say he will send me as soon as the weather is ok to take Emmie out." A few days later she assured an imminent return but, perhaps as part of a subtle effort to persuade her husband to move to North Carolina, she warned that the woman she was bringing along was less than satisfactory "as all the servants have a great horror of S.C." A few months later the Whites (and presumably the servant) moved to Alamance County for good. James's brother queried Emma, "Does Jim long for his native 'sod'? I know that his attachment to this place can never be severed." Clearly Edwin Holt, who sent him four thousand dollars to help settle his affairs, was more persuasive than the Whites in securing James's attachment.[9]

He was equally persuasive with John Lea Williamson. In the fall of 1873, while her husband and stepsons remained on his land to oversee harvesting their corn and selling farm tools and stock, Frances moved back to Alamance County; her father described her as "very comfortable fixed in an humble way." Edwin Holt, however, was not content that his daughters live humbly for very long;

9. Emma White to James White, June 30, 1871, January 30, February 1, 1873, Edwin Holt to James White, September 22, 1871, David White to Emma White, April 9, 1873, White Papers.

in 1874 he had two houses built in Graham for Frances and Emma, each costing over twelve hundred dollars.[10] Once these two daughters returned to Alamance County, Edwin and Emily had all of their children living close by. Some of them lived at Locust Grove for short periods of time; Lawrence's first two children, Erwin and Eugene, were born there. All of the children and grandchildren visited frequently. In 1873 Edwin explained to a son-in-law that "I cant write a letter as am surrounded with children all trying to make as much noise as they can." According to Eugene, however, his grandfather was not always as indulgent as this note indicated. He remembered a patriarch who "was intensely interested" in all of his children and grandchildren but also remembered that "when circumstances justified he could be austere and the fear of his displeasure was a wholesome check on undue frivolity."[11]

Like their parents, this generation of Holts was educated first at home or in small schools and then in private academies. In 1870 Thomas Holt and Dolph Moore hired Eliza Ashe to teach their children. Charles Holt had previously been sent to Graves School in Graham, but his father found its emphasis on the classics "too high grade" for him at an age when the father determined he needed more attention paid to reading and writing. He regretted removing Charles from Graves, however, "as his school is small, & we are anxious to see him prosper." In 1893 Banks hired a teacher from Virginia to live in his home and instruct his youngest daughters. Lawrence first educated his children in a school he helped establish in the St. Athanasius Episcopal Church.[12]

The Holts joined other North Carolina elites in sending their sons and daughters to private boarding schools when they reached their early teens. Ties made as school children continued to play a central role in forging a statewide elite. When Thomas's oldest son Charles outgrew home tutoring, his father sent him to the Bingham School in Mebane, which several of his cousins attended. Founded before the Civil War twelve miles from Hillsborough, Bingham offered an environment and education similar to the Caldwell Institute. Strict rules reinforced the philosophy of making "good scholars

10. John Denny to Edwin Holt, July 3, 1874, White Papers.
11. Edwin Holt to James White, [no month] 13, 1873; Eugene Holt, *Edwin Holt and His Descendants*, 41.
12. Thomas Holt to William Carrigan, March 8, 1870, June 7, 1894, White Papers; Durward T. Stokes, *Company Shops: The Town Built by a Railroad* (Winston-Salem, N.C., 1981), 105; Episcopal Church Records, NCDAH.

and good men." Bingham was the most frequent choice for this generation of Holt boys, but some were educated elsewhere, including Lynch's School and the Davis Military School. When Erwin and Eugene outgrew their local school, Lawrence moved his family to Alexandria, Virginia, so they could attend an Episcopal school there.[13]

A number of Edwin Holt's grandsons attended college, most of them at the University of North Carolina, but a college education continued to take second place to practical training. Most, perhaps all, of them eventually trained to become mill men, either by going north to work in mills or study in business schools or by learning the business from their fathers and uncles.

The granddaughters were also sent to private academies when in their early teens. Most of Banks Holt's daughters went to the Peace Institute in Raleigh. When her youngest daughters were enrolled there, Catherine Holt moved to the capital city for several winters to be near them. Their classmates included some of their cousins. At the age of seventeen, Ada Williamson, Mary's daughter, left Peace to attend school in Baltimore. At least two of Banks's daughters followed her example. Louisa, whose dislike of school prompted frequent changes, finally persuaded her father to send her to the Peabody Conservatory there to study voice.[14]

When Thomas's daughters outgrew home-schooling they attended Miss Nash and Miss Kollock's School in Hillsborough, one of the state's most elite female boarding academies. Its founders had been teachers at Mrs. Burwell's, which Frances Holt and perhaps her sisters had attended in the fifties. Girls at Miss Nash and Miss Kollock's were trained in academic subjects; they also learned to make conspicuous the wealth of their fathers (and eventually their husbands). The curriculum included scripture, orthography, English grammar, geography, mathematics, and music. Thomas and Louisa often traveled by train from Haw River to Hillsborough to hear their daughters in musical performances as well as to see them display their family's wealth. Cora Holt stood out among the girls, all from elite families, as particularly rich and, to some, particularly obnoxious. Mary Belle Mebane, whose family was intermarried with the

13. Pamphlet, "The Bingham School," included in C. Roulhac to Dear Madam, August 6, 1861, Ruffin Papers, Duke; *Alamance Gleaner*, October 8, 1889.
14. *Alamance Gleaner*, October 4, 1893, October 4, 1894, September 19, 1895, October 7, 1886; Interview with Mary Stalter, August 10, 1992.

Holts, wrote her parents, "Cora H speaks much what she thinks (and that isn't the way to be loved by school girls). She is not, tho I love her dearly." But even though professing to love her, Mary Belle was also critical of a girl she saw as privileged and spoiled. She wrote her parents that "Cora Holt got her new hat and cloak and as usual she doesn't like it, as it is trimmed in navy blue, and she says it isn't becoming to her. She has so many nice things and so many advantages and don't know how to appreciate them. I think her hat is beautiful." Months later, after fourteen-year-old Cora received a new dress for a music recital, her classmate reported that, "Cora Holt received her concert dress last week, it is magnificent, that is the only way I can describe it. She received two, both had about fifty yards of real thread lace and inserting. I guess they cost two hundred dollars or more. They are entirely too fine for school girls, it is the finest one in school, without any exception."[15]

Cora's grandfather may have disapproved of the dresses as well. A grandson recalled that he "abhorred ostentation and pretense." His children, however, were products of another culture, one that historian Warren Susman has described as "the culture of abundance," with "a new emphasis on buying, spending, and consuming." They were the Alamance County equivalents of the Newport titans. Thorstein Veblen has best revealed the need of the late-nineteenth-century's industrial elite to display its wealth through conspicuous consumption. Edward Chase Kirkland focused on the ubiquitous big houses built by this class as among the most conspicuous displays of their consumption. Architectural historian Carl Lounsbury's study of houses in Alamance prompted him to conclude that "the frugality of E. M. Holt did not appear in his sons and daughters," and that "in the 1880's and 1890's, as never before, domestic architecture became a symbol or badge of social standing."[16]

This generation of Holts did not compete with the nation's wealthiest "captains of industry"; they did, however, build the finest homes ever seen in Alamance County. Outside architects, craftsmen, and interior decorators were hired to come to Alamance, and

15. "Burwell School"; Mary Belle Mebane to Papa and Mama, November 15, 1773, May 30, June 13, 1774, Mebane Family Papers.
16. Eugene Holt, *Edwin Holt and His Descendants*, 42; Warren I. Susman, *Culture as History: The Transformation of American Society in the Twentieth Century* (New York, 1984), xx–xxiv; Thorstein Veblen, *The Theory of the Leisure Class* (1899; reprint New York, 1987); Edward C. Kirkland, *Dream and Thought in the Business Community* (Ithaca, 1956), 29–49; Lounsbury, *Alamance County Architectural Heritage*, 54.

they brought with them national styles. Mary Alves Long, whose family occasionally visited the Holts, recalled years later that passing through Alamance by train was "a dull prospect except at Haw River, where I always craned my neck for a look at the enchanting though distant view of Mr. Tom Holt's handsome big white house." A newspaper correspondent visiting Alamance County in 1891 described the house she strained to see as a "princely mansion" with grounds so "highly improved and embellished" that they reminded him of Central Park. Thomas divided his time between Linwood and his Haw River mansion, which had eleven rooms as well as an attached kitchen, two bathrooms, large halls, and porches. Water was pumped in by windmill power and a complete gas plant on the lot made gas lighting possible. The nine acres surrounding the house were divided into orchards, vegetable gardens, and carefully cultivated lawn area. Two houses for servants as well as other outhouses were also on the property.[17]

In the 1870s Mary Long also visited Banks and Catherine Holt's home, which she remembered as "a very happy time for me at the Holts, where there was plenty of everything . . . here there was fried chicken almost everyday, peach preserves and Miss Cattie's speciality, mammoth jelly cakes—with four layers." Mary played with the Holt's two oldest daughters who had "lots of toys such as I had never seen."[18] The house she visited was the one Edwin Holt had been born in and which his son Banks had thoroughly renovated.

In 1885, the year after his father died, Banks paid ten thousand dollars for a new house which, the *Gleaner* enthused, was "for beauty of style, comfort and convenience . . . not surpased in middle North Carolina." The mansion was located on five hundred acres; from the cupola on top Banks could survey his estate, including his racetrack. Some of his siblings also replaced their fine homes with finer ones. In 1878 the *Gleaner* described John Williamson's new home as "the finest in the county." After selling his first home in Haw River, Lawrence built a mansion in Burlington, which he named Blythewood. The third generation also built big houses; the Charles Holt home has been described by Lounsbury as "the most ornate textile mansion in Alamance County." The Victorian / Queen Anne–style mansion was intended, another architectural his-

17. Lounsbury, *Alamance County Architectural Heritage*, 54; Long, *High Time to Tell It*, 79; *Atlanta Constitution*, April 9, 1891, quoted in Newby, *Plain Folk in the New South*, 248; Pamphlet, "For Sale: Elegant Country Home of the Late Governor Thomas M. Holt," Weeks Collection.
18. Long, *High Time to Tell It*, 68.

torian suggests, to reveal his position and success "frankly and proudly."[19]

Thomas and Banks particularly fancied themselves country squires as well as mill men. Thomas bought his uncle William Rainey Holt's plantation and inherited his interest in scientific farming. He also followed his uncle in becoming president of the North Carolina Agricultural Society. Thomas won several prizes at the state fair and in 1894 his wheat successfully competed at the World's Fair. Banks was also a prizewinning farmer. In the early eighties the *Gleaner* complimenting his clover and orchard grass, proclaimed "he is a good farmer besides being largely interested in cotton milling." But horse racing was Banks's greatest passion. In 1892 the *Gleaner* reported that "he has taken hold of the horse business in earnest." After hiring a Kentucky trainer, Banks Holt could brag that his horses were the equal of any in the Southeast. The reputation of his stables prompted crowds to come watch his thoroughbreds train on the Alamance County Fairgrounds.[20]

With the exception of Alexander, there is no evidence that Edwin Holt criticized his grown children for their life-styles. There is ample evidence that Edwin Holt's sons and daughters revered him, but several of them moved shortly after his death, suggesting that they may have also chafed under his paternalistic control and avoided the most ostentatious displays of their wealth while he was still alive. Two years after their father died, William moved to Lexington and James to Burlington. Alexander also moved to Burlington, bought a home and together with Minerva Andrews, officially his servant but most likely his mistress or common-law wife, took in a boy to raise.[21]

Big houses served as the most visible symbols of the Holt's elite status in Alamance County. The county paper reinforced the aristocratic image of their mansions with constant coverage of their successful lives. During the summer months, county citizens could read about innumerable Holt family vacations. Guion Griffiths Johnson has explained that by the 1850s spending time at the springs

19. *Alamance Gleaner,* January 28, 1886, April 23, 1878; Whitaker, *Centennial History of Alamance County,* 137; Black, *An Architectural History of Burlington,* 24; Lounsbury, *Alamance County Architectural Heritage,* 56; Catherine Bishir, *North Carolina Architecture* (Chapel Hill, 1990), 351; Chris Faircloth, "The Charles T. Holt / J. A. Long House . . . Haw River's Architectural Treasure," *City-County* 9 (April 1995): 9–12.

20. *Alamance Gleaner,* July 6, 1882, April 14, October 20, 1892, May 18, 1893.

21. Alamance County Wills, Will of Alexander Holt.

served as "a means of distinguishing those who were fashionable in town life from those who were not." The Holts were unquestionably fashionable. In the summer of 1877, Edwin and Emily joined Mary and her two daughters at Catawba Springs. A few years later the *Gleaner* reported that "the venerable Edwin M. Holt and Mrs. Capt. White [Emma] left for the Catawba Springs last week, where they will bask in the mt. breezes of W. North Carolina."[22]

It may have been during one of these visits that Kemp Battle encountered the venerable Holt, an old-fashioned patron of an old-fashioned resort. Every day, boys among the guests were sent along with servants to select sheep for the evening meal. Battle recalled that "old Mr. Edwin Holt, a prosperous farmer and manufacturer, father of Governor Thomas M. Holt, feelingly expressed his indignation: 'It is horrible. They ought to have the sheep in an enclosure, with the fences converging to a corner. Then the animals should be slowly driven into this corner and gently caught and slaughtered. In this way the peculiar odor would not be driven into the flesh.'" Holt, Battle added, "accompanied this advice with a soothing motion of his hands as it he were caressing a grandchild."[23]

This anecdote hints that even as an old man Holt retained ties to his rural past. But several extant letters make clear that even on vacation his mind was more on his family's mills than the fate of sheep. As late as 1882, two years before he died, Holt spent time during his vacation advising his sons-in-law about marketing their goods.[24]

His children and grandchildren were more likely to vacation for leisure at elite resorts. Thomas Holt's family frequented Buffalo Lithia Springs in Mecklenburg County, Virginia, popular with a number of southern political leaders. One North Carolinian who vacationed there as a young man later reminisced that "every season the atmosphere of culture and refinement, together with the virtues of the waters of the Springs as a cure for kidney troubles, would draw together the choicest spirits from all over the South." Among the senators and governors he remembered meeting were Holt of North Carolina and Jones of Alabama. Mornings he joined a group, including the Holts of Haw River and the Lairds of Boydton, that assembled for cards, readings, or bowling until around noon when "the

22. Johnson, *Ante-Bellum North Carolina*, 188; *Alamance Gleaner*, July 17, 1877, July 11, 1881.
23. Kemp Plummer Battle, *Memories of an Old-Time Tar Heel* (Chapel Hill, 1945), 239.
24. Edwin Holt to James White, [?] 1882, White Papers.

juleps were frosty."[25] Clearly the occasions provided an opportunity for courting, for finding partners among the children of the choicest spirits. In 1880 Thomas's daughter Cora married Chambers Laird and fourteen years later her brother Charles married Gena Jones, the daughter of Governor Jones.

Thomas Holt joined his wife and children at the springs but usually for only short periods of time. Men of his generation frequently combined travel with business. Most of them attended the centennial in Philadelphia in 1876 as well as similar expositions. Many of the Holt men, as well as some of their wives and daughters, attended the Chicago World's Fair in the early nineties. Apparently more than his brothers, Banks also traveled simply for recreation. In the summer of 1891 the *Gleaner* reported that he had caught a seventy-five-pound fish at Morehead City. The following winter he went to Lexington, Kentucky, where he bought "fine standard-bred stock." In the next few years Banks returned to Lexington, traveled to several sites in North Carolina for the races, spent a week hunting and fishing at a lodge with a group of men, and took his family on various occasions to the mountains and the coast. He joined his wife on at least two trips to Baltimore and New York. Lawrence was the first of his generation to travel to Europe, the most fashionable destination for America's elite. In 1900 he took his family to the Paris Exposition, which they followed with a two-month tour of the continent.[26]

Travel considered recreational was fashionable; travel for health was both fashionable and necessary. The second and third generations of Holts traveled as often to treat illnesses as they did for business and pleasure. When Laura Holt became ill during a visit to White Sulphur Springs, she remained there for two more months. Her aunt Frances Holt Williamson often traveled there in an effort to restore her health. It was primarily female members of the family who "took the cure," but Frances's son Edwin was only twenty when his poor health prompted a summer in the mountains. Serious illnesses increasingly prompted trips to northern cities. In the late eighties and early nineties, Thomas Holt tried treatment in Philadelphia and rest in Florida in an effort to combat Bright's disease, the kidney ailment that killed him in 1896 as well as both of his sons when they were still young men. Banks's daughter Fannie sought

25. Robert W. Winston, *It's a Far Cry* (New York, 1937), 189–90.
26. *Alamance Gleaner*, August 24, 31, December 14, 1893, July 30, December 10, 1891, July 7, August 25, October 13, 1892, April 26, October 4, 1893, May 11, 1899, September 6, 1900.

treatment in northern cities throughout the nineties for the disease that would end her life at the age of twenty-eight.[27]

The second and third generations of Holts traveled to the same places and for the same reasons, but there are discernible differences in patterns of leisure between the parents and children. Edwin Holt's grandsons easily reconciled their lives as businessmen with their pursuit of conspicuous leisure. They delayed marriage considerably longer than their fathers had. Five of Edwin Holt's sons were married before they were twenty-five. The average age at which his grandsons married was twenty-eight, and twelve were over thirty. By the time they married, most of the males of this generation had become mill men. But work was never as all-consuming for them as it had been for their grandfather and fathers. James's seven sons appeared in the news almost as often for their travels and adventures as Banks's seven daughters did for their parties and weddings. They often traveled around the state to horse shows and the like with their uncle, Alexander. Some also ventured farther afield. The *Gleaner* reported on several of Sam's trips to the West Indies; his brothers Walter and Edwin also sailed, generally along the Atlantic coast, although Edwin did make a trip to Cuba with his cousin James Williamson. Service in such capacities as chief marshal of the state fair gave this generation a statewide profile as being among the leisured elite. In 1889 Edwin represented North Carolina at the International Exposition in Paris and then journeyed throughout Europe. He was so impressed with the Prussian army that on his return he formed a voluntary company, once again drawing on the county's colonial past by naming them the Alamance Regulators, and outfitting them complete with Prussian style uniforms, including spiked metal helmets. When Edwin married, at the age of thirty-one, he turned over command to his younger brother James. When the United States declared war on Spain in 1898, James determined to get the Regulators to Cuba. Despite his effort, as one of his would-be soldiers recalled, "to buy enough men to fill out his company," he failed to come up with the 113 required.[28]

In 1892, a year before he gave up command of his Prussian-style soldiers, Edwin Holt II turned down a request that he serve as grand marshal of the Alamance County Fair on the grounds that it would

27. Ibid., July 17, October 15, 1877, August 20, 1879, May 30, 1889, March 29, 1893, May 7, 1891, March 10, 1892, April 12, 1893.

28. Ibid., July 9, 1891, August 14, 1884, May 28, 1885, August 11, 1886, December 17, 1891, January 7, 1892, July 4, 1889; Whitaker, *Centennial History*, 151–52.

be detrimental to his business. His sister and female cousins did not even need to confront this type of conflict in pursuing an image of conspicuous leisure. Although by the last decades of the nineteenth century, daughters of the middle class were beginning to attend college and take jobs, particularly as teachers, female offspring of the leisured elite almost never did so. On one occasion the *Gleaner* referred to Frances's two daughters and their friends as "a charming quintette these merry innocent girls," a perspective that consistently informed the paper's accounts of what the Holt daughters did. For them vacation often stretched to last a summer. Exhibitions and fairs offered a chance to publicly display their family's wealth and elite status. When Thomas's daughter Ella joined elite young women from around the state "promenading with their beaux" at the state fair, she stood out in her "red silk dress with a train sweeping up the floor." Ella, her sisters, and their female cousins were also frequent prizewinners at the fair for needlework and painting. Like their brothers, they served in honorary positions around the South. James's daughter Daisy represented North Carolina at a large reunion of Confederate veterans, including her uncle Banks, held in Charleston in 1891.[29]

Like their mothers, this generation of females in the Holt family filled up the years between school and marriage with travel. In contrast, however, their travel took them beyond North Carolina to the North and Europe. Banks's wife, Catherine, was particularly adventuresome for her generation and at least some of her daughters followed in her footsteps. As they became old enough, she took them to visit and shop in nearby cities. In the fall of 1887, for example, she and Mary Holt Williamson took some of their daughters on a two-week trip to Baltimore for "business and pleasure." Louisa, Catherine's seventh daughter, went to Europe in her mid-teens with an escorted group. It was a few years after this trip that she persuaded her parents to send her to Baltimore to study voice.[30]

Louisa had time to pursue travel and music because she did not marry until she was twenty-seven, considerably older than her six sisters and most of her female cousins. All twenty-three of the Holt granddaughters who survived childhood married. In contrast to the males of this generation, they married young, thirteen of them be-

29. *Alamance Gleaner,* September 22, 1892, August 2, 1894, April 5, 1883, November 2, 1875, November 8, 1888, April 13, May 11, 1891; Long, *High Time To Tell It,* 203.

30. *Alamance Gleaner,* October 13, 1887; Interview with Mary Graves Stalter, August 10, 1992.

tween the ages of nineteen and twenty-two and only one when she was over the age of thirty. Before marriage, these young women were more independent than their mothers and grandmothers had been. Despite greater freedom to travel unencumbered by male escort, however, the activities of this generation of women were much more tightly proscribed than those of their brothers and male cousins.

Their social activities, especially those of Banks's seven daughters, were constantly reported; when one married, a younger sister took her place in the social columns. Parties and weddings were duly noted. In February 1887 the *Gleaner* described the "elegant supper" that Banks and Cattie Holt held for "the young ladies and gentlemen" their daughters knew. The weddings of these young women became major social occasions. When Thomas's second daughter, Louisa, married Alfred Haywood in 1883, the *Gleaner* called the occasion "a brilliant wedding" and the "social event of the state." The *Gleaner's* description of Kitty Holt's ceremony in 1890 details the lavish weddings of this generation and reveals the widespread coverage they received in the county's only paper. The *Gleaner* described Kitty as "the beautiful bride, attired in an imported gown of pure white faille silk, draped in embroidered lisse and trimmed with garlands of white lilacs." Banks and Catherine Holt's second daughter was married in her parents' home, which "was literally festooned with flowers and evergreens [which] lent enchantment to the scene under the dazzling brightness of the gas light." The couple received "numerous handsome and valuable presents, among them many costly articles of silver and decorated china." When a younger sister married seven years later, the ceremony also took place in "the elegantly appointed home, palatial in its exterior and interior decorations, of our highly esteemed townsman Mr. L. Banks Holt [which] was crowded with friends and relatives from far and near, and the whole presided over in a queenly manner by his cultured wife." Following the wedding Carrie and her husband went on a wedding trip to New York City. Ten years later, her musically inclined younger sister Louisa also spent her honeymoon in New York City where she heard Paderewski and Emma Eames in recitals, as well as Caruso singing in *Aida*.[31]

Edwin and Emily Holt had fit comfortably within the social milieu of rural, nineteenth-century Alamance County. For their chil-

31. *Alamance Gleaner*, May 31, 1883, May 8, 1890, November 25, 1897; Programs in the possession of Mary Stalter Family.

dren and even more so for their grandchildren, society increasingly transcended place. They traveled—to resorts, to the Northeast, some even to Europe—for recreation, for health, to consume, to share in the culture of an elite. Reports on their activities as well as physical monuments to their success reinforced their status as Alamance County's elite. In his diary, Henderson Monroe Fowler, who worked for the Holts for over thirty years, followed their lives almost as religiously as the *Gleaner* did. Neither Fowler nor the paper's editors revealed any resentment of the Holt's wealth or their manifestations of that wealth. Little survives revealing what workers thought. Undoubtedly some admired the Holts as much as the *Gleaner* and Fowler while others deeply resented the discrepancy between their own lives and the people who commanded their labor.

Paul Escott, in his study of "power and privilege in North Carolina," suggests that "men who saw themselves as part of a privileged aristocratic class were not accustomed to establishing real equality or intimacy with their employees." He claims the Holts and their workers as exemplary, pointing out that "whereas workers in the Holt family mills in Alamance County labored long hours six or seven days a week, the owners kept up a life-style characteristic of the state's elite, frequently visiting and meeting with other important North Carolinians."[32]

Escott's observation that "obviously there was little social equality in the Holt mill" is generally accurate for the second and third generations of Holts.[33] Edwin Holt was not socially aloof from the Boons, Albrights, Whitsells, and other descendants of the Germans and Scotch-Irish who had settled the area along with his ancestors and whose children and grandchildren worked in his family's mills. A sense of fundamental white equality, fostered in the revolutionary era, declined, however, in the Gilded Age of conspicuous consumption that the Holt grandchildren grew up in.

Social aloofness, however, did not inform every relationship between owners and workers in the Gilded Age. Supervisors and the most highly skilled workers interacted with the Holts more than Escott allows. He points to the family's opposition to the marriage of Junius Yancey Holt, Alfred's oldest son, with Jin Ashworth, daughter of a skilled machinist who worked for the Holts, as evidence of the strong taboo against social equality between owners and workers. But looked at more closely, the marriage might suggest that the evo-

32. Escott, *Many Excellent People*, 208.
33. Ibid., 209.

lution of rigid class lines was complex but not yet complete in the 1870s.

Not yet six years old when his father died, Junius had grown up in his mother's hometown of Mebane. After completing school at the Bingham Academy, he moved to Locust Grove and began working with his grandfather. As his grandfather made clear in his will, neither Junius nor his two younger brothers, however, conformed easily to the patriarch's ideal of steady, sober businessmen. Whether Junius's choice of a wife added to his grandfather's disappointment is unclear. In the summer of 1878 Henderson Fowler reported that "J Y Holt left here Monday morning . . . with Jin Ashworth to get married." A week after the couple left, Lawrence, who was only a year older than his nephew Junius, went after the couple, perhaps forestalling the wedding. They married soon after, however, and six months later Jin gave birth to a daughter who was named for Junius's mother. It was, Escott claims, "a social calamity for the boy's family," which caused them "mortification."[34] It may well have been this premarital pregnancy that initially upset the Holts. While it appears that Junius did quit working for his grandfather for at least a year, he did not remain estranged from his family. A year after his oldest grandson married the machinist's daughter, Edwin Holt included him in his will as a beneficiary, warning him, along with his brothers, to avoid dissipation, but nevertheless leaving him a handsome legacy. Alfred's youngest son had married a Mebane, a prominent family several Holts had married into; this grandson was also warned that he must conform to his grandfather's standards if he wanted to control his inheritance. Junius's infraction was probably less his marriage to a skilled worker's daughter than his refusal to display the character his grandfather demanded.

Other members of the family also occasionally bridged the social gap between the elite and their workers. In his youth Charley Holt frequently fraternized with mill workers. Bob Holt undermined the symbolic power of big houses when he sold his to a supervisor for little cost. But if Escott misinterpreted the evidence about Junius Holt's marriage, and if examples can be found that class polarization weakened at some points, his analysis remains essentially correct. There was little social equality in the Holt mills, and the working people, whether they admired or despised the Holts, knew it well. When Reid Maynard became a mill worker, he learned that the Holts were a family "who made alot of money" and who had "plenty

34. Fowler Diary, July 16, 1878; Escott, *Many Excellent People*, 209.

of servants." "The women," he was told, "rode around with horses and drivers and umbrellas and all that thing." While women in carriages with parasols symbolized class difference to Maynard, to Dover Heritage, shaving mugs were especially significant. One of his brothers owned a barbershop where rich and poor alike were shaved. He recalled that "all the rich men like the Holts, Gants and Williamsons had their names on their mugs in gold with a brush and soap in them." Dover's family had bought Bob Holt's fine home. His autobiography reveals, however, that he never lost an identity with the mill workers and an edge of resentment toward the owners. "The workers," he recalled, "were so controlled by the owners that if a mill worker dressed in overalls and brogans, met a well-dressed mill owner in a three-piece suit on the street, the worker had to tip his hat and say, 'good morning, Captain.' " "Poor folk," he concluded, "were just like slaves."[35]

Owners, of course, never literally confused their workers with slaves. They hired Anglo-Saxons, who in this racially driven society were privileged by race. They were, however, frequently portrayed as particularly docile and grateful Anglo-Saxons, worthy recipients of the benevolence of their paternalistic owners. Owners carefully cultivated this image of their own paternalism and worker docility. Until recently historians assumed that the image was more or less historically accurate. A 1979 study of the nineteenth-century North Carolina textile industry, for example, concluded that "mill village paternalism at first developed naturally out of planter-industrialists' traditional sense of social responsibility; their dealings with white operatives were guided by the old grammar of master-slave relations."[36] A close look at the Holt family's business and social relations reveals that their motives were often quite the opposite of a paternalistic sense of social responsibility; a close look at their workers reveals that they were as often remiss in playing out their roles of docile and grateful recipients of powerful benevolence.

35. Reid A. Maynard Interview, Southern Oral History Project Papers [hereinafter cited as SOHP], SHC; Heritage, Bivins, and Bolden, *When Shoeshines Were a Nickel*, 17–18.
36. Billings, *Planters and the Making of a "New South,"* 103.

8

Destined to Work

ALAMANCE COUNTY
MILL WORKERS,
1865–1900

Most likely farm laborer Chesley Sutton was never inside a textile mill; perhaps he was not even aware of the early stirrings of industrial transformation in the county he volunteered to defend. In 1861 Sutton left his wife, Nancy, and their two small daughters to join the Confederate army; a year later he died at Antietam. Mary Sutton was six years old when her father died. By the time she reached thirteen she was working in an Alamance County mill in order to support her mother and younger sister as well as an infant boy who may have been her own child. Eli Whitsell, nearly forty when the war came, had accumulated fifty dollars worth of property by working as a day laborer. Although old enough to be exempted from service, Whitsell joined; he died a soldier in 1864, leaving his wife, Nancy, to provide for their three small children as well as her three children from a former marriage. In 1870 Nancy worked in a mill with their nine-year-old son, Franklin, as well as one of her older daughters. Eleven-year-old Roxanna Whitsell, who suffered from a mental or physical handicap, was employed as a servant by James Holt. Ten years later, however, Roxanna, as well as her youngest brother, had joined Franklin and their half-sister as mill workers. With four children to support her, Nancy Whitsell gave up wage work for housework.[1]

1. Eighth Census of the United States, Ninth Census of the United States, Alamance County, 1860, 1870; Jordan, *North Carolina Troops*, vols. 3, 4. Most of the information in this chapter is from the manuscript censuses of the United States for 1870, 1880, and 1900. The 1890 census was destroyed by fire. All families with at least one member working in a textile mill in 1870 and 1880 were included; half of the mill families in 1900 were included. Methods used to analyze census data are described in chapter 3, footnote 33.

For these two war widows and their children the mills did prove to be, if not a haven, at least an alternative to destitution. But widows represented a small minority of the women and children who worked in Alamance mills after the war. Approximately 90 percent of the men from Alamance who enlisted in the army were twenty-five or younger, the majority of them single.[2] Most of the men who died were survived not by wives but parents left to cope with the loss of their labor. The most invisible victims of the slaughter were a generation of young women who would find it difficult to marry in a society that offered them few alternatives to marriage.

Whether or not they buried young men in their family, for most poor southern whites this catastrophic war meant economic hardships whose effects often lingered long after the fighting ended. The transformation of the southern economy, accelerated by war and emancipation, generally harmed white yeoman farmers. Every poor farm family's story was unique; collectively they were victims, especially, of the crop lien, fence laws, and higher taxes, which, as a recent study of textile mill people explains, "added up to a virtual assault on Piedmont yeoman society and eroded its agricultural self-sufficiency." Increasing numbers of yeoman lost their land or were compelled to give up farming on land they rented. Although "there were many paths leading from southern farms to Piedmont cotton mills," these same authors explain, "in one way or another the journey from field to factory had its origins in the transformation of the countryside that was making it more and more difficult to earn an adequate living from the land."[3] In Alamance County, the cotton mills, which had benefited from the war, stood in stark contrast to the impoverished farms that surrounded them. For the first decade after the war, however, the county's mills remained small and few in number, offering only limited opportunity for those not making an adequate living on the land.

They offered almost no opportunity to Alamance's free black population. As discussed in chapter 3, before emancipation slaves were sometimes compelled to run textile machinery alongside white tenders. Decisions against using slave labor were more economically than racially based. As Gavin Wright explains, "By 1860, for reasons having to do with the interaction between the cotton boom and the markets for free and slave labor, the mills had become almost entirely white." After the war as "the core of experienced workers

2. *Confederate Memoirs.*
3. Hall et al., *Like a Family,* 6, 31.

were white, so it made economic sense for the new workers to be white too."⁴ There is almost no evidence revealing how this racial ban developed in Alamance County, but evidence from elsewhere suggests that white workers played the key role. In several southern mills white workers threatened to strike if blacks joined their ranks. The Holts were dependent on their skilled and experienced workers, all of them white. Holt's former slaves, some of whom had helped build the Alamance Factory and village, could not work there, presumably because these key white workers would object. Although former slaves like Caswell and Amy Holt and their family of nine children would most likely have welcomed a chance to earn mill wages, these whites probably said no. Even Republican George Swepson, while offering blacks a refuge on his land, could not offer them a place in his mill.

Five years after the war ended, the composition of Alamance County mill families remained much as it had been ten years before. The number of mill families had grown by only 4, to 73, and included 305 members who were mill workers. Almost all of them had worked in a mill for less than ten years. Only three mill families working in 1860 can be clearly identified in the 1870 census. In 1860 Martha Burch labored in a mill along with her three oldest daughters. The three youngest daughters and two small sons remained at home with their unemployed father, William. Ten years later William had died and Martha had given up mill work for house work. Four of her six daughters, all in their twenties in 1870, lived at home and worked as mill hands. Gooder Murray still supported his family as an artisan in 1870, as he had done ten years before. In 1860 his four oldest children, two girls and two boys who ranged in age from fifteen to twenty-four, were mill workers, while the two youngest remained at home with their mother. In 1870 Gooder, now a widower, continued to supplement his earnings as an artisan with the wages of the two oldest daughters, both with more than a decade of working experience, as well as what the two youngest children brought home. In 1860 laborer Mathew Durham and his wife had two daughters working in a mill and six younger children at home. Ten years later, after the deaths of both parents, the six youngest children lived together and all worked in a mill.

Twenty-three of the seventy-three Alamance mill families were female-headed in 1870, a slightly smaller percentage than found in 1860 but still a much higher percentage than in the general popula-

4. Wright, *Old South, New South*, 188.

tion. Mill families continued to include far more wage-earning daughters (170) than sons (83). The percentage of female workers between twenty-one and twenty-five rose from 67 percent to 72 percent, perhaps reflecting the impact of war on their generation. These figures do not, however, reveal a work force completely reordered by war. Families with a preponderance of daughters had sought mill jobs as an alternative to farming before 1861, and they continued to do so years after the war ended, for the same reasons. The war had increased their numbers by killing sons and by forcing daughters denied marriage to remain longer with their families of origin.

It is impossible to know precisely how the war affected families like that of Martha Burch, but it is possible to speculate. Burch had four daughters. June and Margaret, twenty-seven and twenty-five in 1870, had been workers for more than a decade by that time. Their younger sisters, Martha and Nancy, joined them sometime after 1860. Like the Burches, Susan Row's household also included daughters whose prospects for marriage had been eroded by the slaughter of young men. Twenty-three-year-old Mary, twenty-year-old Martha, sixteen-year-old Eliza, and thirteen-year-old Amanda labored in a mill while their mother kept house and supervised her two young sons. Although none of the daughters in these two families had lost husbands, they joined war widows struggling to provide for themselves in a society that offered women few options to marriage. Families without a male head often depended entirely on the wages of children. Adult women were less likely to work than they had been before the war. War-widow Nancy Whitsell was the only female head of household listed in the census as a mill worker in 1870; her nine-year-old son Franklin was one of the youngest children listed.

Women like Martha Burch, Susan Row, and Nancy Whitsell were particularly vulnerable to the vagaries of an agrarian economy, but male heads of households, particularly those whose working-age children were primarily or exclusively daughters, also increasingly had to consider alternatives to farming. Widower John Underwood, in his forties in 1870, worked in a mill with his daughters, Sarah and Catherine, then twenty and eighteen, as well as his eleven-year-old son, John. Sixteen-year-old Eugenia remained at home with nine-year-old Susan and kept house. Mill work also represented a viable alternative to farming for a family like that of Joseph and Jane Williams. In 1870 they had five teenage daughters at home; their only sons were five and six. Joseph took a mill job along with the five girls. Henry Wansee did not work in a mill himself but supplemented the money he earned as an artisan with the wages of his children, who began to work at an early age. In 1870 James and Carolina Wansee were only eleven and ten; they worked in a mill with their teenage sisters, Sarah and Malinda. The Wansee and Underwood families could count on the wages of an adult male and several working children.

Wesley Baker was also a nine-year-old textile worker in 1870. He and his twelve-year-old sister, Mary, who were probably orphans, boarded with the Wansees. At least from the age of nine, Wesley never lived on a farm. In 1900, some thirty years after beginning work in a mill, he was still there, having risen through the ranks to become a supervisor. Wesley Baker's limited experience with farming would become common for later generations, but it was rare for his own. In the first decades after the war most mill families retained strong ties to the land. In 1870 ten of the seventy-three heads of households listed farming or farm work as their primary occupation. Others included one or more members who were farm laborers. In families that had both sons and daughters of working age, the division between farm and industrial work generally followed gender lines; farm laborers were almost exclusively male while unskilled mill workers were almost two-to-one female.

Nancy and Isiah Leejun owned a farm and $650 worth of property. Because seven of their eight children at home in 1870 were daughters, they predictably sought mill work for some of them to supplement what the family made farming. Emma, Janet, and Nancy, who ranged in age from twelve to twenty in 1870, knew both farm and factory from an early age; while the rest of their family remained oriented to the rhythm of agriculture, they answered the whistle of an Alamance County mill. They were joined by four of the children of Charles and Mary Moize, a couple in their sixties in 1870 who had accumulated one hundred dollars worth of property after decades of farming. Charles continued working the land with the assistance of his oldest son Frederick. The Moize's younger son Joseph worked with his four sisters in a mill.

For some farmers without land, mills were an especially attractive alternative. Lewis Foster was a landless farm worker in 1870; the wages of his two daughters, twenty-year-old Margaret and thirteen-year-old Susan, were critical for the support of the family, which also included their mother and younger brother. Although widow-headed families were more likely to give up farming altogether, some of them also divided their sons and daughters between mill work and farm work. All three of Winiva Simpson's teenage daughters worked in a mill; her only son, twenty-one-year-old Nehemiah, labored on a farm. Margaret Gamby supported her household with the mill wages of three daughters and two sons, but this family also included one farm worker.

Because in the 1870s almost all mill families had only recently left the land, there were few extended families in the villages. Only four of the seventy-three mill families in Alamance County in 1870 included three generations; in each one a member of the oldest generation headed the family. John Merritt and his wife, both in their sixties, lived with their two grown daughters, both mill workers, as well as their two granddaughters. John Walker farmed with the help of his twelve-year-old son. Two of his daughters worked in a mill, while nineteen-year-old Rebecca helped her mother keep house and also cared for her own child.

Three families of siblings represented another kind of exception to the norm of nuclear families found in the mill villages in 1870. Twenty-six-year-old Sarah Roy headed a household that included her three sisters and one brother. Her two youngest sisters and their brother supported the household with mill wages. Through the sixties mill work enabled Alpheus Durham to keep his orphaned brothers and sisters together in the mill village where their parents had brought them before the Civil War.

In 1870 married women with children were less likely to work in a mill than they had been in earlier decades. A number of them, however, augmented their family's income by cooking and cleaning for boarders and by selling produce. Eighteen families, eight of them headed by women, included one or more boarders; most were mill workers. Sometimes Edwin Holt and his sons hired women to run boardinghouses. When Emily and Flora (or Senora) Marshall's parents died around the time of the Civil War, the two young women came to Alamance seeking mill work. Rather than offering them a position tending machines, Edwin Holt asked them to house and feed some of his workers.[5] The Marshalls oversaw at least seven workers, but the large size of many mill families and the small size of mill houses precluded most women from taking in more than one or two people. Eighteen-year-old Elizabeth Albert lived with Charlotte Lashley and worked with her six children in a mill. Albert was one of twenty-nine females living in a mill village with a family other than her own in 1870; only sixteen males boarded. Most male

5. Heritage, Bivins, and Bolden, *When Shoeshines Were a Nickel*, 28–29. Dover Heritage gives his aunt's name as Senora. The 1870 census names the head of a household of boarders as Flora Marshall. I am assuming they were the same person.

and female workers living in boardinghouses were in their teens or early twenties and had left their farming families to seek work in a mill. Occasionally, however, all or several members of a family boarded together. Among the seven people living with the Marshalls were artisan William McDonald and his two children, fourteen-year-old Mary and twelve-year-old Alex, both mill workers. Although none of the forty-five mill village boarders shared a surname with the head of the household in which they lived, it is possible that some were living with kin. Elizabeth Scrags boarded with Sarah Sams and her two children. Both women were in their thirties in 1870, had been born in Virginia, and had subsequently moved to North Carolina. The similarity of their pasts plus the fact that Scrags did not work but helped Sams keep house suggest that the two women were related, probably sisters. Fourteen-year-old Lucinda Hall was the only person living with Sams who worked in a mill.

The southern textile industry grew rapidly in the late 1870s. The number of textile workers, which had remained at around ten thousand for twenty years, grew to seventeen thousand by 1880.[6] In Alamance County, which had experienced only slight growth for nearly half a century, the increase was even more dramatic. Nearly one thousand people worked in the county mills in 1880, over three times as many as a decade before; there was at least one mill worker in 218 families.

The percentage of female-headed households in Alamance rose slightly through the 1870s from 32 percent to 35 percent of the total. War widows continued entering the mill villages in the seventies after failing to find other alternatives to male support. When Mary Sharp's husband David died of pneumonia in 1864, less than a year after enlisting, she was left as the sole support of three children. Although two of them were teenagers in 1870, apparently they did not work in a mill. By 1880, however, Catherine and Robert were mill workers, while their brother Joseph contributed to the family income by teaching.

Mary Sharp's family, like those of Nancy Sutton and Nancy Whitsell, was exactly the type that fueled the image of textile mills as havens for war widows and orphans. Yet this type of mill family remained atypical in 1880. The impact of the war continued to be more indirect in the lives of most mill workers. Both male- and female-headed families continued to be those with a preponderance

6. Edward Ayers, *The Promise of the New South* (New York, 1992), 111.

of daughters at home even though most had not lost sons in the war. In 1880 mill village families included 486 daughters but only 270 sons, a slight increase of males from 1870 to 36 percent of the total. Clearly gender remained a critical factor in the decision to leave the land and relocate in a mill village or to combine the two types of work. Thirty-seven male heads of households, 26 percent of the total, were farmers or farm workers, a percentage that had actually risen slightly in ten years. Thirty-four percent of the heads of household worked in the mills in 1880, also a slight increase over the 32 percent who had done so ten years before. Although the percentage of male heads who farmed did not drop in the seventies, the percentage of sons who were farm workers did. In 1870 seven sons in a mill family worked on a farm; twenty-five worked in a mill. By 1880 the number of sons farming had only risen to thirteen while the number working in a mill had more than quadrupled to 112.

Some families continued to assign their children work strictly according to gender. In 1880 Wesley Lindley farmed with his fourteen-year-old son, James, while his wife, Louisa, kept house and two daughters, eighteen-year-old Dora and ten-year-old Rosanah, worked in a mill. But increasingly the sons of farmers joined their sisters tending machines. D. C. Montgomery farmed with the help of his two oldest sons, both in their early twenties. His youngest son, seventeen-year-old Walter, was a mill worker. Benjamin Brockwell continued to farm after he moved his family from Orange County to Alamance County. Most likely the family decided to move because most of the oldest children were girls. But the only son old enough in 1880 went to work in a mill along with three of his sisters. Mangum Cate also continued to farm after he moved his family from Orange County, but both of his sons joined their six sisters in the mill.

The slaughter of young men on Civil War battlefields continued to shape the lives of women who had to find an economic alternative to marriage well into the eighties. Elizabeth Steele was nineteen in 1865. Most likely she knew some of the young men from Alamance County who died in the war. It is impossible to know if these casualties precluded her marriage, but fifteen years after the war ended she remained single. Steele was one of sixty single women between the ages of twenty-five and thirty-five who worked in an Alamance County mill in 1880. Earning wages by spinning yarn and weaving cloth continued to be one of the few alternatives these women had in a society that continued to assume they would have the economic support of a husband even in the wake of a devastating war.

Women who remained single past their early thirties and continued working in a mill worked alongside the more numerous teenage girls and young women who were likely to quit when they married. Families with a number of teenage daughters continued to be typical mill families. Tempy Allred and her artisan husband, John, had eight daughters and only one son at home in 1880. Nancy and Sarah, both in their early twenties, labored as weavers in the mill; their teenage sisters Mary and Lillie were spinners. The Allreds were able to keep twelve-year-old John in school. Elona Canady's family also exemplifies the type mill owners had traditionally found particularly desirable. A widow, she kept house while her three teenage daughters, Sarah, Sophia, and Maryjane, worked as spinners.

Mill work must have seemed an obvious choice to families like the Allreds and Canadys in the 1880s, but the number of male-headed families and those with a majority of sons that chose to leave the land and enter the factory continued to rise. One study of textile workers in the late nineteenth century explains, "Push came to shove for an increasing number of families headed by men."[7] William Batchman, an occasional laborer, was one of them; the mill wages of his three sons, twenty-one-year-old McCagan and McCagan's younger brothers, Charles and Mitchum, were essential to the family along with those of their teenage sisters, Emily and Sally. Susan Percell was even more dependent on the mill wages of her sons. In 1880 she was the single parent of four boys ranging in age from ten to twenty-one who worked in a mill.

For most women marriage continued to preclude work outside of the home. In 1880 only two of the 132 women whose husbands were heads of their household worked, both of them in a mill. Thirteen mill workers were married women, but eleven of them either boarded along with their husbands or lived separately from them. Mollie Cook and her husband Elias, both in their early twenties, were mill workers; they lived with his two sisters, one of them designated head of household. Once married, most women never again worked, although some divorcees or widows found they had no alternative. Ten of the seventy-three widowed or divorced women living in an Alamance mill village in 1880 were mill workers.

In 1880 most mill families continued to be nuclear ones. Extended families, however, did begin to be more common as parents who had first moved to the mill villages aged, their children married, and their grandchildren were born. Thirty-five children, four

7. Hall et al., *Like a Family*, 33.

times the number in 1870, lived with a grandparent in the mill villages; almost all of these eighteen girls and seventeen boys were too young to work. Seven families included the mother or mother-in-law of the household head. Most working-age kin living in extended families were female. Thirty-three girls or women joined a sibling's family in order to work, while only three boys or men did so. More women than men also came to board in families they were not related to. There were 90 women and 49 men boarding in 1880; 106 of them were mill workers. The greater number of female boarders indicates that although the number of male workers was growing, in 1880 mill work was still considered particularly suitable for females and work they were particularly likely to seek. Males who worked independently of a nuclear family still had far more options than did females. Joe Robertson, for example, was sent by his parents to work in a cotton mill at the age of ten. When he was fourteen, he was able to quit and support himself, first by farming and then by working for the Southern Railroad.[8] For girls and women, mill work remained one of the few means of earning a wage and achieving at least a precarious economic independence.

Unfortunately, the loss of most of the 1890 federal census documents to fire makes it impossible to analyze demographic change through the 1880s. During this decade the southern textile industry was transformed from a string of small factories scattered across the Piedmont into a major component of the region's economy and a rival to New England in productivity. An 1895 study reported that of the 12,000 white people living in Alamance County, 7,000 were "directly interested in the business of cotton manufacturing." In 1900 the North Carolina Labor Bureau offered a profile of Alamance's workers: The county's work force included 1,707 men, 1,444 women, and 521 children. The bureau claimed that 84 percent of the adults and 71 percent of the children could read and write. Most worked for between eleven and twelve hours a day. For a day's work the pay for men ranged from 53 cents to $1.62, for women from 40 cents to $1.02; children averaged 34 cents per day. Most of the these men, women, and children worked for the sons, sons-in-law, and grandsons of Edwin Holt.[9]

In 1900, although a majority of mill families continued to be first generation, parents and children who had personally experienced relocation from field to factory, a solid minority were headed

8. *Alamance County*, vol. 5, 358.
9. Black, *An Architectural History of Burlington*, 23; *Fourth Report . . .*, 1890, 72–73.

by men and women who had grown up in mill villages, married there, and raised children who were mill folk from the time they were born. This second generation of mill families differed significantly in gender composition from the first generation, which so often was composed of daughters who had left the land to seek mill work. Families formed in the villages included as many boys as girls; they had little opportunity to exploit the labor of either sex in any way but by putting them to work in a mill. Furthermore, by 1900, as the number of new mills proliferated, mill owners, driven by their insatiable demand for spinners and weavers, shifted from their traditional preference for "widows with lots of daughters" to families with lots of children, whether boys or girls. One of Andy and Phoebe Ayers's children recalled a mill recruiter from Alamance approaching them in the 1890s because there were fourteen in their family.[10] More and more farm families like the Ayerses, unable to support themselves on the land, became susceptible to the lure of recruiters dispatched by owners to places increasingly distant from Alamance County. In their determination to find alternatives to agriculture, male-headed families with numerous sons came to rival those that were largely female. As generations born after the Civil War became old enough to work, the sex ratio of potential mill workers became virtually equal.

In 1900 men headed approximately 80 percent of the mill families. Although the proportion of female-headed families was still higher than in the general population, it was considerably lower than it had been in the past. By the turn of the century the number of sons and daughters in these families was close to equal, although females between the ages of ten and twenty did continue to slightly outnumber males. In a majority of the Alamance County mill families, a male head continued to be the primary breadwinner, most by working in some capacity for a mill. Frank Owens, a thirty-seven-year-old weaver, was the sole support of his wife and three children under the age of twelve. Rankin Shephard, a weaver the same age as Owens, could augment his own wages with those of thirteen-year-old Laura, a spinner, and eleven-year-old Charles, a doffer, to support his family, which also included his wife and two younger sons. Artisans, day laborers, and other male heads with low-status and low-paying jobs also supplemented their own earnings with the money their children made in the mills.

10. Ethel Bowman Shockley Interview, SOHP.

By 1900 families with some means and standing in the community generally found mill work too disreputable for their children, but there were occasional exceptions. Physician Thomas Lullah had fourteen children, ten living at home in 1900. Quite possibly it was the large size of the family that prompted some of the children to work. Twenty-year-old Carrie and her fifteen-year-old brother Tallisin earned wages in a factory.

Lullah was undoubtedly the primary provider in his family. Some fathers, however, lived entirely off the labor of their children. By the late-nineteenth century a clear stereotype of "mill daddies" or "dinner toters" had evolved. Actually the number of nonworking male heads of household who sent their children to work in a mill was always small. In Alamance County in 1900 only about 5 percent of male heads were unemployed; some of them were disabled. Monroe Pyle took his family of twelve children to Company Shops for mill work after he became blind.[11] Sixty-year-old William Norwood may have been too old to get a mill job; along with his wife, Martha, he depended on the wages of teenage daughters, Sarah, Louise, and Eugenia, to support his family, which also included a younger daughter. Possibly Norwood did nothing more to assure his family's income than to carry his daughters their dinner pails each day. If so, his contribution was atypical, although those of his daughters were not.

Although most male heads of households did work, the shift from subsistence or commercial farming to a family wage economy meant increased emphasis on the contributions of additional family members, particularly teenage children. Some families, particularly those without a male head or viable male labor, were dependent on their teenage children working because it was their sole source of income. Families that included only women and girls continued to appear in the mill villages, although they made up a smaller proportion of the total than they had in the past. Mill work remained an economic alternative they found particularly attractive. In 1900 Nancy McCord's family served as an example of this traditionally ideal mill family. A widow, McCord depended on her three daughters, Bettie, Lydia, and Barbara, all in their twenties, for support. Mary Harden, also a widow, kept house while her three children, eighteen-year-old Maggie and her two younger brothers, Edward and Joseph, supported the family by working as spinners.

Although marriage continued to preclude wage work for most Alamance County women, a higher percentage did work in 1900

11. *Alamance County,* 347.

than had done so since the 1860s. Approximately 28 percent of female workers were married in 1900 compared to only 6 percent in 1880. I. A. Newby, who took a close look at Alamance County in his study of southern mill folk between 1880 and 1915, has found that seventy-one mothers with children under ten years of age were mill workers. Evidence from other parts of the Piedmont indicates that many of these women worked only sporadically.[12] Mollie Bachelor and her husband, Robert, both worked as weavers although they had two small children at home. Possibly Mollie was one such part-time worker who occasionally took over Robert's looms or filled in for other weavers.

Widows still typically did not return to work after their husbands died, but more of these women worked in 1900 than had done so earlier. Approximately 22 percent of widows worked that year, most of them in a mill. Widows who did not head their own households were slightly less likely to work than those who did, because a number of them were elderly and lived with children or other relatives who supported them. Women who were widowed before they had children old enough to support them were sometimes compelled to take a job in a mill themselves. Martha Kinney worked in 1900 as a weaver; her ten-year-old son, Charles, was a doffer in the same mill. Her daughters, nine-year-old Viola and six-year-old Blanche, were not officially employed but may have been among the numerous child "helpers" who spent much of their day in the mill helping a parent or sibling.

Elizabeth Ivens, a widow with four children, worked as a spinner along with Walter, Lula, and Lewis, who were sixteen, thirteen, and ten respectively. Seven-year-old John was not officially employed, but since there was no one at home to supervise him, he most likely spent time in the mill as well. Some of the Holts were more tolerant of young children helping than mill owners elsewhere were. Allie Smith learned to spin by helping her older sister at Saxapahaw. When her family moved to Orange County, a mill owner there refused to allow Allie in his mill.[13]

Taking in boarders continued to be a means for women, especially widows, to remain at home while contributing to their family's support. My sample indicates that approximately 7 percent of workers boarded and a slight majority of them (55 percent) were female. Sixty-four-year-old widow Edna Goins, whose children had all

12. Newby, *Plain Folk in the New South*, 238.
13. Hall et al., *Like a Family*, 62.

left home by 1900, supported herself by housing and feeding mill workers. Mary Badson supplemented the wages of her husband, Wilson, a baler in one of the mills, by taking in boarders even though her own large family included seven children, three of them mill workers.

A majority of male and female boarders were still single and in their late teens or twenties. Because he came to Burlington alone to work at Aurora, Richard Wiles boarded with the Staffords; Sarah Cook, a weaver at Aurora, boarded there as well. In time the two were married in the Staffords' home.[14] Sometimes entire families boarded until they could find housing of their own. The Barbees, a young couple with an infant son, lived with a family that included five children. J. W. was a weaver, while Susan was employed as a servant. Emma and John Stutts and their five-year-old son boarded with Martha Wynn, a widow with two daughters. Both of the Stuttses worked in the mill along with Wynn's teenage daughter Annie.

Since mill families were typically large and their houses small, those who took in boarders usually had room for only a few. Like Flora Marshall thirty years before, Mary Lammy, a widow with no children, was atypical in that she ran a large boardinghouse for nine people. One of them was also a widow who did not work. The others, four men and four women, were all young single mill workers.

Undoubtedly, some of these young men and women had left farms to seek mill work. In 1900 roots to the agrarian past remained strong as the mill villages were constantly repopulated with farm folk. They came for the same reasons as those who came generations before but from farther away and in ever greater numbers. I. A. Newby has estimated that in 1900 one out of every nine mill workers in Alamance County lived in a family headed by a farmer, and that one out of seven families that included at least one mill worker was headed by a farmer, about one-half of whom owned their own land. John Staley, in his mid-sixties in 1900, had farmed all of his life, but since at least 1880 the family income had been supplemented by the mill wages of his children; in 1900 his two teenage daughters, Medda and Maggie, were helping to support the family of twelve. Twenty years later the Staleys had only three of their ten children at home. Ben helped his father farm while John and Lula worked in the mill just as their oldest siblings had done twenty years before. The Cateses' farm was close enough to a mill that they could continue living together for a time while combining farming

14. Bennie Green Wiles Interview, SOHP.

and factory work. When Mr. Cates got work building mill houses, however, the family became entirely dependent on industrial wages.[15]

The Cateses were among a number of families that gradually moved from farm to factory. Many of them were separated, often for years, while they tried to maintain farms and at the same time enjoy the wages factories assured. Sallie Stockard, in her memoir of growing up in Alamance County in the late nineteenth century, recalled that "many farmers, finding their farms less and less productive . . . moved their families to these mill towns so that their children might find work, their wives take in a few boarders, while they themselves travelled back and forth between their farms and town houses." James M. Clapp grew up on his family's farm in rural Alamance County. When he was in his teens he left for Graham and began working in Oneida. One by one the other members of his family joined him there. Isaac Holt, a distant relative of the family that had come to dominate textile manufacturing in Alamance County, also continued farming for some time after the oldest of his ten children left to work in a mill village. One by one the younger children followed their brothers; finally Isaac gave up farming as well and joined his family by finding work as a mill superintendent.[16] The Manor family was not so fortunate. The parents sent their three sons to board and work in Oneida while they remained in Orange County to gather in their crops. Shortly after they arrived the boys became critically ill; eighteen-year-old Hunter and fifteen-year-old Marian died before their parents could join them.

There were migrants who continued to yearn for the land they gave up as well as those who never looked back. Banks Troxler and Daisy Smithey were unusual in rejecting their heritage as mill people even though they had known little else. Banks was born in Altamahaw and went to work in the mill there at an early age, eventually becoming a loom fixer. Daisy was working at Ossipee at the age of eight. Nine years later she married Banks; the couple determined to leave the mills and try farming. Undoubtedly their inexperience was a factor in their first failure; Banks returned to a Rockingham mill as a loom fixer. Several years later, however, he returned permanently to farming despite the difficulties of supporting a family that eventually included sixteen children. B. F. Cates ex-

15. Newby, *Plain Folk in the New South*, 238; Verna Cates Stackhouse Interview, SOHP.

16. Stockard, "Daughter of the Piedmont," 79; Swannie McDaniel Interview, Grace Elizabeth Moore Maynard Interview, SOHP; *Alamance Gleaner*, September 30, 1897.

pressed the ambivalence of a generation. As a young boy he helped his family farm until his father died and he was sent to work in his uncle's sawmill. He recalled of the two years he spent there, "Can't say I liked it very much except that it got me offen the farm." From there he went to Haw River to work in a cotton mill, the first of several mill jobs. Although concluding, "I wuz destined to work in a cotton-mill," he also remembered a yearning "for the independence of farm life," of a love of seeing things growing, and the sun setting "big and red behind the clouds." Others were less willing to concede that they were destined for factory work. William Murray tried it for a time but returned to farming. His son Charles recalled that his father and his mother, Barbara, were both "textilers and farmers" who farmed until "along in the cool times, they moved to textiles." The son speculated of the father that "he just wanted to get out of it, I guess. He was used to being out; I reckon he was raised up that way, used to being out." Eventually, however, William Murray had to give up farming for a second time when it became "too tough"; he returned to mill work, frequently moving from mill to mill because, his son explained, "he just thought the grass was greener over there."[17]

Mill owners were constantly plagued by workers like Murray who returned to farms or sought the greener grass of other mills. By 1900, however, the Holts could count on a core of stable workers. Approximately 10 percent of the mill families in my 1900 sample had lived in an Alamance village in 1880. I. A. Newby has found that at the Alamance Factory fifty of the sixty-seven workers there in 1890 were still there a year later, thirty were there five years later, and seventeen remained ten years later.[18]

John Allred was seventy-two in 1900 and his wife Tempy three years younger. During more than twenty years living in an Alamance mill village they always had children living at home who could contribute mill wages to the family income. In 1890 four of them toiled as weavers with a combined income of approximately fourteen dollars per day.[19] In 1900 Nancy, Sarah, and Lillie continued to support their parents. Through seniority they too had become weavers, the highest paying job available for women. Mary, John, and two of the younger girls had left home. Callie (or Sallie), only four in 1880, had grown up in a mill village. Although she continued

17. *Alamance County*, 453–54; Newby, *Plain Folk in the New South*, 3; Charles Murray Interview, SOHP.
18. Newby, *Plain Folk in the New South*, 176.
19. *Alamance Cotton Mill Time Book*, Alamance Mill Collection.

to live with her parents in 1900, she was not working in the mill with her older sisters. James and Emily Heritage's children also grew up in a mill village. In 1880 James's wages alone supported the family that included four small children. By 1900 their family had grown to include eleven children. Although James had become a supervisor in one of the Holt mills, his wage was inadequate for such a large family. The Heritages, like many mill families, assumed that each child would contribute wages when old enough. The four oldest children had left home by 1900. Albert, only a baby in 1880, twenty years later was helping support his family as a weaver; he was joined in the mill by three siblings, all born after 1880. Three younger children remained at home.

Although women could not anticipate becoming supervisors or taking the highest-paid skilled positions, mill work did allow them to remain financially independent for years. Nancy Andrews, who was fifty in 1900, had by the turn of the century headed a mill household for at least twenty years. In 1880 her sister Susan supported Nancy and two other sisters, Elizabeth and Martha, as well as a six-year-old niece, Frances, with her mill wages. Twenty years later Susan and Frances had left the household; Elizabeth now supported Nancy and Martha as a weaver.

Weaving was the highest-paying position open to women. In 1890 approximately two-thirds of the weavers in the Alamance Factory were female. Although they averaged only slightly more than three dollars a day, less than two-thirds of what the male weavers made, their pay was considerably better than what female spinners earned. Because they were paid equal to the men per cut, some female weavers were able to equal or better their male counterparts. Mary Fogleman and Catherine Isley both occasionally made $4.40 a day in early 1890, equal to or better than four of the male weavers.[20]

Many of the families that remained in the village for a decade and more were able to do so because as older children left home, younger ones replaced them in the mills. Not all of the children left, however; some grew from childhood to middle age supporting their parents as mill workers. In 1880 Alfreda Ward was eighteen; along with her two sisters she worked in a mill to support her widowed mother. Twenty years later her sisters had left home, but Alfreda continued supporting her mother with her mill wages. Fourteen-year-old Georgia Rainey helped her father and two younger sisters support their family of seven in 1880. Her mother stayed home with

20. Ibid.

the two youngest children, three-year-old Daniel and two-year-old Daisy. Twenty years later Georgia still lived with her parents and worked in a mill. She was assisted by Daniel and two younger siblings born since 1880. Daniel's young wife, Cora, also lived with the family and worked in the mill.

Rural kinship networks were strained as the first generation of farm folk left the land for the factory. As a second generation grew up in them, went to work, and established families of their own, new kinship networks developed that were firmly rooted in mill villages. Only two of Martha Carson's seven children remained at home in 1900. Sixteen-year-old Bonnie and nineteen-year-old Daisy worked as weavers in the mill where their father labored as a dyer. Some of the Carson's older children had left the mill village, but their son Willis also had a skilled position in the mill and lived nearby. Although Willis and his wife, Emma, had two small children, Emma also worked in the mill. In 1900 seven mill families including thirty-nine people had the surname Moser; thirteen of them were mill workers. There were nine families of Murrays; their forty-two members included eighteen mill workers.

Family connections bound the villagers together. So did the growing perception of them as a people apart. George Shue, who moved with his family to Graham when "the Holts owned all them cotton mills down there," remembered that "back in them days you know the cotton people was about the lowest class people there was. They called 'em lint heads." This contemporary stereotype was fixed as historically accurate by scholars in the early twentieth century. In the 1920s sociologist Broadus Mitchell enshrined an image of docile cotton mill workers dependent on the paternalistic authority of benevolent mill owners that endured for over half a century. Around the same time Frank Tannenbaum offered an even more devastating portrayal, describing mill folk as "like children . . . who have been lost to the world and have forgotten its existence."[21]

Recent scholarship, particularly books by I. A. Newby, Allen Tullos, and a team of scholars headed by Jacquelyn Hall, all drawing on interviews conducted by the University of North Carolina, Chapel Hill, have offered a much richer portrayal of the men, women, and children who came to work in the mills of Alamance and throughout the southern Piedmont. Their work definitively challenges earlier demeaning stereotypes with more balanced de-

21. George Shue Interview, SOHP; Frank Tannenbaum, "The South Buries Its Anglo-Saxons," *Century* 106 (1923): 210–11.

scriptions of mill people as workers and as members of families and communities. All three studies included Alamance County and imply that it is generally exemplary of their findings.

These studies reveal historic subjects, actors in the industrial transformation of Alamance County. They also make it clear, however, that their stage was a restricted and sometimes disabling one. How restricted and disabling depended to a considerable extent on family composition and per capita income. Families with a male head who held a highly skilled or supervisory position as well as several children of working age could live reasonably comfortably on their family wage. The Heritage family typifies this type of mill family.

Emily Marshall met James Heritage while she helped run a boardinghouse in the Carolina mill village and he worked in the mill. After they married the Heritages moved to a farm near Glencoe; James combined farming and working in the mill. When he was offered a position as superintendent of Windsor, owned by Bob Holt and James Holt Jr., Heritage hired two men to run his farm and moved his family to the two-story house the Holt brothers built for him. The memoir of one of his sons portrays a stable family, able to provide adequately for eleven children. The Heritages enjoyed good relations with the Holts, especially Bob, who established more familiar relations with some of his workers than most of his relatives did. One worker recalled him claiming that he "raised his own help." When Bob's fiancée died on the eve of their wedding, he insisted that James Heritage buy the house he had built for her. Heritage resisted because, his son recalled him saying, "Mr. Holt, you're a rich man. I'm just a poor man working for you. How do you expect me to have a house like that? Besides, I wouldn't feel right living in it." Bob Holt persisted, however, and the Heritages bought the house by making weekly payments totaling twelve hundred dollars. "Our family," Dover Heritage recalled, "had never seen anything like it." Although the Heritages came to live in a house suitable for mill owners, they remained mill folk. Dover recalled that the people who came to his family's fine house for Sunday dinner were mill families. His memoir reveals that even the most successful families of mill workers, those that included men in supervisory positions, perceived themselves and were perceived by others as mill people.[22]

Sallie Stockard's memoir also reveals that despite the degrada-

22. Ethel M. Faucette Interview, SOHP; Heritage, Bivins, and Bolden, *When Shoeshines Were a Nickel*, 34–35, 93.

tion of mill work, many mill folk were determined to use their wages to better their lives. Sallie herself was not allowed to work in a mill because "we were too proud, I suppose," but her mother supplemented the family income by taking in mill workers to board. Sallie recalled that young women with jobs as spinners and weavers were thought to make " 'good money,' as much as three or four dollars a day." She sewed for some of them who had money for nice clothes but not time to make them. Stockard remembered "they were able to obtain some lovely silk or soft, fine linen or shimmering flowered linen."[23]

The *Alamance Gleaner*, the county's sole newspaper through most of the nineteenth century, played a critical role in creating an image of mill families as a distinct and inferior group within white society and of mill work as something the better sort should be too proud to do. Working people were mentioned far less frequently than the Holts. Much of the coverage the mill folk did receive portrayed them as people who lived degraded lives except insomuch as they were uplifted by their employers. While news stories about the Holts featured success, prosperity, education, and leisure, those about their workers emphasized either the benefits of paternalism or unfortunate occurrences such as deaths, crimes, and accidents.

The occasional death notices for mill workers were among their most sympathetic treatment. When Ida Cates died in 1889 at the age of nineteen, she was praised as "an industrious and exemplory young woman" who had worked to help her widowed mother care for her younger children. Joseph Thompson was remembered as "a most worthy man," and Cornelia Blalock, as "highly esteemed by all who knew her."[24]

Workers were most likely to merit press coverage if they were accused of committing a crime or were injured by mill machinery. Crimes were fairly rare, or at least rarely reported; those that were publicized added to an image of a downtrodden people. In 1892 a "Terrible Crime at Carolina Cotton Mills" was reported when two girls there, the oldest only eleven, were raped. Three years later Callie Hall and her brother-in-law were arrested at Glencoe after the body of her infant was found in the millrace.[25] Probably rape and infanticide were rare; certainly the paper, a solid supporter of the Holts and the paternalistic image of their mills as havens for the unfortu-

23. Stockard, "Daughter of the Piedmont," 80.
24. *Alamance Gleaner*, November 21, 1889, December 1, 1897.
25. Ibid., March 11, 1892, June 13, 1895.

nate, had reason to avoid reporting all but the most sensational crimes.

Mill accidents were reported far more often than crimes. Not all were work related; a young man at one factory, for example, "seriously shot himself in the hand," and at Bellemont an Italian boy was slightly wounded when a pistol misfired. Most often, however, workers were victims of the machinery they tended. In 1894, for example, the North Carolina Labor Bureau (NCLB) reported seven disabling accidents in Alamance, all of them attributed by mill owners to carelessness.[26]

The *Gleaner* reported accidents with a sense of morbid curiosity that at times undermined its portrayal of the mills as havens. In the spring of 1889, for example, it reported that Charles Van Story, who was only eight or nine years old, had walked out of a second-story opening while at work on the night shift, falling twelve feet. Although this boy suffered only bruises, numerous other workers, children and adults, were seriously injured and even occasionally killed. A little boy named Perry was caught in the waterwheel at Glencoe; a hand and foot were cut off as he drowned. Daniel Fogleman became "so terribly mangled" in the machinery at Big Falls that he died of blood poisoning. When Gaston Sharp caught his arm in a lapper, it necessitated amputation above the elbow. Isaac Holt's thirteen-year-old son, Luther, was one of the most seriously injured children. His foot was so badly crushed when he caught it in the machinery that it had to be amputated. Another boy had his hand torn off in an accident at Elmira. Children and adults alike most commonly injured and lost fingers. Inexperienced workers were especially at risk. Six days after Henderson Monroe Fowler reported "the Canada famely moved to this place," he had to report that "Mary Canada got her finger hurt in the factory." A year after Em Shoffner started work Fowler noted that she also "got her finger hurt . . . badly hurt."[27]

When workers lost fingers, they usually lost jobs as well. Owners almost always blamed accidents on worker carelessness and assumed no responsibility even when the victims were experienced people who had served them for years. Bettie Ezell had worked for the Holts for at least seven years when she lost a finger as a result of an accident in 1887. Like most injured workers and their families,

26. Ibid., January 8, 1873, August 9, 1883; *Eighth Annual Report . . .*, 1894, 8.
27. Fowler Diary, July 9, 1883, February 17, 1872, April 5, 11, 1879, January 6, May 11, 1876, July 14, 1877; *Alamance Gleaner*, April 5, 1888, February 15, 1894, November 22, 1888.

she was left to cope with the loss of her wages as best she could. Only rarely did the Holts intervene. When Henderson Fowler, who had worked at various jobs for the Holts for thirty years, lost several fingers in a mill accident, he also lost his job. Banks Holt did recommend him for a position with the Internal Revenue, writing that "Mr. Fowler was with my father before the war and since with my brothers and myself and would be with us today but for an accident which rendered him unfit for his profession as a mill man." Holt also suggested that giving this "sober and trustworthy man" a job would "gain the good will of a large number of his fellow laborers."[28]

Mill workers also lost jobs when they made mistakes running the mill machinery. In 1881 Thomas Holt wrote George Taft inquiring about replacing a piece "which one of my men smashed up by the *grocest carelessness.*" He also confided to Taft that "I intend he shall pay the bill and then I expect to discharge him." It was a charge and response Holt made frequently.[29]

Owners routinely dismissed maimed workers and occasionally fired those who erred. Competition for experienced workers, however, prompted them to seek ways to satisfy those who remained healthy and reasonably competent. Paternalism informed the responses of many early textile manufacturers, north and south. Philip Scranton has suggested that "paternalism stands as a transitional form of interaction in the developmental trajectories of industrial capitalism," and that "for the American textile cases at least, it is found, though not universally, in the first stages of factory establishment." Scranton challenges earlier scholarship that claimed mill village paternalism was peculiarly southern. W. J. Cash's *Mind of the South* (1941) has been especially influential in fixing an idea of unique southern paternalism. Cash claimed that "the southern mill man kept himself posted as to their [his workers'] lives as they were lived under his wing; knew their little adventures and scandals and hopes and lives and griefs and joys." Although usually modified, Cash's interpretation continues to inform scholars interested in class relations in southern mills. There is limited evidence, however, that many of the Holts conformed to the familiarity Cash describes. The paternalistic relationship that has come to be viewed as characteristic of southern textile mills was in large part a response to the growing difficulty of maintaining an experienced work force.

28. *Alamance Gleaner,* January 13, 1887; L. Banks Holt to W. H. Yarborough, October 16, 1888, Marmaduke James Hawkins Papers.
29. Thomas Holt to George E. Taft, August 21, 1881 and other letters from Thomas Holt to George E. Taft, Whitin Papers.

From the beginning Edwin Holt built houses for his workers, a practical necessity. Religious facilities were available at least from the mid-forties. After the Civil War charity and recreational facilities grew along with the villages. By the 1890s the *Gleaner* had frequent coverage of ice cream festivals, Christmas entertainments, trips to the circuses and fairs, baseball games, and the like. Mill owners provided entertainment, sometimes complete with political indoctrination. In 1888, for example, Charley and Sam Holt brought workers from their two mills together for music provided by two brass bands, an event the *Gleaner* described as "a gala day, with banners and bandanas flying in the breeze and Cleveland hats in profusion." When all workers at the Juanita Mill were given turkeys for Christmas in 1895, the paper concluded that "good feelings prevailed all around."[30]

Free turkeys and brass bands were obvious short-term efforts to assure loyal, hard-working employees. Influencing the religion and education of workers was a more subtle and long-term effort to achieve the same result. "The villagers wanted churches of their own," I. A. Newby has pointed out, "and helping them get places of worship was a sure way of raising morale." There was more to it than appeasing the workers, however. Newby also points out that "all owners, religious or otherwise, were certain that religious folk were better workers than those who were not." William Holt Williamson clearly stated this opinion when he wrote the labor bureau that "more intelligence and good training, and religious influence would, we think, make better hands and more particular about their work and more attentive." His family made considerable effort to assure the religious environment they believed made better hands. A newspaper correspondent visiting the village around the Granite Factory described "an attractive and comfortable chapel, in which Governor Holt and the operatives worship[ed], and whose pulpit [was] filled at the governor's expense." Other members of the family also gave money for religious facilities and to pay preachers. In 1898 a minister named McCorkle was hired by one of them to deliver a series of sermons to the mill people. He planned to first address the bosses and then the spinners, divided into "boys" and "girls."[31]

30. Philip Scranton, "Varieties of Paternalism," *American Quarterly* 36 (1984): 236–37; Wilbur J. Cash, *The Mind of the South* (New York, 1941), 217; *Alamance Gleaner*, August 23, 1888, January 2, 1896.

31. Newby, *Plain Folk in the New South*, 396; *Ninth Annual Report . . . , 1895*, 70; *Atlanta Constitution*, April 9, 1891, quoted in Newby, *Plain Folk in the New South*, 248; Ethel Faucette Interview, SOHP; Stokes, *Company Shops*, 105; Fowler Diary; North Carolina Church Records, NCDAH; *Alamance Gleaner*, January 27, 1898.

Scholars continue to debate the degree to which religion actually did serve as a means of discipline, of social control, in mill villages. I. A. Newby has effectively challenged earlier work, notably Liston Pope's *Millhands and Preachers,* that claims churches were effectively controlled by owners. He points out that many mill folk attended no church at all; others remained members of churches in the rural areas they left. Monroe Pyle, for example, continued taking his family back to Pyle's Meeting House, the church they had worshiped in before the loss of his sight had forced him to move them to Company Shops for mill work. When queried by the labor bureau whether their workers had good religious facilities, mill owners in Alamance almost always answered "yes." Banks Holt, however, once revealed that efforts to indoctrinate workers by religion were not altogether successful. In 1894 he complained that whereas his workers "have reasons to feel grateful, as they have the same church and school facilities as others . . . they do not avail themselves of their advantages as seems to their interest, their disposition being to wander to churches at a greater distance from their homes than their own." The disposition of workers to wander to churches of their own choosing generally took them to rural ones but occasionally even to those of the owners. Class lines were clear but not rigid. Verna Stackhouse occasionally attended the Episcopal church in Burlington; years later her strongest memory was of seeing the Holts there.[32]

In the last two decades of the nineteenth century, more emphasis was placed on the efficacy of education in creating a more orderly and stable work force. Lynn Banks Williamson, for example, promoted education on the practical grounds that when workers "become interested in their school work they will not always be moving from pillow to post, then back to pillow, spending whatever they have accumulated in transportation." Similar to their response about religious facilities, mill owners uniformly told the labor bureau that educational facilities in the county were adequate. Sometimes in more candid and detailed discussion of the schooling of mill children, however, owners acknowledged that educational opportunity was really less than adequate; they occasionally admitted that schools were too far for children to attend in the winter or that night schools and libraries were nonexistent. Prior to the mid-1890s there

32. Newby, *Plain Folk in the New South,* 390–95; *Alamance County,* 347; *Eighth Annual Report . . . ,* 1894, 73; Verna Cates Stackhouse Interview, SOHP.

was only one mill school in Alamance County. In 1890 one owner explained to the bureau the need for a public school for the mill children but complained that "the county board seems loath to give it," despite his offer of a cash donation. Another owner acknowledged that "a day school is kept up from October to May each year but the average attendance is small, about thirty."[33]

Mill parents made decisions about educating their youngsters based on a number of variables, including the availability of schools and the demands of the family economy. Gender was also a factor. In 1860 only 5 of the 30 Alamance County mill village girls between the ages of ten and fifteen attended school; 10 of the 18 boys in that age bracket did so. Ten years later the number of children in that age group remaining in school had actually dropped to 9, 6 girls and 3 boys, although the total number of village children of those ages had grown to 81. In 1880 there were 223 children between ten and fifteen, a nearly threefold increase in a decade. Their number in school had increased to 73, eight times as many as a decade before. As in 1860, gender influenced parental decisions about education; 38 of 94 boys in this age group attended school while 35 of the 129 girls did. A sample of villagers living in Alamance County in 1900 reveals that the gender gap in education remained approximately the same through the nineteenth century.

By the 1890s, as compulsory schooling emerged as a major issue in the South, mill parents struggled to retain the prerogative to determine whether their children would go to school or to work. The Holts generally supported state laws that required young children to go to school. In 1896 Banks made an especially impassioned plea, demanding that decisions concerning compulsory education be left to neither "the eager, and sometimes heartless, manufacturer," or "the ignorant, custom-taught, and needy parent or guardian." More unusual for this southern manufacturer than acknowledgment of the greed of capitalists was his demand that it be a national rather than a state law that determine the age when children could work. But generally the Holts joined the chorus of mill owners who insisted that "the great trouble is with the parents." In the 1890s Bob Holt complained that "parents of cotton-mill help, especially, are apt to neglect educating their children."[34] Clearly many mill parents in Alamance County as elsewhere

33. *Sixteenth Annual Report . . .*, 1902, 163; John Harrison Cook, *A Study of the Mill Schools of North Carolina* (New York, 1925), 4; *Fourth Annual Report . . .*, 1890, 27; *Sixth Annual Report . . .*, 1892, 23.

34. *Tenth Annual Report . . .*, 1896, 87–89; *Eleventh Annual Report . . .*, 1897, 247.

either actively opposed or were indifferent to their children's formal
education. Opposition was prompted by a variety of factors, cultural
and practical. For many families the wage of a child even as young as
ten was a crucial addition to the family income.

The paternalistic system, whether dispensing free turkeys or
building churches and schools, was intended to keep workers and to
keep them working. Many of the recipients of this paternalistic giving considered the greatest problem they faced to be long hours. Until
the mid-eighties a mill job meant approximately seventy hours a
week at work. A gradual reduction in hours was in large part a response to the constant problem of turnover. In 1896 James Nathaniel
Williamson and his son William complained to the NCLB that the
greatest problem with southern mill help was their "continually
shifting around." "They do not," the Williamsons claimed, "stay, as
a rule, long enough to make themselves useful or try to advance
themselves." In September 1886 Henderson Monroe Fowler reported
"L. S. Holt adopted the 11 hour System Monday Sept 6, 1886 without
their [the workers] asking or demanding it." Several of Lawrence's
relatives followed suit. When fourteen years later most of the workers employed went out on strike, a spokesman for the family recalled
this reduction and, in words echoing Fowler, claimed "we gave our
help this reduction of hours without their asking or demanding it."[35]

Many workers may have opposed a reduction of hours because
they feared a reduction in pay; they also assumed periodic breaks
from work. In the 1890s the weaving room at the Alamance Factory
was idle for an average of forty-five days a year and the spinning
room for an average of forty-two days. There were also days when
the mill was closed for part of a day or a portion of the workers were
laid off. Inclement weather, especially rain, caused work stoppages
throughout the year. Henderson Fowler frequently reported that
work was stopped for a few days when the mill was flooded or covered in mud. In April 1884 he described the "biggest freshet ever
here," with water "over the looms heavy damage to looms & to
flower & corne." Two years later he wrote that the "hardest raine
ever fell the first day of July 1886 water in the factory 2 ft deep &
lots of mud." Ice halted work from time to time in the winter. Repairs or installation of new machinery could result in even longer
work stoppages. For the first two weeks of 1884, workers at the Alamance Factory were idle while the mill was covered with tin. Occa-

35. *Tenth Annual Report . . .* , 1896, 85; Fowler Diary, September, 1886;
Raleigh News and Observer, December 16, 1900.

sionally funerals also resulted in time off. On April 19, 1882, for example, the Alamance Factory was closed for the funeral of Lura Holt, the first of William and Amelia Holt's infant twin daughters to die that year. The appearance of the circus and, in the nineties, the fair was another excuse for a holiday. Weather, repairs, funerals, and shows were unpredictable causes of lost work. Holidays were regular breaks assumed almost as firmly as Sunday. Three or four days were typically given at Christmas as well as a day for Easter Monday, Thanksgiving, and the Fourth of July. When the mills were run on Easter Monday 1879, Fowler recorded that "such was never the case before hands all mad & not much good done that day 1879."[36] In subsequent years the Easter holiday was restored.

Some workers also added breaks of their own choosing. In 1876 Daniel Overby was fired for refusing to follow rules established for use of the single bathroom, rules he considered demeaning. He later recalled that

> Holt and Moore had a little rack hanging by the door that the hands had to take when they went out to do their business; when the rack is gone no one can go until it is hung back again; so I refused taking this rack. I told Mr. Holt I did not want to equalize myself with the little boys to take a stick when I went out; Mr. Holt says "this is Mr. Moore's orders." He said when Moore gave an order it had to be carried out.

Overby, who quit rather than allow them to fire him, claimed that Holt and Moore tried to prevent him from getting a job elsewhere although eventually George Swepson hired him. A few years later a worker name Hubbert "got drunk lost his hat fell in the creek got turned off the 20th." The next day he was given his looms back, but he "got drunk again [and] left for good Sunday 22th 1878." In 1884, Henderson Fowler reported that Alamance Factory workers "Jim May John May John Isley Bob Clapp L Anderson Bob Sharp all went without leaf," because "there was an exhibition at Oake dale the 30th of May." As a result four of the men "was turned out of a job next morning 1884." They may have carefully calculated the risk breaking rules entailed in mills where demand for skilled male workers was so high. Most, and perhaps all, of the men would work again for the Holts. Another Alamance worker, John Allred "took 7 hands out of the Mill Monday Morning Oct 11th 1886 on ac of a lit-

36. Newby, *Plain Folk in the New South*, 158; Fowler Diary, April, 1884, July, 1886, August 31, 1884, April 19, 1882, April, 1879.

tle fuss between his son John & Webb out side of the mill about a dog." Allred and his family were soon back at work.[37]

Workers also established some control by frequently moving. There was less movement within Alamance County than to other counties because the Holt family owned most of the mills; discontented workers, however, did at least have the alternative of Swepson's mill as Daniel Overby discovered. Henderson Fowler recorded the movement of several others who moved between the Holt mills and their rival Swepson's Big Falls as well. When Banks Holt turned Linda Lankford out of his mill, her family moved to Swepsonville less than a month later. Other workers left the county altogether. In the seventies Ruth Culberson moved her five children from Alamance to Bynum. Most likely the Holts gained as many transient workers as they lost; Gaston Hart moved his family from Bynum to Alamance sometime in the nineties.[38]

In 1891 a correspondent for the *Atlanta Constitution* visited Haw River and described the mill village he saw as one of "well-constructed and neatly painted brick and frame dwellings" plus "a beautiful and conveniently arranged office," "sundry store and ware houses," and "an attractive and comfortable chapel." The correspondent concluded that the operatives lived in "a large, thrifty and beautiful village." By 1900 the majority of workers lived in houses built by the Holts along streets leading up to the factories. Most of those in Ossipee and near the Granite Factory were one story, sometimes including only three rooms. Two front rooms served as parlor and bedroom while the one in back was used as a kitchen and dining room. Houses in Glencoe and Bellemont were more commodious, often including a second story, with a one-story wing or detached structure for the kitchen. A recent study of the Piedmont mill villages points out that these designs "had long been common in the Piedmont countryside, and they gave the village [Glencoe] the appearance of a rural hamlet more than a manufacturing settlement." "If work in the mill seemed alien to men and women fresh off the farm," this study concludes, "at least the village offered the comfort of familiar surroundings."[39]

---

37. *Alamance Gleaner,* February 8, 1876, April, 1884; Fowler Diary, September 22, 1878, October, 1886.

38. Fowler Diary, March 29, April 22, 1880; Douglass DeNatale, "Traditional Culture and Community in a Piedmont Textile Mill Village" (M.A. thesis, University of North Carolina at Chapel Hill, 1980), 522–23.

39. *Atlanta Constitution,* April 9, 1891; Lounsbury, *Alamance County Architectural Heritage,* 51–52; Hall et al., *Like a Family,* 115–16.

Not all contemporary descriptions of Alamance mill villages were as sanguine as the one offered by the Atlanta correspondent. Twenty-two years after the Haw River village was described as "thrifty and beautiful," state health workers determined that although Alamance was one of the state's wealthiest counties, "in the matter of public health, however, the county is very backward." Many homes, especially those owned by the mills, were found to have "dirty, loathsome, unsanitary, open-back privies." Haw River was described as especially unsanitary. Conditions may have deteriorated badly in the two decades between these starkly different observations, years in which Thomas and James Holt died as well as both of Thomas's sons. Most likely, however, workers had long endured deplorable conditions hidden from visiting reporters and rarely defined as a public problem until progressive reformers defined a new era. Mill village paternalism was a facade of good will, an attempt to mask the reality of long hours, unsafe working conditions, inadequate housing, and seething resentment.

Undoubtedly some people did become the docile and contented workers management wanted them to be. But many more did not. In 1890 a worker reported to the labor bureau that unless conditions were improved for workers in the state, "it will be plebian and patrician or lords and peasants. The people of this country have tasted liberty and they will never submit to be enslaved by a few. A revolution must come."[40] Ten years later the mill workers of Alamance County staged the largest strike seen in the state to that time.

40. Benjamin Washburn, *The Hookworm Campaign in Alamance County, North Carolina* (Raleigh, 1914), 6, 13, 28; *Fourth Annual Report . . .*, 1890, 34–35.

9

Citizens of a Common Country

THE ALAMANCE COUNTY
STRIKE OF
1900

In 1899 Greensboro mill owner Julian Shakespeare Carr gave a speech honoring the Holt family in which he praised Alamance County for its "contented homes of busy workers, who love their country, esteem their employers, fear no trusts with their blight, engage in no strike, turn out honest work that goes with credit and confidence throughout the world." Benjamin R. Lacy, North Carolina commissioner of labor in 1900, expressed an equally sanguine view of class relations when he assured a U.S. House of Representatives committee investigating industrial relations that "I never heard of any friction between the cotton operators" and "never heard a demand made." The cotton mill workers did not complain, he reported, because "they are very well treated in North Carolina."[1]

Less than a year after Carr and Lacy offered their assurances of class harmony, the majority of the men, women, and children who ran the machinery in the mills owned by the heirs of Edwin Holt went out on strike. The gap between the images and the realities of class relations was always present, but it was rarely made so blatantly clear. Especially after the Civil War, the Holts and their supporters, along with most of the state's mill men, carefully cultivated an image of their own paternal benevolence and of their workers' contentment. In part this was propaganda to promote industrialization by southerners who recognized in defeat the necessity of change. Like their northern counterparts described by Thomas Cochran, southern textile entrepreneurs "naturally wished to make the lesser seem the greater good, the private seem the national

---

1. *Alamance Gleaner,* January 25, 1900; U.S. Congress, House Documents, No. 476, vol. 7, 502.

profit." Sending little girls to work was rationalized as enhancing the greater good. When in 1888 the *Manufacturers' Record* proclaimed that "every cotton mill or kindred enterprise employing girls or women that is started in the South becomes really a philanthropic institution, as well as a wealth-producing investment," it was echoing a rationale with roots deep in the antebellum period. For the Holts such rationalizing helped sanction their great profits; it was also a response to the harsh criticism they had received during and just after the war when they were accused of profiteering at the expense of the poor as well as the common cause. In public sources, the press, histories and biographies, and in promotional literature, first Edwin Holt, and eventually his sons, were presented as men to be admired, as models to emulate. In 1875 the *Carolina Household*, for example, described Thomas Holt as "a model master" and claimed that "the highest compliment to the generous heart of the owner, as well as his clear brain, is visible in the cheerful and contented faces of the employees," and that "unlike many mills . . . here there is quiet peace and cheerful content." Samuel Ashe, in his *Biographical History of North Carolina* written three decades later, praised Edwin Holt for his "benevolence and patience and tenderness," and "the highly honest and honorable principles that governed his relations with his fellows always." At one point the *Gleaner* even reprinted an article suggesting that Holt, like most of his fellow industrial leaders, was born poor and had grown rich only through his own unrelenting efforts. No one claimed such a Horatio Alger background for his sons, but otherwise they were praised much as their father was. Although the Holts could depend on the media and other supporters to build the images they wanted, sometimes they took up the task themselves. In 1899, when James Williamson was asked about the needs of working people, he responded, "The situation, as far as the laborer is concerned, is in such a healthful state that there is no remedy needed at all." "The average cotton mill operative in North Carolina," he claimed, "is, and I think ought to be, almost as happy and contented an individual as can be found anywhere."[2] The only improvements in labor conditions that the Holts would concede were limiting child labor and offering greater access to education for the children of working families.

2. Cochran and Miller, *Age of Enterprise*, 123; *Manufacturers' Record*, June 23, 1888; *Carolina Record*, April 1875, 75; Ashe, *Biographical History of North Carolina*, vol. 7, 188; *Alamance Gleaner*, August 17, 1882; *Twelfth Annual Report . . .*, 1898, 229.

Maintaining quiet peace required not only loyal workers but loyal Democrats as well. A team of historians has explained that "in North Carolina, the Democratic Party remained firmly in the hands of an 'aggressive aristocracy' of lawyers, bankers, and manufacturers." The Holts were prominent among them. The race issue was the dominant tactic used by this oligarchy to assure that whites of lesser means, including the rapidly growing population of male mill folk, voted Democratic. They could not entirely prevent concerns of these folk from becoming political, but through the 1880s the Democratic Party was generally successful in persuading workers to remain loyal. Among the county's mill communities only Swepsonville, owned by Republican George Swepson, consistently reported a Republican majority. Dover Heritage claimed years later that for a time

> [Burlington] was run by the rich mill owners. They controlled everything, [and] at election time they closed their mills down for an hour, handed the workers, some of them little children 10, 12, 15 years old, a paper with names written on it. These papers were dropped in a box and the box was taken to town where the votes were counted. Anybody could vote. No one had to be registered. Problem was, the poor mill workers had to vote as the mill owners directed.

To the end of his career Thomas Holt remained confident that the poor workers would remain politically loyal; during the campaign of 1894 he requested to "speak at all the Factorys in particular."[3]

By that time, however, enough adult male mill workers were becoming so emboldened and determined to use politics to address their grievances that political candidates began to identify a cotton mill bloc. According to Cliff Kuhn, who has analyzed voting in Alamance County, white male workers did increasingly reject "the party of the fathers" more often than their rural counterparts and began voting Republican. Dover Heritage claimed that political coercion by the mill owners lasted only until men like his father fought back. James Heritage's son recalled that "a few people began to get together after work and talk about how much better off they would be if they got their own kind of people in office. My father and Bill Bivins were two of the leaders in this. They were a step higher than

---

3. Hall et al., *Like a Family*, 121; Cliff Kuhn, Untitled Paper, 16–17; Heritage, Bivins, and Bolden, *When Shoeshines Were a Nickel*, 17; Thomas Holt to R. W. Scott, September 5, 1894, Robert W. Scott Papers, NCDAH.

the average mill worker. They could read and write. They were smart, hard-working men." He remembered Bivins as a man who "wouldn't take his hat off to anybody. He was independent and everybody knew it. He was a good man who had a lot of fun in him, had a lot of jokes to tell." Bivins and Heritage spent hours on the front porch of the fine home Heritage had bought from Bob Holt, discussing which political candidates would best serve the needs of mill people. Their talk inspired a determination to change politics in Alamance County. Dover remembered that

> my daddy, Bill Bivins, Wesley Cates, Bill Hall and a few others decided to bust things up in Burlington. They held secret meetings at night up in Burlington. They held secret meetings at night or after work in the mill workers' homes and told them that they didn't have to vote like the mill owners said. They told the workers that they could vote downtown at the mayor's office and could vote for someone else.

Since the mill owners were Democrats, men like Bivins and Heritage became Republicans. According to Dover, "The rich people tried to fight the change but they saw they couldn't do anything or they might lose all their help." He concluded that "little by little the common working man began to have a voice in the town's government" and that "when the working people got a voice in the government, the town started to grow."[4]

Close to 80 percent of the county's eligible voters voted in the 1890s, the years Dover Heritage described. In 1896 the Republicans won a narrow victory in Alamance County; two years later, however, the *Gleaner* could celebrate a Democratic victory described as "redemption from negro domination."[5] Although the majority of mill workers, highly susceptible to threats of black empowerment, voted Democratic, a sizable majority were willing to buck the dictates of the Holts and the appeal of a racist argument to join Heritage and Bivins in voting Republican. In parts of the county with a large number of mill workers, nearly one-third voted Republican in 1898.

The specter of poor black and poor white collusion always loomed as a particularly deplorable threat to the Democratic elite. In 1899 North Carolina joined other southern states in precluding the possibility by disfranchising its black population. Voters were asked to consider an amendment to the constitution that would require

4. Kuhn, Untitled Paper, 17–18; Heritage, Bivins, and Bolden, *When Shoeshines Were a Nickel*, 18–19.

5. *Alamance Gleaner*, November 9, 1998.

passing a literacy test and payment of a poll tax to vote as well as stricter residency requirements and denial of the vote to those with a criminal record. Inspired by Louisiana's infamous "grandfather clause," the amendment also included a proviso that no voter whose descendants were eligible before January 1, 1867, would be affected. "White Supremacy" clubs founded in Graham and Elon College worked to win support by emphasizing white solidarity and the importance of black disfranchisement to all whites. Election results suggest that many of Alamance County's poorer white voters were not convinced. The amendment was narrowly defeated in the county although it won by over forty thousand votes in the state. In some mill communities there was a drop in the vote from the previous year, but in Haw River there was a large turnout with the majority of votes cast opposing the suffrage amendment.[6]

Beginning in 1887 the North Carolina Bureau of Labor offered working people another means of expressing their dissatisfaction with the status quo in the state. Every year the bureau issued an annual report; the first ones were generally uncensored and revealed publicly more tension-laden class relations than the Holts and other industrialists cared to admit. In 1887 W. H. T., who described himself as a working man acquainted with both owners and workers, reported "a general feeling of distrust with both parties and in some instances much bitterness. The laborer does not think that he gets a fair share of the profits, and the capitalist disposed to keep him down to the lowest figures." A mechanical engineer who frequently worked in the mills observed that the major complaint of workers was the long hours "but as the labor is mostly females and boys, the thing is not much agitated."[7]

The bureau was successfully endorsed by the Knights of Labor, the first labor union that attempted to organize southern textile workers and teach them to agitate. Founded in Philadelphia in 1869, the Knights were successfully organizing throughout the South within a decade; in 1879 the first organizer was commissioned in North Carolina. The Knights' emphasis on utopian reformism rather than class struggle had considerable appeal in the South where the focus on racial division generally overwhelmed the reality of class division. Early in 1885 Terrence V. Powderly, president of the national organization, spoke in Raleigh. John Ray, an organizer from

6. Kuhn, Untitled Paper, 18–20.
7. *First Annual Report . . . ,* 1887, 32; *Second Annual Report . . . ,* 1888, 50.

Massachusetts, moved to the Raleigh-Durham area and made it the center of union activity in the state. The small isolated mill communities in Alamance County were difficult to organize, but by 1886 there were several locals there. That year the Knights demonstrated the potential of their organization when state master workman John Nichols was elected to Congress as an Independent from the Fourth District, which included Alamance County. Despite Powderly's warning to remain strictly nonpartisan, the Knights endorsed labor candidates like Nichols. Although his opponent carried Alamance, the close vote indicates that Nichols commanded much of the mill vote. Thomas Holt only narrowly won in the county his family dominated economically, revealing the limits to the Holts' control of the workers' vote.[8]

Initially Thomas Holt attempted to control rather than to exclude the Knights. On the Fourth of July 1887, he spoke to a gathering of union members in Graham. Ultimately, however, his determination to maintain Democratic power and prevent unionization made any compromise impossible. The prospect of political success emboldened the Knights in Alamance. In October W. A. Fogleman, master workman of the Company Shops local, wrote Powderly that superintendents there were discriminating against union members and that the [unnamed] mill owner "would not give us no satisfaction and says he will not do nothing so we ask your advice." Fogleman assured the union president that his local was strong enough to close the mill and suggested that they should do so, as "we have got to come down to 11 hours per day," Powderly, however, warned him to neither lead a strike nor ask that any superintendent be fired. Instead, he advised the union to continue secretly organizing while doing nothing overt that would risk getting members fired.[9]

During the 1888 campaign a member of the Knights from Altamahaw condemned the "tyrannical yoke of oppression that so many poor factory hands and others have been wearing for the past twenty years"; he was also bold enough to announce his support of the Union Labor Party. The *Fayetteville Messenger*, the official Knights of Labor paper in the state, claimed that when workers in one Alamance mill were polled to determine how they intended to

8. Melton McLaurin, *The Knights of Labor in the South* (Westport, Conn., 1978), 44, 47–48, 82–85; McLaurin, *Paternalism and Protest.*
9. *Alamance Gleaner*, June 30, 1887; McLaurin, *Paternalism and Protest*, 78.

vote, Thomas T. Taylor also asserted his independence by refusing to confirm his support for Thomas Holt. According to Taylor's own interpretation, he was fired for his political apostasy. When the *Messenger* condemned Holt for political coercion, two other Knights, however, challenged Taylor's accusation, claiming that he was really fired for getting drunk and cursing. Taylor had the final word in the *Messenger*, claiming that "the bosses are cutting up" about his claim, which, he assured the paper, he could prove.[10] There is no way to know whether Taylor was fired for drinking or for refusing to vote for Thomas Holt. Most likely, however, the mere suggestion that they could lose their jobs was enough to convince some adult male workers not as bold as Bivins, Heritage, or Taylor that it was expedient to remain politically loyal to the party of their bosses.

The Burlington Knights heeded Powderly's advice, but despite the national leadership's reluctance, union members in Swepsonville went on strike in 1887 in an effort to get the work week reduced from seventy-five to sixty-six hours. There was also a brief strike that year at Ossipee for reasons that are not clear. Defeat of the Swepsonville strikers brought the defeat of that local, a warning of the likelihood that a strike would fail and could destroy the fragile union organization.[11]

The following year Nichols ran again, this time against Benjamin H. Bunn, president of a mill in Rocky Mount, a town approximately seventy-five miles east of Burlington. Sobered by Nichols's unexpected victory in 1886, the Democrats became more aggressive in their determination to win. The campaign revealed the power of an appeal to racism as a tactic to defeat reform. Conservative papers around the state successfully tied the Knights to black political power, warning that the victory of a party they endorsed would restore the "horrors" of Reconstruction.

This campaign also revealed the political power of wealthy industrialists like the Holts. The *Messenger* charged that Bunn was "merely the tool of the plaid trust," a thinly disguised charge that he was the tool of the Holt family. During the 1888 campaign the Holts were also accused of firing workers who did not vote Democratic.[12]

Nichols and most candidates the Knights of Labor supported in North Carolina were defeated in 1888. Subsequently the Knights

10. *Fayetteville Messenger*, July 23, 1888, September 28, October 3, 6, 12, 1888.
11. Fowler Diary, May 1, 1887; McLaurin, *Knights of Labor*, 73.
12. *Fayetteville Messenger*, September 28, October 12, 1888.

steadily lost members until the union's complete collapse in the 1890s. Although unionization had made a promising start in Alamance County, the adamant opposition of the Holts proved decisive. Melton McLaurin, the leading historian of the southern Knights of Labor, points out that labor organization was also stymied by the position of industrial workers as a minority in an area populated largely by discontented farm workers, by racial division, and by inept leadership overly concerned with politics, as well as by general ignorance of organizing labor.[13]

For a decade after their short-lived success organizing, textile workers in Alamance County reverted to more individual ways of protesting. But as McLaurin also explains, the years of success "disproved the claims of industrialists and politicians that there was no friction between capital and labor within the region."[14] These years also disproved the claim that a special brand of southern white individualism precluded unionization. The Alamance workers had seen their personal grievances collectivized and publicized, and they had learned something about organization.

After unionization failed, elections continued to offer adult male mill workers only limited means of challenging the domination of the Holts. The majority of mill workers, however, were denied the franchise by age and sex. By 1898 unionism was again presenting them with another vehicle for collective protest. In 1890 the National Union of Textile Workers (NUTW) was founded in the North as an affiliate of the American Federation of Labor (AFL). Seven years later division between socialists and trade unionists in the North resulted in the election of a southerner, Prince Greene, who worked as a weaver in Georgia, as president; NUTW headquarters followed him south. Like the Knights, the NUTW was most successful in urban centers of manufacturing, but it also formed locals in small mill villages, including those that dotted Alamance County.[15]

Low wages and, especially, long hours remained the fundamental grievances that drove workers to organize. In the 1884 campaign Thomas Holt's opponent announced his support of a law limiting the workday in factories to ten hours. The Democratic *Gleaner* condemned the proposal as not in the workers' best interest on the grounds that it would force a reduction in their wages. By 1899,

13. McLaurin, *Paternalism and Protest*, 114.
14. McLaurin, *Knights of Labor*, 189.
15. McLaurin, *Paternalism and Protest*, 134–39.

however, a mechanic polled by the Bureau of Labor could claim that a ten-hour law "is the wish of nearly all of the working people, though many are not willing to express themselves openly." W. W. Oakes, president of the local founded at Altamahaw, proclaimed that he fought against wages "too low for the average man, woman and child who are toiling day by day for their daily bread" and hours so long that they turned women into "skin and bones" and children into "dwarfs."[16]

The NUTW began efforts to organize in the South in 1895, but it was not until several years later that unions were again a presence in Alamance County. According to Labor Commissioner Benjamin Lacy, NUTW workers from South Carolina, who came to Graham after they were fired and blacklisted there, brought a determination to unionize back to Alamance. In March 1900 Lacy speculated that the small local in the county was the only one in North Carolina. In reality the NUTW was by this time involved in clandestine organization all over the Piedmont. In June 1899, AFL organizer C. P. Davis held a meeting in Haw River as he traveled through the area. By the spring of 1900 NUTW locals had been established there as well as in Burlington and Altamahaw. Successful organization was enhanced by the NUTW's clandestine methods. The first hint that it would successfully close or curtail work in most of the mills in Alamance County came in May when workers at Elmira struck. The *Gleaner* did not record the reason these strikers gave, only that in three days they were back at work. The paper was confident that so would end labor strife in Alamance since both owners and workers "are home people."[17] But the Holts had clear warning that a union was again threatening their control.

The threat was realized in the fall of 1900 when a strike forced closure or reduced work in all of the Holt mills. The strike began in the T. M. Holt Manufacturing Company, which since Thomas Holt's death had been owned by his children. Tension in this mill ran particularly high as a growing number of workers there joined the union that owners found so odious. Skilled adult males, whose support was critical to the success of the union, were markedly divided; some led the resistance while others identified with the owners. Jim May, who had worked for the Holts since he was a boy, was among those who refused to join the union. Sometime after he was fired in 1886

16. *Alamance Gleaner*, October 30, 1884; *Thirteenth Annual Report . . . ,* 1899, 133; *Fifteenth Annual Report . . . ,* 1901, 420.
17. U.S. Congress, Industrial Commission, House Reports, 497; McLaurin, *Paternalism and Protest*, 154–56; *Alamance Gleaner*, May 10, 1900.

for leaving work without permission, May had returned to T. M. Holt and was eventually made boss weaver. He had no use for the NUTW, but many of the weavers he supervised, including Annie Whitesell, whose German ancestors had settled near the Holts along the Haw River over a century earlier, joined.[18]

The tension between union and nonunion workers on the weave room floor at T. M. Holt came to a head when May chastised Whitesell for leaving her looms to go to the quilling room for more filling; he claimed that she already had a sufficient supply and threatened to fire her for leaving her work too often. Whitesell reportedly "flew into a passion, denying his charges and scorning his threat," and insisted that she "would go when she pleased, where she pleased." May fired her and offered her looms to nonunion worker Johnie Pope, a young woman with no means of support but her own wages. Despite the higher pay it offered, Pope first refused the promotion to weaver after union members explained that replacing a fired worker was against union rules. When Pope rejected his offer, it was May who "waxed wroth"; he warned Pope that unless she took the job, she would be fired as well. According to a neutral observer writing about the strike a year later, Pope, "being an orphan having to choose between giving up her job and incurring the frowns of her union friends, she did not know what to do and burst into tears." She finally determined that she had no choice but to take Whitesell's looms. The other weavers on the floor, most of them adult males, both union and nonunion, became indignant at the treatment of both Whitesell and Pope and demanded that May, whom they claimed had a history of brutality toward women and children, be the one fired. The mill owners predictably refused any ultimatum from workers. On the night of September 27, the Haw River local met and planned to announce a strike if management refused to meet their demand. The next day employees of T. M. Holt went out on strike and within an hour were joined by workers from Cora and the Granite Factory; all three mills were owned by the descendants of Thomas M. Holt.[19]

The strikers would not have won the widespread sympathy they eventually received throughout the Piedmont if the mill owners had done nothing more than refuse to fire Jim May. But, perhaps predict-

18. William T. Whitsett, *A Brief History of Alamance County, North Carolina: With Sketches of the Whitesell Family and the Huffman Family* (Whitsett, N.C., 1926), 14–15. The family name was spelled in a variety of ways including Whitsett and Whitsell.

19. Jerome Dowd, "Strikes and Lockouts in North Carolina," *Gunton's Magazine* 20 (1901): 136–41.

ing that a more widespread and protracted strike would have the desired result, the Holts determined to use the incident to destroy the union once and for all. It is unclear what family members assumed leadership as they confronted the strike. Apparently neither Banks nor Lawrence, the only two sons of Edwin Holt still living in Alamance County, was actively involved. Lawrence, who had just returned from a two-month trip to Europe when the strike erupted, was often away and was relatively aloof from politics and local affairs even when he was home. A young mill worker interviewed years later remembered that Lawrence Holt "stayed away a good deal, and when I came along he was probably away a good bit." Ordinarily Banks was more actively engaged, but one of his daughters was critically ill when the strike began and died shortly after it started, undoubtedly leaving him more detached than usual. Charles Holt was suffering from the same disease that killed his father; he died in December. Emily Holt's death in October at the age of ninety-two also distracted the family. Thomas's son-in-law, Alfred A. Haywood, who had given up the practice of law to become vice president of T. M. Holt, clearly emerged as one spokesman. He met with several other family members, possibly the other sons-in-law of Thomas Holt, in Burlington shortly after the first workers walked out to coordinate their response. Family representatives refused, in what was described as "a rather slack manner," to meet with a committee appointed by the NUTW, insisting that they would deal with their workers only on an individual basis. Instead of negotiating they announced that the mills could not be run without "the necessary harmony" and gave workers notice in every mill in the county except for the two they did not control. The notice distributed at T. M. Holt read:

> In accordance with notice posted on the 4th inst. we propose starting this mill next Monday morning at the usual hour with non-union help. No one belonging to labor unions will be allowed to enter the mill Monday morning. We respectfully request that all who have decided to remain in labor unions will give notice today to the superintendent of the mill in which he or she works.[20]

This heavy-handed tactic was ultimately successful, but initially it resulted in increased union membership and considerable

20. Verna Cates Stackhouse Interview, SOHP; *Alamance Gleaner,* October 5, 1900.

sympathy for the strikers. On October 16 striking mill workers and their supporters marched from Haw River to Graham where they joined a crowd estimated at between 700 and 1,500 for a rally at the courthouse. A committee representing the NUTW sent a letter to the *Gleaner* defending the union's action and asking, "Is it right that mill owners shall organize, meet together, fix prices on their yarns, their loom product, and regulate wages, and then say to the laborer: 'You take what we give you, do what we tell you, and say nothing'?" Even the *Gleaner*, which sometimes read almost as the official paper of the Holt family, was critical of the manner in which the mill owners responded, rejoining that "both classes are citizens of a common country."[21] Union membership soared as hundreds joined; according to the *Gleaner* they were joining to protest management's refusal to even meet with union leadership. By November approximately five thousand workers were out on strike, closing or forcing cutbacks in production in all of the Holt mills.

Not all Alamance County mill workers or their parents, however, were convinced that joining a union was in their best interest. The *Gleaner* reported that not only was there much bitterness between employers and employees but also between union and nonunion workers. Probably in most cases decisions about whether to join the union and support the strike were made by heads of households for the entire family but not always. A reporter for a Raleigh paper found one case of a mother and her two children, all three workers in the Granite Factory, divided because the children had been persuaded to join and strike against their mother's wishes; she continued to work and support them with her wages. Two sisters who supported their invalid father found themselves on opposite sides when one decided to join while the other refused, explaining that she would not go against the owners' wishes because "they have been my friend and now I'm going to stand by them." She further explained that "I have never been to the office of the company or to its store when in need of anything and failed to get it. Once last winter we needed a considerable sum of money and I asked Mr. Charlie Holt to let me have it. He did it without making me sign a paper. I've paid him back, but that doesn't make me forget his kindness."[22] For the strike to succeed the NUTW had to convince workers that it was unionization rather than the style of paternalism displayed by Charlie Holt that would best serve their

21. *Alamance Gleaner*, October 10, 11, 1900.
22. Ibid., October 20, 1900.

interests. The national union sent agents to persuade these Alamance County workers to coordinate their strikers and arrange for provisions to feed them. When mill owners retaliated by evicting union members and their families from their homes, the union assured the homeless that they would be supplied with tents.[23]

As the strike continued, each side accused the other of resorting to violence. The Holts tried, with limited success, to bring in nonunion workers from elsewhere. Burwell Summerlin, a Virginian who took a job in the Granite Factory, claimed that he had to sleep in the mill and have his food delivered there due to threats he received. When a new worker arrived from Gibsonville, just across the county line, the *Gleaner* reported that armed deputies were sent to the train depot to meet him. Spokesmen for the workers retaliated with claims that it was the owners who were armed and that the worst they had to fear from strikers was "the cry of 'scab' from the union girls and women whenever they see a non-union operative."[24]

As the strike moved into its second month, Fred Merritt, a *Raleigh News and Observer* reporter increasingly sympathetic to the strikers, predicted that although they should win, the owners ultimately would. Union leaders had been extremely successful in eliciting verbal support but in assuring practical support were hardly successful at all. I. A. Newby's assessment of NUTW strikes throughout the South in this period as "unplanned and therefore unprepared for" rings true of the Alamance strike. He claims that "the strikers had no strategy, no resources for sustaining themselves, no organization or experienced leaders." By late November some striking workers, especially those in families with neither the resources to move out of state nor prospects of alternative support, renounced union membership and returned to work. Others, probably a majority, determined to continue the strike into the winter. A third group, estimated by the *Gleaner* in late November to be around three hundred, left Alamance and sought jobs elsewhere in the state or in Virginia, South Carolina, or Georgia. Finding another job in North Carolina, where the Holts had widespread contacts with both politicians and mill owners was more difficult. Union leaders added blacklisting to their list of grievances. Striking Alamance workers were clearly refused employment at the Erwin Mill, managed by William Erwin, who had left his partnership with Lawrence Holt to relocate in Durham, and in Fayetteville, where two of James Holt's

23. Ibid., November 15, 1900.
24. Ibid., October 20, 1900.

sons had mills; most likely they were blacklisted elsewhere in the state as well. Mill owners in other states were less likely to be concerned with hiring away Holt employees; a mill in Georgia successfully recruited unemployed North Carolinians. The *Atlanta Constitution* reported in December that "two [rail] cars were sidetracked here yesterday, another this morning and still another is expected tomorrow morning containing families from the cotton mill regions of North Carolina, principally from Graham, North Carolina." Others went to Columbus, Georgia, the home of NUTW President Prince Greene. Among those who left the state, the Alamance paper claimed, "are a great many excellent people who prefer to go elsewhere rather than surrender rights and privileges which they as citizens deem their own and should enjoy."[25]

The strike was led by a minority of workers, most of them skilled adult males; they were joined by adult females who shared their sense of injustice, if not always for the same reasons. Their entitlement to the rights of equal citizenship was especially clear to adult male workers. According to Edward Johnson, president of one of the locals, "the privileges of free men" was the first demand; he claimed that the demand for the removal of May for his brutal treatment of women was secondary. Sustaining a strike around an ideology of equality was difficult, however, when the majority of workers were women and children. Some women, including Annie Whitesell, shared with men the sense that they were being deprived of fundamental rights. Generally, however, females had been successfully trained to be dependent and were confined to the lowest paid and most powerless jobs; they were accordingly less likely to define the exclusion of unions or blacklisting as an affront to their essential equality. Children were even less likely to develop a concept of equal rights. Apparently children under the age of sixteen were ineligible to join the union and few of them would have joined the strike out of a clear sense of principle in any case. Probably a majority of those classified as adult but still in their teens or early twenties and still living at home did as their parents wished. For many parents providing food and housing was more compelling than abstractions about the privileges of free men. Gender, age, and family income were primary determinants of how workers responded to abstracted ideals. All the Alamance County mill workers understood well enough, however, that the Holts were rich and

25. Newby, *Plain Folk in the New South*, 563, 235–36, 99; *Alamance Gleaner*, November 29, 1900.

they were poor. One adult male employee spoke for the strikers in language accessible to even the youngest workers when he condemned mill owners who "are making enormous profits on our labor, building new mills, buying new machinery and other things and living in extravagant luxury, and ease, while we toil almost day and night for them, for a meagre living, with no hope for a home we can call our own." The strike was primarily about one thing, he concluded: "We only ask a fair share of the profits produced by our labor."[26]

On October 30 union members were given the choice of leaving the union or finding themselves evicted from company housing. The NUTW responded by vowing to support the strike all winter if necessary, but in reality their limited resources made it impossible to provide for the evicted workers. In late November Merritt reported that "the union is going to pieces." Soon after the NUTW reversed itself and announced that it was withdrawing support.[27]

The failure of the 1900 strike brought an end to union organizing in Alamance County for several decades. Thomas Shatterly, secretary of Local 198 in Haw River, tried to keep the memory of the union and what it had done in 1900 alive. He called on working people to "come together and not be frightened away because some boss looks mad at you and advises you not to join a union. . . . I believe," he continued, that "a man who does not believe in a union does not believe in the Bible and he should be called an infidel."[28]

The Holts and their allies determined that, to the contrary, the very idea of unionization was a heresy to be obliterated. Accounts written about the Holts and their mills in the early twentieth century rarely mentioned the strike. The image of the textile industry as owned and managed by benevolent paternalists and tended by docile, contented, and grateful workers was carefully reconstructed. Eight years after the strike, Samuel Ashe, historian and friend of many industrial leaders, described Thomas Holt as "a model master"; although

> inflexible in his requirements, compelling industry and painstaking care on the part of servants and employees, he was yet kind, sympathetic, and generous in his dealings with all. He was ever ready to aid the well deserving, and by every means sought to stimulate in them the virtues of self-respect, thrift,

26. *Greensboro Patriot*, November 14, 1900.
27. McLaurin, *Paternalism and Protest*, 161.
28. *Fifteenth Annual Report . . .* , 1901, 425.

honesty, industry, and self-reliance. A strike was never so much as proposed among the faithful people who served him.[29]

The Battle of the Regulators in 1771 and the strike of 1900 remain seminal events in Alamance County history; both occurred on property owned by the Holt family. In both conflicts members of this family, separated by four generations, were central figures in the effort first to defeat poor, aggrieved peasants and then poor, aggrieved mill hands trying to challenge fundamental power relations. In 1771 Michael Holt II was among the elite men in Alamance "severely whipped" by "poor industrious peasants" determined to challenge elite privilege. Over a hundred years later poor industrial proletarians tried again, using the more modern tactic of a union-led strike to challenge elite privilege. In his contest with powerful men, one of the regulators questioned "what can be expected from those who have ever discovered a Want of good Principles, and whose highest Study is the Promotion of their Wealth; and with whom the Interest of the Publick, when it comes in Competition with their private Advantages, is suffered to sink nothing less than the ruins of the Publick?"[30] This agrarian farmer, living in a time now called premodern, would have not understood much about machinery and mills, but he could have clearly articulated a justification for his ideological heirs struggling a century later.

29. Ashe, *Biographical History of North Carolina*, vol. 7, 192–93.
30. Quotation from William K. Boyd, ed., *Some Eighteenth-Century Tracts Concerning North Carolina* (Raleigh, 1927), 303.

10

The Day Spencer Love Came to Town

Today the birthplace of Edwin Holt is included on the National Register of Historic Places and houses the Alamance County Historical Museum. Most of the museum's furnishings, including some that belonged to members of the Holt family, are in the style of the 1870s and 1880s, the period in which Banks Holt remodeled his grandfather's home and lived there with his family. The Holt family graveyard behind the house is carefully preserved; Edwin and Emily are buried there, along with their son Alexander, Edwin's parents, and several of his siblings. In nearby Graham a large obelisk that dominates the cemetery marks the grave of Banks Holt; the graves of Thomas Holt and other family members are there as well. Across Highway 62 from the Banks Holt home, Locust Grove still stands but in a dilapidated state and closed to the public. Less than a mile away from the two houses a historical marker identifies the location of the Alamance Factory. The Alamance Battleground nearby commemorates the eighteenth-century regulators. The Edwin M. Holt School, between the mill site and the historical museum, is a modern reminder of the importance of the Holts in nineteenth-century Alamance County. Beyond the county, however, they are hardly remembered. Asked about preeminent industrial families from the past century, North Carolinians would almost invariably name the Dukes, not the Holts.

A woman whose family had worked for the second generation of Holts reflected years later on their aloofness from the county they had so profoundly influenced. Verna Stackhouse remembered that "they were not particularly interested in it [Burlington]" and rarely involved themselves in civic affairs. In the 1980s Reid Maynard, a prominent hosiery manufacturer in Alamance County in the mid-twentieth century, also reminisced about the Holts and reflected on why the family dynasty, so successful for decades, ultimately failed. He recalled, "It was the Holts and Williamsons who had run the old plaid cotton mills. And they had let them go down. They were at a low ebb, a lot of them closed, some of them bankrupt, the others just took their money out and quit." The reason for the failure, Maynard concluded, was "there wasn't any broad stock, there was just family." Maynard, remembering people he had known in his youth, added that "of course, the Holts went out and the Williamsons closed them out or done something. They had plenty of things on the side, none of those people died poor, they were well fixed, but the old mills, they just give them up. That was the day Spencer Love came to town."[1]

Love came to town by way of Cambridge, Massachusetts. But this was no Yankee carpetbagger come South. The history of J. Spencer Love's family is reminiscent of the Holt genealogy. Loves, who were Scotch-Irish Presbyterians, migrated into the North Carolina Piedmont about the same time the Holts came; they moved to the southern border of North Carolina, to what would become Gaston County. Here, as in Alamance, Germans and Scotch-Irish first separated themselves out but soon intermingled and intermarried. Grier Love, Spencer's grandfather, married Susan Rhyne, from a German family. In 1850 her father, Moses Rhyne, built the Pinhook Factory, the second mill in Gaston County. After the war his sons built additional mills there and in surrounding counties. Grier Love became a partner in one of the Rhyne mills and later built his own. Some of his sons followed his example, but one of them, Lee, later recalled that "in 1887, when my father built the first cotton mill of the long series of mills afterward established in the town of Gastonia, I was not in the least tempted to give up my teaching and join him." Two years later Lee Love joined the faculty of Harvard where for over twenty years he taught mathematics. But the ambition to build mills in North Carolina had only skipped one generation. Lee's son Spencer Love was born and grew up in Cambridge but frequently visited his North Carolina relatives. He graduated from Harvard, then served in the army during World War I. A few years later, Reid Maynard recalled, the twenty-seven-year-old veteran "came home and worked to get in the textile business. He and his daddy bought this old rundown cotton mill in Gastonia. I don't know what got him to Burling-

---

1. Verna Cates Stackhouse Interview, SOHP; Tullos, *Habits of Industry*, 113–14.

ton. The Chamber of Commerce, I think, went after him." Love first sought to revitalize one of his uncle's Gaston County mills but within a few years determined on a fresh start in a new location. Around the same time that Love was planning to leave, Alamance County promoters were watching with envy as Gaston County's textile industry prospered while their own mills declined. In competition with several other sites, the Burlington Chamber of Commerce agreed to underwrite a stock sale of $250,000 if Love would move his mill there. Love accepted the offer, moved to Burlington, and rented one of the fine Holt homes, still standing as testimony to the family's former prestige, for three hundred dollars a month. "Everybody in Burlington thought he was crazy," Maynard recalled, because "nobody else paid over twenty-five dollars."

J. Spencer Love more than successfully revived the textile industry in Alamance County. Eventually he built Burlington Industries, the largest textile corporation in the United States.[2]

Edwin Holt and his sons probably knew the Rhynes and Loves, at least by reputation; they were all mill men in nineteenth-century North Carolina. I have found only one documented example of contact between the two families. Spencer Love's grandmother Cornelia Phillips Spencer recalled in her memoir that in 1880 she worked with Thomas Holt to organize a dinner for the one hundred or so convicts who had built the tracks connecting Chapel Hill to the main railroad line. Probably there were other encounters; perhaps children attended the same boarding schools; business brought men in both families to Charlotte and possibly to meetings elsewhere as well.[3]

Neither Loves nor Holts, however, could have predicted the transfer of economic power and social prestige that would occur less than one hundred years after Edwin Holt built his first factory. His grandsons were successful mill men, but successful only on a small scale. As Allen Tullos has explained, the Holt mills, "because of their small size and inconvenient locations . . . were eclipsed, near the century's end, by a new era in Carolina Piedmont manufacturing." The eclipse was virtually complete the day Spencer Love came to town. In 1953 a textile journal described the builder of Burlington Industries as "impelled by a merciless, relentless, driving force that knows no abatement."[4] Spencer Love was the final heir of Edwin Holt.

2. Tullos, *Habits of Industry*, 86–122.
3. Hope Summerell Chamberlain, *Old Days in Chapel Hill: Being the Life and Letters of Cornelia Phillips Spencer* (Chapel Hill, 1926), 248–51; Tullos, *Habits of Industry*, 89, 93–94.
4. Tullos, *Habits of Industry*, 20, 122.

APPENDIX

Holt Family Tree

PREPARED BY BILL MARTIN

SOURCE: Eugene Holt, *Edwin Michael Holt and his Descendants, 1807–1948* (Private printing, 1949). Death dates after 1950 not available.

APPENDIX

Edwin Michael Holt 1807–1884
Emily Farish 1808–1900

Alfred Augustus Holt 1829–1858
Elizabeth Ann Mebane 1827–1895
- Junius Yancey Holt 1852–1911
- Thomas Franklin Holt 1854–1931
- George Edwin Holt 1856–1931

Thomas Michael Holt 1831–1896
Louisa Moore 1833–1899
- Alice Linwood Holt 1856–1857
- Charles Thomas Holt 1858–1900
- Cora May Holt 1859–1942
- Louisa Moore Holt 1861–?
- Ella Moore Holt 1862–?
- Thomas Michael Holt, Jr. 1871–1897

James Henry Holt 1833–1897
Laura Cameron Moore 1835–1901
- Ida Cameron Holt 1857–1861
- Walter Lawrence Holt 1859–1913
- Edwin Cameron Holt 1861–1944
- Samuel Michael Holt 1862–1924
- James Henry Holt, Jr. 1864–1928
- Robert Lacy Holt 1866–1923
- William Irwin Holt 1868–?
- Mary Louise Holt 1870–1882
- Ernest Augustus Holt 1873–?
- Laura Alice Holt 1875–1875
- Glen Holt 1876–1876
- Lelia Daisy Holt 1879–?

Alexander Holt 1835–1892

218

Frances Ann Holt 1837–1918
1st T.L. Slade ?–1864
2nd John Lea Williamson
1823–1904

- Edwin Holt Williamson 1866–1934
- Emma Virginia Williamson 1868–1942
- Lawrence Augustus Williamson 1870–?
- Finley Lea Williamson 1872–1947
- James Walter Williamson 1874–1940
- Lynn Banks Williamson 1878–?

William Edwin Holt 1839–1917
Amelia Lloyd Holt 1850–1938

- Claudia de Bonheur Holt 1872–?
- William Edwin Holt, Jr. 1873–?
- Ethel Holt 1878–?
- Lora Frances Holt 1881–1882
- Lura Eugene Holt 1881–1882
- Lois Amelia Holt 1882–?
- Maud Farish Holt 1885–?
- Emily Louise Holt 1889–?

Lynn Banks Holt 1842–1920
Mary Catherine Mebane
1844–1924

- Mary Virginia Holt 1867–?
- Elizabeth Mebane Holt 1869–1938
- Frances Yancey Holt 1872–1900
- Infant daughter 1874–1874
- Caroline Banks Holt 1876–1942
- Cora Alice Holt 1878–1905
- Emily Louisa Holt 1880–?
- Martha Lynn Holt 1886–1920

Mary Elizabeth Holt 1844–1935
James Nathaniel Williamson
1842–1921

- William Holt Williamson
  1867–1926
- Ada Virginia Williamson 1869–1898
- James Nathaniel Williamson, Jr.
  1872–1945
- Mary Blanche Williamson
  1874–1947

Emma Virginia Holt 1847–1904
James Wilson White 1839–1887

- Emily Holt White 1872–1873
- Joseph Harvey White 1875–1946
- William Elliott White 1877–1936
- Edwin Michael Holt White
  1880–1908
- Mary Adelaide White 1886–1937

Lawrence Shackleford Holt
1851–1937
Margaret Locke Erwin 1852–1918

- Erwin Allen Holt 1873—?
- Eugene Holt 1875–1948
- Emily Farish Holt 1877–1882
- Margaret Erwin Holt 1879–1938
- Florence Elvira Holt 1881–?
- Lawrence Shackleford Holt, Jr.
  1883–?
- Bertha Harper Holt 1888–?

BIBLIOGRAPHY

MANUSCRIPT COLLECTIONS

Alamance County Historical Museum, Haw River, North Carolina
Collections

Catholic University, Washington, D.C.
Knights of Labor Collection

Duke University, Perkins Library, Manuscripts Division
William A. Carrigan Papers
Washington Duke Papers
Erwin Mills Papers
Fuller-Thomas Papers
Grasty-Rison Papers
Mark Morgan Papers
Edward Oldham Papers
Samuel Finly Patterson Papers
Pilot Cotton Mills Correspondence
Thomas Ruffin Papers
William L. Scott Papers

Harvard University, Baker Library
Dun and Bradstreet Papers
Lowell Machine Company Papers
Whitin Machine Company Papers

Massachusetts Historical Society, Boston
New England Manufacturers Association Papers

Moravian Archives, Winston-Salem
Francis Fries Papers
Salem Manufacturing Company Papers

North Carolina Division of Archives and History, Raleigh
Samuel Ashe Papers
Cedar Falls Manufacturing Company Day Book, 1854–1865
Walter Clark Papers
Calvin J. Cowles Letterbook
Fries Papers
Marmaduke James Hawkins Papers
Military Collection
North Carolina Church Records
Patterson Papers

Edward W. Phifer Jr. Collection
Thomas M. Pittman Collection
Robert W. Scott Papers
Tolar-Hart Mill Village Scrapbook
Jonathan Worth Papers

University of Georgia, Special Collections Division
DeRenne Collection

University of North Carolina at Chapel Hill, Wilson Library, Southern Historical Collection
Alamance Cotton Mill Records
John Mebane Allen Papers
Battle Family Papers
Beall-Harper Papers
Henderson Monroe Fowler Diaries
Francis Fries Papers
Graves Family Papers
Heartt-Wilson Papers
McBee Family Papers
McLaws Papers
Mebane Family Papers
George Phifer Papers
Leonidas Lafayette Polk Papers
James Pugh Papers
Elizabeth Nims Rankin Papers
W. C. Rankin Papers
Andrew Rike Papers
Thomas Ruffin Papers
Archibald Smith Papers
Southern Oral History Project Papers
Zebulon Baird Vance Papers
James W. White Papers
Calvin Wiley Papers

University of South Carolina, South Caroliniana Room
Graniteville Cotton Mill Papers
William Gregg Papers
Hammett Papers

GOVERNMENT DOCUMENTS
North Carolina
NORTH CAROLINA BUREAU OF LABOR AND PRINTING
Annual Reports, 1887–1901.

NORTH CAROLINA DEPARTMENT OF ARCHIVES AND
HISTORY, RALEIGH
Wills, Alamance County: Alexander Holt, Edwin Holt, Emily Holt.
Wills, Orange County: Michael Holt II.
Wills, Rockingham County: Thomas T. Slade.

United States
U.S. Bureau of the Census. Seventh–Twelfth Manuscript Censuses, Alamance County.
———. Seventh Manuscript Census, Caswell County.
———. Eighth Manuscript Census, Davidson County.
———. Third–Seventh Manuscript Censuses, Orange County.
———. Eighth Manuscript Census, Rockingham County.
U.S. Congress, Senate Reports, 42d Cong., 1st sess., no. 1.

PUBLISHED MANUSCRIPTS
Boyd, William K., ed. *Some Eighteenth-Century Tracts Concerning North Carolina.* Raleigh: Edwards and Broughton, 1927.
Brooks, Aubrey Lee, and Hugh T. Lefler, eds. *The Papers of Walter Clark.* Chapel Hill: University of North Carolina Press, 1948.
Hamilton, J. G. de Roulhac, ed. *The Papers of Thomas Ruffin.* Raleigh: Edwards and Broughton, 1918.
Johnston, Frontis W., ed. *The Papers of Zebulon Baird Vance.* Raleigh: North Carolina Department of Archives and History, 1963.
Saunders, William L., ed. *The Colonial Records of North Carolina.* Raleigh: North Carolina Department of Archives and History, 1886–90.
Tolbert, Norbert J., ed. *The Papers of John W. Ellis.* Raleigh: North Carolina Department of Archives and History, 1964.

NEWSPAPERS AND PERIODICALS
Alamance Gleaner
Atlanta Constitution
Carolina Watchman
Charlotte Observer
Fayetteville Messenger
Greensboro Patriot, 1900
Hillsborough Recorder
Manufacturers' Record
Raleigh News and Observer, 1900

BOOKS

Alamance County: The Legacy of Its People and Places. Greensboro: Greensboro Legacy Press, 1984.

Allmendinger, David F. *Ruffin: Family and Reform in the Old South.* New York: Oxford University Press, 1990.

Anderson, Jean Bradley. *Piedmont Plantation: The Bennehan-Cameron Family and Lands in North Carolina.* Durham, N.C.: Historic Preservation Society of Durham, 1985.

Anderson, Lucy London. *North Carolina Women of the Confederacy.* Fayetteville, N.C.: Cumberland Printing, 1926.

Ashe, Samuel A., ed. *Biographical History of North Carolina: From Colonial Times to the Present.* Greensboro, N.C.: Charles L. Van Noppen, 1905–17.

Ayers, Edward. *The Promise of the New South.* New York: Oxford University Press, 1992.

Battle, Kemp Plummer. *Memories of an Old-Time Tar Heel.* Chapel Hill: University of North Carolina Press, 1945.

Beardsley, Edward H. *A History of Neglect: Health Care for Blacks and Mill Workers in the Twentieth-Century South.* Knoxville: University of Tennessee Press, 1987.

Beecher, George. *Science and Change in Alamance County.* Graham, N.C.: Alamance County Schools, 1938.

Billings, Dwight. *Planters and the Making of a 'New South': Class, Politics, and Development in North Carolina, 1865–1900.* Chapel Hill: University of North Carolina Press, 1979.

Bishir, Catherine W. *North Carolina Architecture.* Chapel Hill: University of North Carolina Press, 1990.

Black, Allison Harris, comp. *An Architectural History of Burlington, North Carolina.* Burlington, N.C.: City of Burlington, 1987.

Bremner, Robert. *The Public Good: Philanthropy and Welfare in the Civil War Era.* New York: Alfred A. Knopf, 1980.

Brown, Richard D. *Modernization: The Transformation of American Life, 1600–1865.* New York: Hill and Wang, 1976.

Burton, Orville Vernon. *In My Father's House Are Many Mansions: Family and Community in Edgefield, South Carolina.* Chapel Hill: University of North Carolina Press, 1985.

Bynum, Victoria. *Unruly Women: The Politics of Social and Sexual Control in the Old South.* Chapel Hill: University of North Carolina Press, 1992.

Carlton, David. *Mill and Town in South Carolina, 1880–1920.* Baton Rouge: Louisiana State University Press, 1982.

Cash, Wilbur J. *The Mind of the South.* New York: Vintage, 1941.

Cathy, Cornelius O. *Agricultural Development in North Carolina, 1783–1860.* Chapel Hill: University North Carolina Press, 1956.

Cecil-Fronsman, Bill. *Common Whites: Class and Culture in Antebellum North Carolina.* Lexington: University of Kentucky Press, 1992.

Censer, Jane Turner. *North Carolina Planters and Their Children, 1800–1860.* Baton Rouge: Louisiana State University Press, 1984.

Chamberlain, Hope Summerell. *Old Days in Chapel Hill: Being the Life and Letters of Cornelia Phillips Spencer.* Chapel Hill: University of North Carolina Press, 1926.

Chandler, Alfred D. Jr. *The Visible Hand: The Managerial Revolution in American Business.* Cambridge, Mass.: Harvard University Press, 1972.

Clark, Walter, ed. *Histories of the Several Regiments and Battalions from North Carolina in the Great War, 1861–65.* Goldsboro, N.C.: Nash Brothers, 1901.

Cobb, James C. *Industrialization and Southern Society, 1877–1984.* Lexington: University of Kentucky Press, 1984.

———. *The Most Southern Place on Earth: The Mississippi Delta and the Roots of Regional Identity.* New York: Oxford University Press, 1992.

Cochran, Thomas C. *Frontiers of Change: Early Industrialization in America.* New York: Oxford University Press, 1981.

Cochran, Thomas C., and William Miller. *The Age of Enterprise: A Social History of Industrial America.* New York: Macmillan, 1942.

Confederate Memoirs: Alamance County Troops of the War Between the States, 1861–1865. Centennial Edition. N.p., n.d.

Cook, John Harrison. *A Study of the Mill Schools of North Carolina.* New York: Teachers College, Columbia University, 1925.

Creely, Richard Benburg. *Grandfather's Tales of North Carolina History.* Raleigh: Edwards and Broughton, 1901.

Dublin, Thomas. *Women at Work: The Transformation of Work and Community in Lowell, Massachusetts, 1826–1860.* New York: Columbia University Press, 1979.

Durden, Robert F. *The Dukes of Durham, 1865–1929.* Durham, N.C.: Duke University Press, 1975.

Durrill, Wayne K. *War of Another Kind: A Southern Community in the Great Rebellion.* New York: Oxford University Press, 1990.

Eaton, Clement. *A History of the Old South.* New York: Macmillan, 1949.

Escott, Paul D. *Many Excellent People: Power and Privilege in North Carolina, 1850–1900.* Chapel Hill: University of North Carolina Press, 1985.

Farnham, Christie Anne. *The Education of the Southern Belle: Higher*

Education and Student Socialization in the Antebellum South. New York: Oxford University Press, 1994.

Fink, Gary M., and Merl E. Reed, eds. *Race, Class, and Community in Southern Labor History.* Tuscaloosa: University of Alabama Press, 1994.

Flamming, Douglas. *Creating the Modern South: Millhands and Managers in Dalton, Georgia, 1884–1984.* Chapel Hill: University of North Carolina Press, 1992.

Foner, Eric. *Reconstruction: America's Unfinished Revolution, 1863–1877.* New York: Harper and Row, 1988.

Fox-Genovese, Elizabeth. *Within the Plantation Household: Black and White Women of the Old South.* Chapel Hill: University of North Carolina Press, 1988.

Freedly, Edwin T. *Philadelphia and Its Manufacturers.* Philadelphia: Edward Young, 1859.

Genovese, Eugene D. *The Political Economy of Slavery: Studies in the Economy and Society of the Slave South.* New York: Random House, 1961.

———. *The World the Slaveholders Made.* New York: Pantheon Books, 1969.

Gibbs, George Sweet. *The Saco-Lowell Shops: Textile Machinery Building in New England, 1813–1849.* Cambridge, Mass.: Harvard University Press, 1950.

Hadley, Wade Hampton, Doris G. Horton, and Nell Craig Stroud. *Chatham County, 1771–1971.* Durham, N.C.: Moore, 1976.

Hahn, Steven. *The Roots of Southern Populism: Yeoman Farmers and the Transformation of the Georgia Upcountry, 1850–1890.* New York: Oxford University Press, 1983.

Haley, Alex. *Roots.* Garden City, N.Y.: Doubleday, 1976.

Hall, Jacquelyn Dowd, et al. *Like a Family: The Making of a Southern Cotton Mill World.* Chapel Hill: University of North Carolina Press, 1987.

Hearden, Patrick. *Independence and Empire: The New South's Cotton Mill Campaign, 1865–1901.* DeKalb: Northern Illinois University Press, 1982.

Heritage, Dover G., Corinne E. Bivins, and Gail Cox Bolden. *When Shoeshines Were a Nickel: An Oral History of Alamance County, North Carolina.* Burlington, N.C.: G. Bolden–C. Bivins, 1986.

Holt, Eugene. *Edwin Michael Holt and His Descendants, 1807–1948.* Private Printing, 1949.

Hughes, Julian. *Development of the Textile Industry in Alamance.* Burlington, N.C.: Burlington Letter Shop, 1965.

Iobst, Richard, and Louis H. Manarin. *The Bloody Sixth: The Sixth North Carolina Regiment, Confederate States of America.* Raleigh: North Carolina Centennial Commission, 1965.

Jacobs, William Plummer. *The Pioneer.* Clinton, S.C.: Jacobs, 1934.

Janiewski, Dolores E. *Sisterhood Denied: Race, Gender and Class in a New South Community.* Philadelphia: Temple University Press, 1985.

Jeffery, Thomas E. *State Parties and National Politics: North Carolina, 1815–1861.* Athens: University of Georgia Press, 1989.

Jeremy, David John. *Transatlantic Industrial Revolution: The Diffusion of Textile Technologies Between Britain and America, 1790–1830s.* Cambridge, Mass.: MIT Press, 1981.

Johnson, Guion Griffiths. *Ante-Bellum North Carolina: A Social History.* Chapel Hill: University of North Carolina Press, 1937.

Johnson, Paul. *A Shopkeeper's Millennium: Society and Revivals in Rochester, New York, 1815–1837.* New York: Hill and Wang, 1978.

Jordan, Weymouth T., comp. *North Carolina Troops, 1861–65.* Raleigh: North Carolina Department of Archives and History, 1973.

Kasson, John. *Civilizing the Machine: Technology and Republican Values in America, 1776–1900.* New York: Grossman, 1976.

Kessler-Harris, Alice. *Out to Work: A History of Wage-Earning Women in the United States.* New York: Oxford, 1982.

Kirkland, Edward Chase. *Dream and Thought in the Business Community.* Ithaca, N.Y.: Cornell University Press, 1956.

Konkle, Burton Alva. *John Motley Morehead and the Development of North Carolina, 1796–1866.* Philadelphia: William J. Campbell, 1922.

Kruman, Marc W. *Parties and Politics in North Carolina, 1836– 1865.* Baton Rouge: Louisiana State University Press, 1983.

Kulikoff, Alan. *The Agrarian Origins of American Capitalism.* Charlottesville: University of Virginia Press, 1992.

Lefler, Hugh Talmage, and Albert Ray Newsome. *North Carolina: The History of a Southern State.* Chapel Hill: University of North Carolina Press, 1953.

Leiter, Jeffrey, Michael D. Schulman, and Rhonda Zingrafe, eds. *Hanging by a Thread: Social Change in Southern Textiles.* Ithaca, N.Y.: ILR Press, 1991.

Lemert, Ben F. *The Cotton Textile Industry of the Southern Appalachian Piedmont.* Chapel Hill: University of North Carolina Press, 1933.

Leonard, Jacob C. *Centennial History of Davidson County, North Carolina.* Raleigh: Edwards and Broughton, 1927.

Leyburn, James G. *The Scotch-Irish: A Social History.* Chapel Hill: University of North Carolina Press, 1962.

Long, Mary Alves. *High Time to Tell It*. Durham, N.C.: Duke University Press, 1950.

Lossing, Benson. *The Pictorial Field-Book of the Revolution*. Vol. 2. New York: Harper and Brothers, 1860.

Lounsbury, Carl Ravis. *Alamance County Architectural Heritage*. Graham, N.C.: Alamance County Historical Properties Commission, 1980.

Luraghi, Raimondo. *The Rise and Fall of the Plantation South*. New York: New Viewpoints, 1978.

McHugh, Cathy L. *Mill Family: The Labor System in the Southern Cotton Textile Industry, 1880–1915*. New York: Oxford University Press, 1988.

McLaurin, Melton Alonza. *Paternalism and Protest: Southern Cotton Mill Workers and Organized Labor, 1875–1905*. Westport, Conn.: Greenwood Press, 1971.

———. *The Knights of Labor in the South*. Westport, Conn.: Greenwood Press, 1978.

———. *Celia: A Slave*. Athens: University of Georgia Press, 1991.

McPherson, James M. *Battle Cry of Freedom: The Civil War Era*. New York: Oxford University Press, 1988.

Manarin, Louis H., *North Carolina Troops, 1861–1865: A Roster*. Raleigh: North Carolina Division of Archives and History, 1971.

Mathews, Donald G. *Religion in the Old South*. Chicago: University of Chicago Press, 1977.

Mitchell, Broadus. *The Rise of Cotton Mills in the South*. Baltimore: Johns Hopkins University Press, 1921.

———. *William Gregg: Factory Master of the Old South*. Chapel Hill: University of North Carolina Press, 1928.

Mitchell, George Sinclair. *Textile Unionism and the South*. Chapel Hill: University of North Carolina Press, 1931.

Montgomery, David. *Workers' Control in America: Studies in the History of Work, Technology, and Labor Struggles*. New York: Cambridge University Press, 1979.

Moore, Barrington. *Social Origins of Dictatorship: Lord and Peasant in the Making of the Modern World*. Boston: Beacon Press, 1966.

Navin, Thomas R. *The Whitin Machine Works Since 1831: A Textile Machinery Company in an Industrial Village*. Cambridge, Mass.: Harvard University Press, 1950.

Newby, I. A. *Plain Folk in the New South: Social Change and Cultural Persistence, 1880–1915*. Baton Rouge: Louisiana State University Press, 1989.

Oakes, James. *The Ruling Race: A History of American Slave Holders*. New York: Alfred A. Knopf, 1982.

Owsley, Frank. *Plain Folk of the Old South.* Baton Rouge: Louisiana State University Press, 1949.

Perman, Michael. *The Coming of the American Civil War.* Lexington, Mass.: D. C. Heath, 1993.

Porter, Glenn. *The Rise of Big Business, 1860–1910.* Arlington Heights, Ill.: Harlan Davidson, 1973.

Powell, William S. *When the Past Refused to Die: A History of Caswell County, North Carolina, 1777–1977.* Durham, N.C.: Moore, 1977.

———. *North Carolina Through Four Centuries.* Chapel Hill: University of North Carolina Press, 1989.

Powell, William S., James Huhta, and Thomas J. Farnham. *The Regulators in North Carolina: A Documentary History, 1759–1776.* Raleigh: North Carolina Department of Archives and History, 1971.

Prude, Jonathan. *The Coming of Industrial Order: Town and Factory Life in Rural Massachusetts, 1810–1860.* New York: Cambridge University Press, 1983.

Rabinowitz, Howard N. *The First New South, 1865–1920.* Arlington Heights, Ill.: Harlan Davidson, 1992.

Rable, George C. *Civil Wars: Women and the Crisis of Southern Nationalism.* Urbana: University of Illinois Press, 1989.

Raper, Charles L. *The Church and Private Schools of North Carolina.* Greensboro, N.C.: Joseph J. Store, 1898.

Raper, Horace W. *William W. Holden: North Carolina's Political Enigma.* Chapel Hill: University of North Carolina Press, 1985.

Rogers, Daniel T. *The Work Ethic in Industrial America, 1850–1920.* Chicago: University of Chicago Press, 1974.

Scott, Ann Firor, *The Southern Lady: From Pedestal to Politics, 1830–1930.* Chicago: University of Chicago Press, 1970.

Scranton, Philip. *Proprietary Capitalism: The Textile Manufacture at Philadelphia, 1800–1885.* New York: Cambridge University Press, 1983.

Sellers, Charles. *The Market Revolution: Jacksonian America, 1815–1846.* New York: Oxford University Press, 1991.

Shanks, Henry T., ed. *The Papers of Willie Person Mangum.* 5 vols. Raleigh: North Carolina Division of Archives and History, 1950–56.

Shirley, Michael. *From Congregation Town to Industrial City: Culture and Social Change in a Southern Community.* New York: New York University Press, 1994.

Spencer, Cornelia Phillips. *The Last Ninety Days of the War in North Carolina.* New York: Watchman, 1866.

Spruill, Julia Cherry. *Women's Life and Work in the Southern Colonies.* Chapel Hill: University of North Carolina Press, 1938.

Stockard, Sallie Walker. *The History of Alamance.* 1900. Reprint Haw River, N.C.: Alamance County Historical Museum, 1986.

Stokes, Durward T. *Company Shops: The Town Built by a Railroad.* Winston-Salem: John F. Blair, 1981.

Studley, Miriam J. *Historic New Jersey Through Visitors' Eyes.* Princeton: D. Van Nostrand, 1964.

Susman, Warren. *Culture and History: The Transformation of American Society in the Twentieth Century.* New York: Pantheon Books, 1984.

Thomas, Emory. *The Confederate Nation: 1861–1865.* New York: Harper and Row, 1979.

Thompson, E. P. *The Making of the English Working Class.* New York: Vintage Books, 1966.

Thompson, Holland. *From the Cotton Field to the Cotton Mill: A Study of the Industrial Transition in North Carolina.* New York: Macmillan, 1906.

Trachtenberg, Alan. *The Incorporation of America: Culture and Society in the Gilded Age.* New York: Hill and Wang, 1982.

Trelease, Allen. *The North Carolina Railroad, 1849–1871, and the Modernization of North Carolina.* Chapel Hill: University of North Carolina Press, 1991.

Trotter, William R. *Silk Flags and Cold Steel: The Civil War in North Carolina: The Piedmont.* Winston-Salem, N.C.: John F. Blair, 1988.

Tullos, Allen. *Habits of Industry: White Culture and the Transformation of the Carolina Piedmont.* Chapel Hill: University of North Carolina Press, 1989.

Turner, Herbert Snipes. *Church in the Old Fields: Hawfield Presbyterian Church and Community in North Carolina.* Chapel Hill: University of North Carolina Press, 1962.

———. *The Dreamer: Archibald DeBow Murphy, 1777–1832.* Greensboro, N.C.: McClure Press, 1972.

Veblen, Thorstein. *The Theory of the Leisure Class.* 1899. Reprint New York: Penguin Books, 1987.

Washburn, Benjamin. *The Hookworm Campaign in Alamance County, North Carolina.* Raleigh: E. M. Uzzell, 1914.

Whitaker, Walter, in collaboration with Stanley A. Cook and Howard A. White. *Centennial History of Alamance County, 1849–1949.* Burlington, N.C.: Burlington Chamber of Commerce, 1949.

Whitsett, William T. *A Brief History of Alamance County, North Carolina: With Sketches of the Whitesell Family and the Huffman Family.* Whitsett, N.C.: Saber and Song, 1926.

Wiener, Jonathan M. *Social Origins of the New South: Alabama, 1860–1885.* Baton Rouge: Louisiana State University Press, 1978.

Winston, George Tayloe. *A Builder of the New South: Being the Story of the Life Work of Daniel Augustus Tompkins.* Garden City, N.Y.: Doubleday, Page, 1920.

Winston, Robert Watson. *It's a Far Cry.* New York: Henry Holt, 1937.

Wood, Gordon S. *The Radicalism of the American Revolution.* New York: Alfred A. Knopf, 1992.

Woodward, C. Vann. *The Origins of the New South, 1877–1913.* Baton Rouge: Louisiana State University Press, 1951.

Wright, Gavin. *The Political Economy of the Cotton South: Households, Markets, and Wealth in the Nineteenth Century.* New York: W. W. Norton, 1978.

————. *Old South, New South: Revolutions in the Southern Economy Since the Civil War.* New York: Basic Books, 1986.

Yearns, W. Buck, and John Barrett, eds. *North Carolina Civil War Documentary.* Chapel Hill: University of North Carolina Press, 1980.

ARTICLES

Auman, William T., and David D. Scarboro. "The Heroes of America in Civil War North Carolina." *North Carolina Historical Review* 58 (October 1981): 327–63.

Beatty, Bess. "Textile Workers in the North Carolina Piedmont: Mill Owner Images and Mill Worker Response, 1830–1900." *Labor History* 25 (Fall 1984): 485–503.

————. "The Edwin Holt Family: Nineteenth-Century Capitalists in North Carolina." *North Carolina Historical Review* 63 (October 1986): 511–35.

————. "Lowells of the South: Northern Influences on the Nineteenth-Century North Carolina Textile Industry." *Journal of Southern History* 53 (February 1987): 37–62.

Boyte, Harry. "The Textile Industry: Keel of Southern Industrialization." *Radical America* 6 (March–April 1972): 4–49.

Carlson, Leonard A. "Labor Supply, the Acquisition of Skills, and the Location of Southern Textile Mills, 1880–1900." *Journal of Economic History* 41 (March 1981): 65–73.

Carlton, David. "The Revolution from Above: The National Market and the Beginnings of Industrialization in North Carolina." *Journal of American History* 77 (September 1990): 445–75.

"Catalogue of Bingham School, Mebaneville, 1873." *Hillsborough Historical Society Newsletter* 25 (January 1966).

Collins, Herbert. "The Idea of a Cotton Textile Industry in the South,

1870–1900." *North Carolina Historical Review* 34 (July 1957): 358–92.

Denson, C. B. *An Address in Memory of Thomas M. Holt.* Raleigh: Bynum and Christopher, 1899.

Dowd, Jerome. "Strikes and Lockouts in North Carolina." *Gunton's Magazine* 20 (February 1901): 136–41.

Durrill, Wayne. "Producing Poverty: Local Government and Economic Development in a New South County, 1874–1884." *Journal of American History* 71 (March 1985): 764–81.

Faircloth, Chris. "The Charles T. Holt / J. A. Long House . . . Haw River's Architectural Treasure." *City-County* 9 (April 1995): 9–12.

Fries, Adelaide. "One Hundred Years of Textiles in Salem." *North Carolina Historical Review* 27 (January 1950): 1–19.

Gehrke, William H. "The Ante-Bellum Agriculture of the Germans in North Carolina." *Agricultural History* 9 (July 1935).

Goldfarb, Stephen. "A Note on Limits to the Growth of the Cotton-Textile Industry in the Old South." *Journal of Southern History* 68 (November 1982): 545–58.

Griffin, Richard W. "Reconstruction of the North Carolina Textile Industry, 1865–1885." *North Carolina Historical Review* 41 (January 1957): 15–35.

———. "The Civil War and Cotton Manufacturing in North Carolina." *Cotton History Review* 2 (1961): 152–61.

Griffin, Richard W., and Diffie W. Standard. "The Cotton Textile Industry in Antebellum North Carolina, Part I: Origin and Growth to 1830." *North Carolina Historical Review* 34 (January 1957): 15–35.

———. "The Cotton Textile Industry in Antebellum North Carolina, Part II: An Era of Boom and Consolidation, 1830–1860." *North Carolina Historical Review* 34 (April 1957): 131–64.

Hall, Jacquelyn Dowd. "Disorderly Women: Gender and Labor Militancy in the Appalachian South." *Journal of American History* 73 (September 1986): 354–82.

Hine, Darlene Clark. "Rape and the Inner Lives of Black Women in the Middle West." *Signs* 14 (Summer 1989): 912–20.

Lebergott, Stanley. "Why the South Lost: Commercial Purpose in the Confederacy, 1861–1865." *Journal of American History* 70 (June 1983): 58–74.

Price, Charles L. "The Railroad Schemes of George W. Swepson." *Essays in American History.* Vol. 1 (Greenville, N.C.: College Publication in History, 1964).

Ramsdell, Charles W. "The Control of Manufacturing by the Confederate Government." *Mississippi Valley Historical Review* 8 (December 1921): 231–49.

Reid, Richard. "A Test Case of the 'Crying Evil': Desertion Among North Carolina Troops During the Civil War." *North Carolina Historical Review* 58 (July 1981): 234–55.

Scranton, Philip. "Varieties of Paternalism." *American Quarterly* 36 (Summer 1984): 235–57.

Sellers, Charles. "Who Were the Southern Whigs." *American Historical Review* 54 (January 1954): 335–46.

Sitterson, J. Carlyle. "Business Leaders in Post–Civil War North Carolina, 1865–1900." *Studies in Southern History* 39: 111–21.

Tannenbaum, Frank. "The South Buries Its Anglo-Saxons." *Century* 106 (June 1923): 205–15.

Terrill, Tom E. "Eager Hands: Labor for Southern Textiles, 1850– 1860." *Journal of Economic History* 36 (March 1976): 84–101.

Thompson, E. P. "Time, Work-Discipline, and Industrial Capitalism." *Past and Present* 38 (December 1967): 56–97.

Webb, Elizabeth Yates. "Cotton Manufacturing and State Regulation in North Carolina, 1861–65." *North Carolina Historical Review* 9 (April 1932): 117–37.

Welter, Barbara. "The Cult of True Womanhood: 1820–1860." *American Quarterly* 18 (Summer 1966): 151–74.

Wright, Gavin. "Cheap Labor and Southern Textiles Before 1880." *Journal of Economic History* 39 (September 1979): 655–80.

———. "Cheap Labor and Southern Textiles, 1880–1930." *Quarterly Journal of Economics* 96 (November 1981): 605–29.

DISSERTATIONS, THESES, AND UNPUBLISHED PAPERS

Briggs, Martha. "Mill Owners and Mill Workers in an Antebellum County." M.A. thesis, University of North Carolina at Chapel Hill, 1975.

Carrigan, Robert. "Richard Caswell." Senior thesis, University of North Carolina at Chapel Hill, 1855.

Carrigan, William. "Beyond the Mississippi." Senior thesis, University of North Carolina at Chapel Hill, 1852.

DeNatale, Douglass. "Traditional Culture and Community in a Piedmont Textile Mill Village." M.A. thesis, University of North Carolina at Chapel Hill, 1980.

Ferguson, C. V. "Educational Growth in Alamance County." M.A. thesis, University of North Carolina at Chapel Hill, 1931.

Freeze, Gary Richard. "Agricultural Origins of Piedmont Cotton Mill Families, 1880–1900: The Case of the Forest Hill Community, Concord, North Carolina." Seminar paper, University of North Carolina at Chapel Hill, 1981.

Fries, Henry. "Reminiscences of Confederate Days." typescript, North Carolina Division of Archives and History, n.d.

Goebbel, W. B. "A Brief History of Manufacturers in North Carolina Before 1865." M. A. thesis, Duke University, 1925–26.

Holt, Rachel. "Edwin Michael Holt, 1807–1884." M.A. thesis, University of North Carolina at Chapel Hill, 1969.

Kuhn, Cliff. Research paper, no title, no institutional affiliation.

Mebane, B. H. "Address at Unveiling of Portrait of L. Banks Holt." typescript copy in the North Carolina Collection, 1927.

Murphy, Mary. "Burlington, North Carolina." Working paper, Southern Oral History Program, University of North Carolina at Chapel Hill, 1974.

Pierpont, Andrew. "Development of the Textile Industry in Alamance County, North Carolina." Ph.D. dissertation, University of North Carolina at Chapel Hill, 1953.

Robinson, Blackwell P. "Thomas Ruffin." Unpublished manuscript, copy in the North Carolina Collection, University of North Carolina at Chapel Hill, 1992.

Stockard, Sallie. "Daughter of the Piedmont: Chapel Hill's First Co-ed." Unpublished paper, copy in the North Carolina Collection, University of North Carolina at Chapel Hill, n.d.

MISCELLANEOUS

"Plan of the Caldwell Institute, Presbytery of Orange County, North Carolina, October 1835." Copy in the North Carolina Collection, Richmond, 1836.

Pamphlet. "The Burwell School in Historic Hillsborough, North Carolina." Historic Hillsborough Commission, 1965.

Circular and Catalogue. Mr. and Mrs. Burwell's Female School, Hillsborough, North Carolina, Term 1848–51. Copy at the Hillsborough Historic Society.

INTERVIEWS

Carrigan, Joanne. January 3, 1996, Atlanta.

Stalter, Mary. August 10, 1992, Seattle.

Vincent, Bill. January 3, 1990, Burlington, N.C.

INDEX

Blacks: political rights for, 109–10, 115; Ku Klux Klan violence against, 110–16, 121; population of, in Alamance County, 110; in Republican Party, 111, 115; free blacks barred from mill work, 169–70; disfranchisement of, 200–201. *See also* Slavery
Blalock, Cornelia, 187
Boarders and boardinghouses, 173–74, 177, 180–81
Bracon, Josiah and Libby, family, 69
Brandt, George, 90
Breckinridge, John C., 76–77
Brockwell, Benjamin, 175
Brown, John, 74
Brown, Richard D., 51–52
Bunn, Benjamin H., 203
Burch, Martha, 70, 170, 171
Burlington Industries, xiii, 215
Burlington mill, 145
Bynum, Victoria, 88
Byrd, William II, 59

Caldwell Institute, 36–39, 42, 155
Cameron, Paul C., 13, 76, 98, 103–104, 107, 142
Canada, Mary, 188
Canady, Elona, 176
Cane Creek Factory, 15, 23, 27. *See also* Granite Factory/Mills
Carlton, David, 134
Carolina Mill, 124
Carr, Julian Shakespeare, 197
Carrigan, Alfred, 35, 41
Carrigan, Cora Moore, 96
Carrigan, Elizabeth, 63–64
Carrigan, James (Nancy's son), 35, 96
Carrigan, James (William's brother), 63
Carrigan, John, 35, 39, 50, 64, 77, 96
Carrigan, Nancy Holt, 6, 17, 35
Carrigan, Robert, 35, 38–39
Carrigan, William (father): move to Arkansas by, 13, 41, 108; partnership of, with Holt in Alamance Factory, 17–18, 21–25, 27, 33, 65; sale of share of Alamance Factory to Holt, 27, 28, 41, 63; children of, 35, 36, 38, 40, 41; and wife's death, 35; as slaveowner, 62; relationship with Elizabeth Carrigan, 63; sons of, in Civil War, 94, 100; during Reconstruction, 108

Carrigan, William, Jr. (son), 35, 41–42, 43–44
Carrigan, William A. (nephew), 36, 39, 40, 42, 44, 63
Carson, Martha, family, 185
Cash, W. J., xvii, 133, 189
Cate, Mangum, 175
Cates, B. F., 182–83
Cates family, 181–83
Cecil-Fronsman, Bill, 85
Cedar Falls Mill/Factory, 15, 23, 62–63, 85
Censer, Jane Turner, 30–31, 34, 44
Centennial Celebration, 131–32
Chandler, Alfred, 149
Chicago World's Fair, 161
Children. *See* Education; Mill families; Mill workers
Churches. *See* Religion
Civil War: cause of, 8; Holt family members in, 75, 79, 93–97, 98, 100–101, 105; beginning of, 78; exemption from conscription in, 79, 81, 82–83, 101; and textile mills in South, 79–86; mill workers during, 81, 85–89; profiteering during, 84–85, 88, 92–93, 99, 198; poor southern whites' attitude toward, 85–87; women's protests during, 87–89; mill owners' complaints during, 89–92; scarcities and high prices during, 89, 99–100, 103; Union blockade during, 89–90; desertion rate during, 90, 103; battles of, 93, 94, 95, 96, 103; elite southern women during, 97–99; social life during, 98; differences for wealthy and poor men in, 100–101; Kilpatrick's entry into Lexington, 100; age of soldiers in, 101–102; single status of soldiers in, 101–102, 169; casualties in generally, 102–103, 169, 175; Confederate defeat in, 103–105; in Piedmont, 103–104. *See also* Confederate States of America
Clapp, James M., 182
Clark, Henry T., 81–82
Class. *See* Elite families; Mill workers
Clay, Henry, 25–26
Cochrane, Thomas, 22, 197–98
Commission houses, 123, 127, 134–35, 147

Retail stores, 21, 39, 42, 65, 127
Revolutionary War. *See* American Revolution
Reynolds, R. J., 127*n*9
Rhode Island model, 54
Rhyne, Moses, 214
Rhyne, Susan, 214
Rike, B. L., 106
Robertson, Ben, 145
Robertson, Joe, 177
Row, Susan, 171
Roy, Sarah, 173
Ruffin, Edmund, 77, 78
Ruffin, John, 76
Ruffin, Thomas: and financial assistance to family members and friends, xv, 12, 17; as president of North Carolina Agricultural Society, 14; children of, 76; as Unionist initially, 77–78; during Civil War, 80, 83, 83*n*25, 98, 103; death of, 107; during Reconstruction, 107; and financial losses due to Civil War, 107, 118; opposition to Ku Klux Klan by, 110
Ruffin family, 19, 34

Salem Cotton Manufacturing Company, 15, 16
Salem Factory, 54
Sams, Sarah, 174
Saxapahaw Factory, 22, 134, 143, 144
Scales, Junius, 141
Scheible, Elizabeth, 2
Schenck, Michael, 10
Schools. *See* Education
Scott, Ann, 59
Scraggs, Elizabeth, 174
Scranton, Philip, 189
Secession, 77–78. *See also* Confederate States of America
Sellers, Charles, 12
Sharp, Gaston, 188
Sharp, Mary, family, 174
Shatterley, Thomas, 211
Shephard, Rankin, 178
Sherman, William T., 103, 104
Shoffner, Em, 188
Shue, George, 185
Sibling exchange marriage, 44, 47
Siddall, Thomas, 24, 57, 114
Simpson, Winiva, 172–73

Slade, Frances Holt. *See* Holt, Frances Ann
Slade, Thomas, 49, 95, 98, 101, 101*n*63
Slater, John, 54
Slavery: Edwin Michael Holt as slaveowner, xiii, 13, 14, 29, 30–31, 34, 55, 61–62, 72, 114; Genovese on, xiv; in eighteenth-century Piedmont, 3; Michael Holt III as slaveowner, 6, 7, 8, 9; defense of, 7, 8, 57; Wright on, 28; sexual vulnerability of female slaves, 45–46; mill work for slaves, 55, 61–62, 114, 169; Jeffersonian view of, 73; and Compromise of 1850, p. 74; and Kansas-Nebraska Bill, 74, 76; Holt's emancipation of slaves, 110. *See also* Abolitionism; Blacks
Smithey, Daisy, 182
Social life: of Holt family, 34–35, 48, 98, 138, 151, 163; of mill workers, 190
Southern Railroad, 177
Southern Textile Manufacturers Association, 147
Spanish-American War, 162
Spencer, Cornelia Phillips, 99, 215
Stackhouse, Verna, 191, 213
Staley, John, 181
Steam power, 131, 132, 133
Steele, Elizabeth, 175
Stockard, Sallie, 106, 182, 186–87
Stoneman, George, 103, 104
Stores. *See* Retail stores
Stowe, Harriet Beecher, 73
Stowe, Jasper, 91–92
Strike of 1900, xix, xx, 205–12
Strikes of 1887, p. 203
Stutts, John and Emma, 181
Summerlin, Burwell, 209
Susman, Warren, 157
Sutton, Chesley and Nancy, 168
Swepson, George, 110, 116–20, 125, 131, 170, 194, 195

Taft, C. A., 135
Taft, George, 136–37, 189
Tannenbaum, Frank, 185
Tate, Thomas, 82–83
Taylor, Thomas T., 203
Teaching profession, 163
Telephones, 132